American Constitutional Development

GOLDENTREE BIBLIOGRAPHIES
In American History
under the series editorship of
Arthur S. Link

American Constitutional Development

compiled by

Alpheus Thomas Mason
Princeton University

and

D. Grier Stephenson, Jr.
Franklin and Marshall College

AHM Publishing Corporation
Arlington Heights, Illinois 60004

PRINTED IN THE UNITED STATES OF AMERICA
737

For Claire

Contents

CONTENTS

CONTENTS

Editor's Foreword

Goldentree Bibliographies in American History are designed to provide students, teachers, and librarians with ready and reliable guides to the literature of American history in all its remarkable scope and variety. Volumes in the series cover comprehensively the major periods in American history, while additional volumes are devoted to all important subjects.

Goldentree Bibliographies attempt to steer a middle course between the brief list of references provided in the average textbook and the long bibliography in which significant items are often lost in the sheer number of titles listed. Each bibliography is, therefore, selective, with the sole criterion for choice being the significance — and not the age — of any particular work. The result is bibliographies of all works, including journal articles and doctoral dissertations, that are still useful, without bias in favor of any particular historiographical school.

Each compiler is a scholar long associated, both in research and teaching, with the period or subject of his volume. All compilers have not only striven to accomplish the objective of this series but have also cheerfully adhered to a general style and format. However, each compiler has been free to define his field, make his own selections, and work out internal organization as the unique demands of his period or subject have seemed to dictate.

The single great objective of *Goldentree Bibliographies in American History* will have been achieved if these volumes help researchers and students to find their way to the significant literature of American history.

Arthur S. Link

Preface

American constitutional development is a maze of crucial historic events, basic documents, underlying principles, governmental pronouncements and decisions, as well as analyses and interpretations, both official and unofficial. All are shaped by implacable social, economic, and political forces. The orientation, predominantly legal, reflects the Founding Fathers' initial decision to control government power and conduct "by an overruling Constitution." James Wilson (1742–1798) called this "an improvement in the science and practice of government reserved to the American States."

The accumulated literature is well-nigh boundless. Our effort to be both comprehensive and selective has not been easy; certain criteria had perforce to govern. Choices have been inspired primarily by the belief that American constitutionalism can best be understood in terms of theory. Justice Holmes' pointed observation concerning the most fruitful approach to the study of law is applicable to political life generally: "Theory is the most important part of the dogma of the law, as the architect is the most important man who takes part in the building of a house. . . . It is not to be feared as unpractical, for, to the competent, it simply means going to the bottom of the subject." Hopefully, the titles listed in this bibliography meet this test.

Our thanks go to Jean Grosjean Kerich, who assisted with the index and the citations, and Janet Nelson Stephens, who assisted in checking citations; to Peter Young of the Fackenthal Library of Franklin and Marshall College, who patiently answered questions on reference and bibliographic materials; and to Bobbie Brooks, who typed the manuscript. Funds for manuscript preparation were made available by Franklin and Marshall College through a grant from the Shell Oil Corporation.

Alpheus Thomas Mason
D. Grier Stephenson, Jr.

Abbreviations

Trans Ala Hist Soc	Transactions of the Alabama Historical Society
Alb L J	Albany Law Journal
Am Assoc U Prof Bull	American Association of University Professors Bulletin
Am Bar Assoc J	American Bar Association Journal
Am Hist Rev	American Historical Review
Am J Int L	American Journal of International Law
Am J Leg Hist	American Journal of Legal History
Am J Pol Sci	American Journal of Political Science
Am L Mag	American Law Magazine
Am L Reg	American Law Register
Am L Rev	American Law Review
Am Lit	American Literature
Am Pol Sci Rev	American Political Science Review
Am Q	American Quarterly
Ann Am Acad Pol Soc Sci	Annals, American Academy of Political and Social Science
Ariz L Rev	Arizona Law Review
Atl Month	Atlantic Monthly
Bay L Rev	Baylor Law Review
Bos Q Rev	Boston Quarterly Review
Bos U L Rev	Boston University Law Review
Buff L Rev	Buffalo Law Review
Calif L Rev	California Law Review
Cath Hist Rev	Catholic Historical Review
Cincin L Rev	Cincinnati Law Review
Colum L Rev	Columbia Law Review
Colum U Q	Columbia University Quarterly
Conn Bar J	Connecticut Bar Journal
Const Rev	Constitutional Review
Corn L Q	Cornell Law Quarterly
Corn L Rev	Cornell Law Review
Dart Alum Mag	Dartmouth Alumni Magazine
Dick L Rev	Dickinson Law Review
Duke L J	Duke Law Journal
Eco L Q	Ecology Law Quarterly
Fed Bar J	Federal Bar Journal
Ford L Rev	Fordham Law Review
Geo L J	Georgetown Law Journal
Geo Wash L Rev	George Washington Law Review
Ga L Rev	Georgia Law Review
Ga	Georgia Reports

Harv Civ R—Civ Lib L Rev	Harvard Civil Rights—Civil Liberties Law Review
Harv L Rev	Harvard Law Review
Hist	The Historian
Ill L J	Illinois Law Journal
Ill L Rev	Illinois Law Review
Ind	The Independent
Ind L J	Indiana Law Journal
Ind L Rev	Indiana Law Review
Int & Comp L Q	International and Comparative Law Quarterly
Iowa L Rev	Iowa Law Review
J Am Hist	Journal of American History
J Am Jud Soc	Journal of the American Judicature Society
J Ill State Hist Soc	Journal of the Illinois State Historical Society
J L & Econ	Journal of Law and Economics
J Leg Stud	Journal of Legal Studies
J Neg Hist	Journal of Negro History
J Phil, Psy, & Sci Meth	Journal of Philosophy, Psychology, and Scientific Method
J Pol Econ	Journal of Political Economy
J Pol	Journal of Politics
J Pub L	Journal of Public Law
J Soc Iss	Journal of Social Issues
J Soc Phil	Journal of Social Philosophy
J So Hist	Journal of Southern History
J Urb L	Journal of Urban Law
Kan L Rev	Kansas Law Review
Ky L J	Kentucky Law Journal
Lab Hist	Labor History
L & Cont Prob	Law and Contemporary Problems
L & Soc Rev	Law and Society Review
L & Soc Ord	Law and the Social Order
L Lib J	Law Library Journal
L Quad N	Law Quadrangle Notes
La L Rev	Louisiana Law Review
Md L Rev	Maryland Law Review
Proc Mass Hist Soc	Proceedings of the Massachusetts Historical Society
Mass L Q	Massachusetts Law Quarterly
Merc L Rev	Mercer Law Review
Mich L Rev	Michigan Law Review
Midw J Pol Sci	Midwest Journal of Political Science
Minn L Rev	Minnesota Law Review
Miss Val Hist Rev	Mississippi Valley Historical Review
Mod L Rev	Modern Law Review
Nat Bar J	National Bar Journal
Neb L Rev	Nebraska Law Review
N Eng Q	New England Quarterly

N Y	New York Reports
N Y State Bar J	New York State Bar Journal
N Y Times Mag	New York Times Magazine
N Y U L Q Rev	New York University Law Quarterly Review
N Y U L Rev	New York University Law Review
N Am Rev	North American Review
N C L Rev	North Carolina Law Review
N D L Rev	North Dakota Law Review
Northe L Rev	Northeastern Law Review
Northw U L Rev	Northwestern University Law Review
Not Dame Law	Notre Dame Lawyer
O State L J	Ohio State Law Journal
Ore L Rev	Oregon Law Review
Penn Bar Assoc Q	Pennsylvania Bar Association Quarterly
Phil & Pub Aff	Philosophy and Public Affairs
Pol Sci Q	Political Science Quarterly
Princeton Rev	Princeton Review
Proc Am Acad Arts & Sci	Proceedings of the American Academy of Arts and Sciences
Proc N Y State Bar Assoc	Proceedings of the New York State Bar Association
Pub Ad Rev	Public Administration Review
R Rel L Rep	Race Relations Law Reporter
Ry & Corp L J	Railway and Corporation Law Journal
Reg Ky Hist Soc	Register of the Kentucky Historical Society
Rep Am Bar Assoc	Report of the American Bar Association
Rep Am Hist Assoc	Report of the American Historical Association
Rep N Y State Bar Assoc	Report of the New York State Bar Association
Rev Pol	Review of Politics
Rut L Rev	Rutgers Law Review
Sci & Soc	Science and Society
S Atl Q	South Atlantic Quarterly
S C L Rev	South Carolina Law Review
So Calif L Rev	Southern California Law Review
So Rev	Southern Review
Sw Pol & Soc Sci Q	Southwestern Political and Social Science Quarterly
Stan L Rev	Stanford Law Review
State Govt	State Government
Suf U L Rev	Suffolk University Law Review
S Ct Rev	Supreme Court Review
Syr L Rev	Syracuse Law Review
Tem L Q	Temple Law Quarterly
Tex L Rev	Texas Law Review
Tul L Rev	Tulane Law Review
UCLA L Rev	U. C. L. A. Law Review
U S	United States Reports

ABBREVIATIONS

U Chi L Rev	University of Chicago Law Review
U Cin L Rev	University of Cincinnati Law Review
U Fla L Rev	University of Florida Law Review
U Miami L Rev	University of Miami Law Review
U Mo Stud	University of Missouri Studies
U Penn L Rev	University of Pennsylvania Law Review
U Pitt L Rev	University of Pittsburgh Law Review
U S News & World Rep	U. S. News and World Report
Vand L Rev	Vanderbilt Law Review
Vill L Rev	Villanova Law Review
Va L Rev	Virginia Law Review
Va Mag Hist & Biog	Virginia Magazine of History and Biography
Va Q Rev	Virginia Quarterly Review
Vit Speeches	Vital Speeches
Wash L Rev	Washington Law Review
Wash & Lee L Rev	Washington and Lee Law Review
Wash U L Q	Washington University Law Quarterly
West Pol Q	Western Political Quarterly
Wm & M L Rev	William and Mary Law Review
Wm & M Q	William and Mary Quarterly
Wis L Rev	Wisconsin Law Review
Yale L J	Yale Law Journal
Yale Rev	Yale Review
Yale Rev L & Soc Act	Yale Review of Law and Social Action

NOTE: The publisher and compiler invite suggestions for additions to future editions of this bibliography.

I. General Sources

A. Bibliographical Guides

1 *Advance Bibliography of Contents: Political Science and Government.* Santa Barbara, Calif., 1969.

2 American Historical Association. *Writings on American History.* 46 vols. Washington, D.C., 1902–1964.

3 AMES, J. G. *Comprehensive Index to the Publications of the United States Government, 1881–1893.* 2 vols. Washington, D.C., 1905.

4 *An Index to Legal Periodical Literature* (–1937). Boston, Indianapolis, and Los Angeles, 1888–1939.

5 BASLER, Roy P., *et al.,* eds. *A Guide to the Study of the United States of America: Representative Books Reflecting the Development of American Thought and Life.* Washington, D.C., 1960.

6 BEERS, Henry P. *Bibliographies in American History: Guide to Materials for Research.* New York, 1942.

7 BOYD, Anne Morris. *United States Government Publications.* 2nd ed., rev. New York, 1941.

8 BROOKS, Alexander D. *A Bibliography of Civil Rights and Civil Liberties.* New York, 1962.

9 BROWNE, Cynthia E. *State Constitutional Conventions from Independence to the Completion of the Present Union 1776–1959; A Bibliography.* Westport, Conn., 1973.

10 BUCHANAN, William W., and Edna M. KANELY. *Cumulative Subject Index to the Monthly Catalog of United States Government Publications 1900–1971.* Washington, D.C. 1973–.

11 *Bulletin of the Public Affairs Information Service.* New York, 1915–.

12 *Catalogue of the Public Documents* (1893–1940). 25 vols. Washington, D.C., 1896–1945.

13 CRAVEN, Wesley Frank. *The American Revolution: A Guide for Independent Study.* Princeton, N.J., 1973.

14 *Dissertation Abstracts: A Guide to Dissertations and Monographs Available in Microfilm.* Ann Arbor, Mich., 1938–.

15 *Doctoral Dissertations Accepted by American Universities.* 22 vols. New York, 1934–1955.

16 *Essay and General Literature Index.* New York, 1934–.

17 FREIDEL, Frank, ed. *Harvard Guide to American History.* Rev. ed., 2 vols. Cambridge, Mass., 1974.

18 George Washington University. Division of Library Science. *The Supreme Court: Its Power of Judicial Review.* Washington, D.C., 1937.

GENERAL SOURCES

19 *Government Publications Review: An International Journal.* Elmsford, N.Y., 1973–.

20 HAINES, Charles G. "Histories of the Supreme Court of the United States Written from the Federalist Point of View." *Sw Pol & Soc Sci Q,* 4 (1923), 1–35.

21 HALLAM, H. C., Jr., and Edward G. HUDON. "United States Supreme Court Records and Briefs: A Union List." *L Lib J,* 40 (1947), 82–84.

22 HAMER, Philip M., ed. *A Guide to Archives and Manuscripts in the United States.* New Haven, 1961.

23 HOLLER, Frederick L. *The Information Sources of Political Science.* Santa Barbara, Calif., 1971.

24 *Index to Legal Periodicals* (1907–). Chicago and New York, 1908–.

25 *International Index to Periodicals.* New York, 1916–.

26 JOHNSON, Julia. *Reorganization of the Supreme Court.* New York, 1937.

27 LARNED, J. N., ed. *The Literature of American History: A Bibliographical Guide.* Boston, 1902.

28 MECHANIC, Sylvia. *Annotated List of Selected United States Government Publications Available to Depository Libraries.* New York, 1971.

29 *Monthly Catalog of U.S. Public Documents* (1895–). Washington, D.C., 1895–.

30 *National Union Catalogue of Manuscript Collections.* Ann Arbor, Mich., 1962–.

31 *Poole's Index to Periodical Literature* (1802–1902). 6 vols. Boston, 1882–1908.

32 POORE, B. P. *A Descriptive Catalogue of the Government Publications of the United States, September 5, 1774–March 4, 1881.* Washington, D.C., 1885.

33 *Readers' Guide to Periodical Literature.* New York, 1900–.

34 SCHUBERT, Glendon A. "Behavioral Research in Public Law." *Am Pol Sci Rev,* 57 (1963), 433–445.

35 SCHUBERT, Glendon A. "Judicial Process and Behavior, 1963–1971." *Political Science Annual: An International Review.* Ed. J. A. Robinson. Vol. III. Indianapolis, 1972.

36 SEDDIG, Robert G. "Toward a Political Jurisprudence: Recent Writing in Public Law." *Am J Pol Sci,* 17 (1973), 441–456.

37 SERVIES, James A. *A Bibliography of John Marshall.* Washington, D.C., 1956.

38 SPECTOR, Robert M. "Judicial Biography and the United States Supreme Court: A Bibliographical Appraisal." *Am J Leg Hist,* 11 (1967), 1–24.

39 TOMPKINS, Dorothy Campbell. *The Supreme Court of the United States: A Bibliography.* Berkeley, Calif., 1959.

40 United States Library of Congress. *List of Works Relating to the Supreme Court of the United States* (with supplements). Washington, D.C., 1909, 1912, 1916, 1922.

41 United States Library of Congress. Division of Bibliography. *List of References on the Popular Election of Supreme Court Judges, State and Federal.* Washington, D.C., 1924.

42 United States Library of Congress. Division of Bibliography. *List of References on the Supreme Court of the United States with Particular Reference to the Doctrine of Judicial Review.* Washington, D.C., 1935.

43 United States Library of Congress. Division of Bibliography. *The Supreme Court Issue; A Selected List of References.* Washington, D.C., 1938.

44 Yale University Law School. *Louis Dembitz Brandeis, 1856–1941: A Bibliography.* New Haven, 1958.

B. Reference Works and Public Documents

45 *American State Papers. Documents, Legislative and Executive, of the Congress of the United States.* 38 vols. Washington, D.C., 1832–1861.

46 *Annals of the Congress of the United States* (1789–1824). Washington, D.C., 1834–1856.

47 BLACK, Henry Campbell. *Black's Law Dictionary.* 4th ed., rev. St. Paul, Minn., 1968.

48 *Book of the States* (1935–). Chicago, 1935–.

49 CHASE, Harold W., and Craig DUCKETT, eds. *Corwin's Constitution and What It Means Today.* 13th ed. Princeton, N.J., 1973.

50 *Code of Federal Regulations.* Washington, D.C., 1949–.

51 *Congressional Digest.* Washington, D.C., 1921–.

52 *Congressional Globe* (1833–1873). Washington, D.C., 1834–1873.

53 Congressional Quarterly Service. *Congress and the Nation* (1945–1972). 3 vols. Washington, D.C., 1965–1973.

54 Congressional Quarterly Service. *Guide to the Congress of the United States.* Washington, D.C., 1971.

55 *Congressional Quarterly Weekly Report* (1945–). Washington, D.C., 1945–.

56 *Congressional Record* (1873–). Washington, D.C., 1874–.

57 CORWIN, Edward S., *et al.,* eds. *The Constitution of the United States, Analysis and Interpretation.* Rev. ed. Washington, D.C., 1964.

58 COX, Edward F. *State and National Voting in Federal Elections, 1910–1970.* Hamden, Conn., 1972.

59 DAVIS, J. C. Bancroft. *Appendix to the Reports of the Decisions of the Supreme Court of the United States from September 24, 1789 to the End of October Term 1888.* New York, 1889.

60 EWING, Cortez A. M. *The Judges of the Supreme Court, 1789–1937.* Minneapolis, 1938.

61 FLANDERS, Henry. *The Lives and Times of the Chief Justices.* New York, 1875.

62 FRIEDMAN, Leon, and Fred L. ISRAEL, eds. *The Justices of the United States Supreme Court, 1789–1969. Their Lives and Major Opinions.* 4 vols. New York, 1969.

63 *Historical Statistics of the United States: Colonial Times to 1957.* Washington, D.C., 1960.

64 JOHNSON, Allen, and Dumas MALONE, eds. *Dictionary of American Biography.* 23 vols. New York, 1928–1974.

GENERAL SOURCES

65 *Journal of the Executive Proceedings of the Senate of the United States, 1789–1905.* 90 vols. Washington, D.C., 1828–1948.

66 *Journal of the House of Representatives of the United States.* Philadelphia and Washington, D.C., 1789–.

67 *Journal of the Senate of the United States.* Philadelphia and Washington, D.C., 1789–.

68 KENNEDY, Lawrence F., comp. *Biographical Directory of the American Congress, 1774–1971.* Washington, D.C., 1971.

69 MacDONALD, William, ed. *Documentary Source Book of American History, 1603–1913.* New York, 1916.

70 MacDONALD, William, ed. *Select Documents Illustrative of the History of the United States, 1776–1861.* New York, 1898.

71 MORRISON, Stanley E., ed. *Sources and Documents Illustrating the American Revolution, 1764–1788.* Oxford, 1929.

72 *National Journal* (1969–). Washington, D.C., 1969–.

73 *Register of Debates in Congress* (1824–1837). Washington, D.C., 1825–1837.

74 RICHARDSON, J. D. *A Compilation of the Messages and Papers of the Presidents, 1789–1902.* 20 vols. Washington, D.C., 1917.

75 SELIGMAN, E. R. A., and Alvin W. JOHNSON, eds. *Encyclopedia of the Social Sciences.* 15 vols. New York, 1930–1935.

76 SILLS, David L., ed. *International Encyclopedia of the Social Sciences.* 17 vols. New York, 1968.

77 THORPE, Francis Newton, ed. *The Federal and State Constitutions, Colonial Charters and Other Organic Laws.* 7 vols. Washington, D.C., 1909.

78 UMBREIT, Kenneth Bernard. *Our Eleven Chief Justices; A History of the Supreme Court in Terms of Their Personalities.* New York, 1938.

79 *United States Code Service.* Rochester, N.Y., 1972–.

80 United States Library of Congress. Congressional Research Service. *Digest of Public General Bills and Resolutions.* Washington, D.C., 1936–.

81 United States Library of Congress. Division of Bibliography. *List of References on Judicial Legislation by Decisions of the United States Supreme Court Declaring Laws Unconstitutional* (with supplement). Washington, D.C., 1922, 1924. For an updating of these decisions through 1969, see 62, pp. 3240–3256, vol. 4.

82 *United States Reports* (1790–). Vols. 1–4 (Dallas), 5–13 (Cranch), 14–25 (Wheaton), 26–41 (Peters), 42–65 (Howard), 66–67 (Black), 68–90 (Wallace), 91–(U.S.). Washington, D.C., 1875–.

83 *United States Statutes at Large.* Washington, D.C., 1848–.

84 *Who's Who in American Politics* (1967–). New York, 1971–.

85 WIRE, G. E. "Index to Memoirs, Orders and Rules of Court, Admissions to the Bar and Other Interesting Material Found in United States Supreme Court Reports, Volumes 1–291." *L Lib J,* 28 (1935), 27–39.

C. General Works

86 ABRAHAM, Henry J. *The Judicial Process.* 3rd ed. New York, 1975.

87 Association of American Law Schools. *Selected Essays in Anglo-American Legal History.* 3 vols. Boston, 1907.

88 Association of American Law Schools. *Selected Essays on Constitutional Law.* 4 vols. Chicago, 1938.

89 BADGER, William V. *A Systematic Analysis of the United States Supreme Court Cases Dealing with Education, 1790–1951.* Ann Arbor, Mich., 1953.

90 BALDWIN, Henry. *A General View of the Origin and Nature of the Constitution and Government of the United States.* New York, 1970 (reprint of 1837 ed.).

91 BARRETT, Edward L., Jr., *et al.,* eds. *Selected Essays on Constitutional Law, 1938–1962.* St. Paul, Minn., 1963.

92 BAUER, Elizabeth K. *Commentaries on the Constitution, 1790–1860.* New York, 1965.

93 BETH, Loren P. *Development of the American Constitution, 1877–1917.* New York, 1971.

94 BETH, Loren P. *Politics, the Constitution, and the Supreme Court.* New York, 1962.

95 BISHOP, Joseph W., Jr. *Obiter Dicta: Opinions, Judicious and Otherwise, on Lawyers and the Law.* New York, 1971.

96 BLACK, Charles L., Jr. *Structure and Relationship in Constitutional Law.* Baton Rouge, La., 1969.

97 BLACK, Hugo L. *A Constitutional Faith.* New York, 1969.

98 BOUDIN, Louis B. *Government by Judiciary.* 2 vols. New York, 1968 (reprint of 1932 ed.).

99 BRACKENRIDGE, Hugh Henry. *Law Miscellanies.* Philadelphia, 1814.

100 BROWNSON, Orestes A. *The American Republic, Its Constitution, Tendencies and Destiny.* New York, 1866.

101 BRYCE, James. *The American Commonwealth.* 2nd ed., rev. 2 vols. London, 1891.

102 BUTLER, Charles Henry. *A Century at the Bar of the Supreme Court of the United States.* New York, 1942.

103 COMMAGER, Henry Steele, ed. *Documents of American History.* 7th ed. New York, 1963.

104 CONANT, Michael. *The Constitution and Capitalism.* St. Paul, Minn., 1974.

105 COOLEY, Thomas M. *A Treatise on Constitutional Limitations.* Boston, 1868.

106 CORWIN, Edward S. *American Constitutional History.* Eds. Alpheus T. Mason and Gerald Garvey. New York, 1964.

107 CORWIN, Edward S. "The Basic Doctrine of American Constitutional Law." *Mich L Rev,* 12 (1914), 247–276.

108 CROSSKEY, William W. *Politics and the Constitution in the History of the United States.* 2 vols. Chicago, 1953.

GENERAL SOURCES

109 DEWEY, Donald O. *Union and Liberty: A Documentary History of American Constitutionalism.* New York, 1969.

110 DIETZE, Gottfried, ed. *Essays on the American Constitution. A Commemorative Volume in Honor of Alpheus T. Mason.* Englewood Cliffs, N.J., 1964.

111 FLEMING, Donald, and Bernard BAILYN, eds. *Perspectives on American History: Law in American History.* Vol. 5. Cambridge, Mass., 1971.

112 FRIEDMAN, Lawrence M. *A History of American Law.* New York, 1973.

113 FRIEDMANN, Wolfgang. *Law in a Changing Society.* London, 1959.

114 GARRATY, John A. *Quarrels That Have Shaped the Constitution.* New York, 1966.

115 GARVEY, Gerald. *Constitutional Bricolage.* Princeton, N.J., 1971.

116 *The Gaspar G. Bacon Lectures on the Constitution of the United States 1940–1950.* Boston, 1953.

117 GRAHAM, Howard Jay. *Everyman's Constitution: Historical Essays on the Fourteenth Amendment, the "Conspiracy Theory," and American Constitutionalism.* Madison, Wis., 1968.

118 HARLAN, John M. "Government under the Constitution." *Law Notes,* 11 (1908), 206–208.

119 HART, H. L. A. *The Concept of Law.* Oxford, 1961.

120 HAZARD, Geoffrey C., Jr. *Social Justice Through Civil Justice.* Chicago, 1969.

121 HAZARD, John N. *Legal Thought in the United States of America under Contemporary Pressures.* Brussels, 1970.

122 HENDRICK, Burton J. *Bulwark of the Republic; A Biography of the Constitution.* Boston, 1937.

123 HOCKETT, Homer Carey. *The Constitutional History of the United States, 1776–1876.* 2 vols. New York, 1939.

124 HOLMES, Oliver Wendell, Jr. *The Common Law.* Boston, 1881.

125 HOWE, Mark A. DeWolfe, ed. *Readings in American Legal History.* New York, 1971.

126 KELLY, Alfred H., and Winfred A. HARBISON. *The American Constitution: Its Origins and Development.* 4th ed. New York, 1970.

127 KENT, James. *Commentaries on American Law.* 5th ed. 3 vols. New York, 1844.

128 KURLAND, Philip B., ed. *The Supreme Court Review.* Chicago, 1960–.

129 LEVY, Leonard W., ed. *American Constitutional Law. Historical Essays.* New York, 1966.

130 LEVY, Leonard W., ed. *Judgments; Essays on American Constitutional History.* Chicago, 1972.

131 McCLOSKEY, Robert G., ed. *Essays in Constitutional Law.* New York, 1957.

132 McILWAIN, Charles H. *Constitutionalism, Ancient and Modern.* Ithaca, N.Y., 1940.

133 McLAUGHLIN, Andrew C. *A Constitutional History of the United States.* New York, 1935.

134 McLAUGHLIN, Andrew C. *Foundations of American Constitutionalism.* New York, 1932.

135 MARSHALL, Geoffrey. *Constitutional Theory.* Oxford, 1971.

136 MASON, Alpheus T. "Constitutional Limitations in a World of Continuing Crisis." *Continuing Crisis in American Politics.* Ed. Marian D. Irish. Englewood Cliffs, N.J., 1962.

137 MASON, Alpheus T., and William M. BEANEY. *American Constitutional Law.* 5th ed. Englewood Cliffs, N.J., 1972.

138 MATTESON, David M. *The Organization of the Government under the Constitution.* New York, 1970 (reprint of 1943 ed.).

139 MENDELSON, Wallace, ed. *The Constitution and the Supreme Court.* 2nd ed. New York, 1965.

140 MERRYMAN, John Henry. *The Civil Law Tradition.* Stanford, Calif., 1969.

141 MILLER, Arthur S. "Toward the 'Techno-Corporate' State?—An Essay in American Constitutionalism." *Vill L Rev,* 14 (1968), 1–73.

142 MILLER, Samuel F. *Lectures on the Constitution of the United States.* New York, 1893.

143 MURPHY, Paul L. *The Constitution in Crisis Times, 1918–1969.* New York, 1972.

144 MURPHY, Walter F., and Joseph TANENHAUS. *The Study of Public Law.* New York, 1972.

145 PADOVER, Saul. *The Living U.S. Constitution.* New York, 1963.

146 POWELL, Thomas Reed. "The Logic and Rhetoric of Constitutional Law." *J Phil, Psy, & Sci Meth,* 15 (1918), 645–658.

147 POWELL, Thomas Reed. *Vagaries and Varieties in Constitutional Interpretation.* New York, 1956.

148 PRITCHETT, C. Herman. *The American Constitution.* 2nd ed. New York, 1968.

149 READ, Conyers, ed. *The Constitution Reconsidered.* New York, 1938.

150 SCHMIDHAUSER, John R., ed. *Constitutional Law in the Political Process.* Chicago, 1963.

151 SCHUBERT, Glendon A. *Constitutional Politics.* New York, 1960.

152 SCHUBERT, Glendon A. *The Constitutional Polity.* Boston, 1970.

153 SCHWARTZ, Bernard. *A Commentary on the Constitution of the United States.* 5 vols. New York, 1963–1968.

154 SCHWARTZ, Bernard, et al. *Statutory History of the United States.* 3 vols. New York, 1970.

155 SMITH, J. Allen. *The Spirit of American Government; A Study of the Constitution: Its Origin, Influence, and Relation to Democracy.* New York, 1907.

156 SMITH, James, and Paul L. MURPHY, eds. *Liberty and Justice: A Historical Record of American Constitutional Development.* 2d ed. 2 vols. New York, 1968.

157 STORY, Joseph. *Commentaries on the Constitution of the United States.* 3 vols. New York, 1970 (reprint of 1833 ed.).

158 SUTHERLAND, Arthur E. *Constitutionalism in America: Origins and Evolution of Its Fundamental Ideas.* New York, 1965.

159 SUTHERLAND, Arthur E., ed. *Government under Law: A Conference Held at Harvard Law School on the Occasion of the Bicentennial of John Marshall.* Cambridge, Mass., 1956.

160 SWISHER, Carl B., *American Constitutional Development.* 2nd ed. Boston, 1954.

161 THORPE, Francis Newton. *The Constitutional History of the United States.* 3 vols. Chicago, 1901.

162 TUCKER, St. George. *Blackstone's Commentaries with Notes of Reference to the Constitution and Laws of the Federal Government of the United States and the Commonwealth of Virginia.* 5 vols. Clifton, N.J., 1969.

163 VON HOLST, Hermann E. *Constitutional and Political History of the United States.* 7 vols. Chicago, 1876–1892.

164 WILLOUGHBY, Westel Woodbury. *The Constitutional Law of the United States.* 3 vols. New York, 1924.

165 WILSON, Woodrow. *Constitutional Government in the United States.* New York, 1908.

166 WRIGHT, Benjamin F. *The Growth of American Constitutional Law.* New York, 1942.

II. Origins

167 ARONSON, Jason. "Shaftesbury on Locke." *Am Pol Sci Rev,* 53 (1959), 1101–1104.

168 BECKER, Carl. *The Heavenly City of the Eighteenth Century Philosophers.* New Haven, 1961.

169 CHESNIN, Harold, and Geoffrey C. HAZARD, Jr. "Chancery Procedures and the Seventh Amendment: Jury Trial of Issues in Equity Before 1791." *Yale L J,* 83 (1974), 999–1021.

170 CORWIN, Edward S. *The "Higher Law" Background of American Constitutional Law.* Ithaca, N.Y., 1955.

171 DUMBAULD, Edward. "State Precedents for the Bill of Rights." *J Pub L,* 7 (1958), 323–344.

172 DWIGHT, Theodore D. "Harrington and His Influence upon American Political Institutions and Political Thought." *Pol Sci Q,* 2 (1887), 1–45.

173 FOSTER, H. D. "The Political Theory of Calvinists before the Puritan Exodus to America." *Am Hist Rev,* 21 (1916), 481–503.

174 GOOCH, G. P. *The History of English Democratic Ideas in the Seventeenth Century.* Cambridge, England, 1898.

175 GOUGH, J. W. "Harrington and Contemporary Thought." *Pol Sci Q,* 45 (1930), 395–404.

176 GOUGH, J. W. *John Locke's Political Philosophy.* Oxford, 1950.

ORIGINS

177 GREENE, Jack P. "Political Nemesis: A Consideration of the Historical and Cultural Roots of Legislative Behavior of the British Colonies in the Eighteenth Century." *Am Hist Rev,* 75 (1969), 337–360.

178 HARRINGTON, James. *The Commonwealth of Oceana.* London, 1777.

179 HASTINGS, William G. "Montesquieu and Anglo-American Institutions." *Ill L Rev,* 13 (1918–1919), 419–430.

180 HOOKER, Thomas. *Survey of the Summe of Church Discipline.* London, 1648.

181 HOWARD, A. E. Dick. *Road from Runnymede: Magna Carta and Constitutionalism in America.* Charlottesville, Va., 1968.

182 JUDSON, Margaret. *The Crisis of the Constitution: An Essay in Constitutional and Political Thought in England, 1603–1645.* New York, 1964 (reprint of 1949 ed.).

183 KAMMEN, Michael. *People of Paradox: An Inquiry Concerning the Origins of American Civilization.* New York, 1972.

184 KATZ, Stanley N. "The Origins of American Constitutional Thought." *Perspectives in American History,* 3 (1969), 474–490.

185 KENDALL, Willmoore, and George W. CAREY. *Basic Symbols of the American Political Tradition.* Baton Rouge, La., 1970.

186 LEAVELLE, Arnaud B. "James Wilson and the Relation of the Scottish Metaphysics to American Political Thought." *Pol Sci Q,* 57 (1942), 394–410.

187 LOCKE, John. *Two Treatises of Government.* Ed. Thomas I. Cook. New York, 1947.

188 McILWAIN, Charles H. "Due Process of Law in Magna Charta." *Colum L Rev,* 14 (1914), 27–51.

189 McKEON, R. "The Development of the Concept of Property in Political Philosophy: A Study of the Background of the Constitution." *Ethics,* 48 (1938), 297–366.

190 MacPHERSON, C. *The Political Theory of Possessive Individualism: Hobbes to Locke.* Oxford, 1962.

191 DE MONTESQUIEU, Charles-Louis de Secondat. *The Spirit of the Laws.* (Thomas Nugent, tr.) 4th ed. London, 1766.

192 MULFORD, Elisha. *The Nation: The Foundations of Civil Order and Political Life in the United States.* New York, 1870.

193 PALLISTER, Anne. *Magna Carta: The Heritage of Liberty.* Oxford, 1971.

194 PHILLIPS, N. C. "Political Philosophy and Political Fact: The Evidence of John Locke." *Liberty and Learning: Essays in Honor of Sir James Hight.* Christchurch, New Zealand, 1950.

195 POOKE, Florence A. *Fountain-Sources of American Political Theory, a Study of the Origin and Meaning of the Democratic Political Theories in the American Declaration of Independence.* New York, 1930.

196 ROSSITER, Clinton. *Seedtime of the Republic: The Origin of the American Tradition of Political Liberty.* New York, 1953.

197 SABINE, George. *A History of Political Theory.* New York, 1937.

198 SANDOZ, Ellis. "The Civil Theology of Liberal Democracy: Locke and His Predecessors." *J Pol,* 34 (1972), 2–36.

199 SARTORI, Giovanni. *Democratic Theory.* New York, 1965.

200 SCHUYLER, Robert L. *Parliament and the British Empire.* New York, 1929.

201 SMITH, H. F. Russell. *Harrington and His Oceana: A Study of a 17th Century Utopia and Its Influence in America.* Cambridge, England, 1914.

202 SPURLIN, Paul Merrill. *Montesquieu in America, 1760–1801.* Baton Rouge, La., 1940.

203 SWINDLER, William F. *Magna Carta: Legend and Legacy.* Indianapolis, 1967.

204 VAN CAENEGEM, R. C. *Birth of the English Common Law.* Cambridge, England, 1973.

205 WOODHOUSE, A. S., ed. *Puritanism and Liberty, being the Army Debates (1647–1649) from Clarke Manuscripts with Supplementary Documents.* London, 1938.

206 WORMUTH, Francis. *The Origins of Modern Constitutionalism.* New York, 1948.

207 WRIGHT, Benjamin F. "The Early History of Written Constitutions in America." *Essays in History and Political Theory in Honor of C. H. McIlwain.* Cambridge, Mass., 1936.

III. Political, Social, Economic, and Intellectual Context

A. General

208 ALLEN, Walter. *The Urgent West; The American Dream and the Common Man.* New York, 1969.

209 BASKIN, Darryl. "American Pluralism: Theory, Practice, and Ideology." *J Pol,* 32 (1970), 71–95.

210 BELL, Daniel. *Marxian Socialism in the United States.* Princeton, N.J., 1967.

211 BENSON, Lee. *Turner and Beard: American Historical Writing Reconsidered.* Glencoe, Ill., 1960.

212 BENTLEY, Arthur F. *The Process of Government.* Chicago, 1908.

213 BERNSTEIN, Marver H. *Regulating Business by Independent Commission.* Princeton, N.J., 1955.

214 BERTHOFF, Rowland. *An Unsettled People: Social Order and Disorder in American History.* New York, 1971.

215 BLAISDELL, Donald C. *Government and Agriculture: The Growth of Federal Farm Aid.* New York, 1940.

216 BOK, Derek C., and John T. DUNLOP. *Labor and the American Community.* New York, 1970.

217 BONNIE, Richard J., and Charles H. WHITEBREAD, II. "The Forbidden Fruit and the Tree of Knowledge: An Inquiry into the Legal History of American Marijuana Prohibition." *Va L Rev,* 56 (1970), 971–1203.

CONTEXT

218 BOORSTIN, Daniel. *The Americans.* 3 vols. New York, 1958–1973.

219 BOORSTIN, Daniel. *The Genius of American Politics.* Chicago, 1953.

220 BRADY, Robert A. *Business as a System of Power.* New York, 1947.

221 BROWN, Harrison. *The Challenge of Man's Future.* New York, 1954.

222 BULLOCK, Henry A. *A History of Negro Education in the South: From 1619 to the Present.* Cambridge, Mass., 1967.

223 BURNHAM, James. *The Managerial Revolution.* New York, 1941.

224 CAMPBELL, Angus, *et al. The American Voter.* New York, 1960.

225 CLARK, Thomas D., and Albert D. KIRWAN. *The South Since Appomattox.* New York, 1967.

226 COMMAGER, Henry Steele. *The American Mind: An Interpretation of American Thought and Character since the 1880's.* New Haven, 1950.

227 CRAVEN, Avery O. *Democracy in American Life.* Chicago, 1941.

228 CURTI, Merle. *Growth of American Thought.* New York, 1943.

229 DAHL, Robert A. *A Preface to Democratic Theory.* Chicago, 1956.

230 DESVERNINE, Raoul E. *Democratic Despotism.* New York, 1936.

231 DIETZE, Gottfried. *In Defense of Property.* Baltimore, 1971.

232 DIGGINS, John P. *The American Left in the Twentieth Century.* New York, 1973.

233 DIGGINS, John P. "Ideology and Pragmatism: Philosophy or Passion?" *Am Pol Sci Rev,* 64 (1970), 899–906.

234 DORSEN, Norman, and Stephen GILLERS. *None of Your Business; Government Secrecy in America.* New York, 1974.

235 DRAPER, Theodore. *The Roots of American Communism.* New York, 1963.

236 EATON, Clement. "The Jeffersonian Tradition of Liberalism in America." *S Atl Q,* 43 (1944), 1–10.

237 EISENSTEIN, James. *Politics and the Legal Process.* New York, 1973.

238 FERGUSSON, Harvey. *People and Power: A Study of Political Behavior in America.* New York, 1947.

239 FORD, Henry Jones. *Rise and Growth of American Politics.* New York, 1898.

240 FRANKEL, Charles. *The Case for Modern Man.* New York, 1956.

241 FRANKEL, Charles. *The Democratic Prospect.* New York, 1962.

242 FREUND, Paul A. *On Law and Justice.* Cambridge, Mass., 1968.

243 FRIEDMANN, Wolfgang. *The State and the Rule of Law in a Mixed Economy.* London, 1971.

244 GABRIEL, R. H. *The Course of American Democratic Thought.* New York, 1940.

245 GLAZER, Nathan. *The Social Bases of American Communism.* New York, 1961.

246 GLAZER, Nathan, and Daniel P. MOYNIHAN. *Beyond the Melting Pot.* Cambridge, Mass., 1963.

247 GOLDMAN, Eric F. *Rendezvous with Destiny: A History of Modern American Reform.* New York, 1952.

11

248 GOODRICH, Carter. *Government Regulation of American Canals and Railroads: 1800–1890.* New York, 1960.

249 GORER, Geoffrey. *The American People: A Study in National Character.* Rev. ed. New York, 1964.

250 GRAHAM, Hugh D., and Ted R. GURR. *Violence in America: Historical and Comparative Perspectives.* 2 vols. Washington, D.C., 1969.

251 GRISWOLD, A. Whitney. *Farming and Democracy.* New York, 1948.

252 GUSFIELD, Joseph R. *Symbolic Crusade: Status Politics and the American Temperance Movement.* Urbana, Ill., 1966.

253 HACKER, Louis M. *Alexander Hamilton in the American Tradition.* New York, 1957.

254 HALL, Thomas Cuming. *The Religious Background of American Culture.* Boston, 1930.

255 HAND, Learned. *The Spirit of Liberty. Papers and Addresses.* Ed. Irving Dilliard. New York, 1953.

256 HARTZ, Louis. *Economic Policy and Democratic Thought: Pennsylvania, 1776–1860.* Cambridge, Mass., 1948.

257 HARTZ, Louis. *The Liberal Tradition in America: An Interpretation of American Political Thought Since the Revolution.* New York, 1955.

258 HENDERSON, G. C. *The Position of Foreign Corporations in American Constitutional Law.* Cambridge, Mass., 1918.

259 HOFSTADTER, Richard. *The American Political Tradition and the Men Who Made It.* New York, 1948.

260 HOFSTADTER, Richard. *Anti-Intellectualism in American Life.* New York, 1963.

261 HOFSTADTER, Richard. *The Paranoid Style in American Politics.* New York, 1965.

262 HOOK, Sidney. *Political Power and Personal Freedom.* New York, 1962.

263 HOWE, Irving, and Levin COSER. *The American Communist Party.* New York, 1962.

264 HUNTINGTON, Samuel P. "Paradigms of American Politics: Beyond the One, the Two, and the Many." *Pol Sci Q,* 89 (1974), 1–26.

265 HURST, James Willard. *The Growth of American Law.* Boston, 1950.

266 HURST, James Willard. *Legitimacy of the Business Corporation in the Law of the United States, 1780–1970.* Charlottesville, Va., 1970.

267 HYMAN, Harold M., and Leonard W. LEVY, eds. *Freedom and Reform: Essays in Honor of Henry Steele Commager.* New York, 1967.

268 JORDAN, Winthrop D. *White over Black: American Attitudes Toward the Negro, 1550–1812.* Chapel Hill, N.C., 1968.

269 KAUPER, Paul G. "The Higher Law and the Rights of Man in a Revolutionary Society." *L Quad N,* 18 (winter 1974), 8–17.

270 KELLOGG, Charles Flint. *NAACP: A History of the National Association for the Advancement of Colored People.* Vol. 1. Baltimore, 1967.

271 LERNER, Max. *America as a Civilization.* New York, 1957.

272 LIPSET, Seymour Martin. *The First New Nation.* New York, 1963.

273 LIPSET, Seymour Martin. *Political Man: The Social Bases of Politics.* 1st ed. Garden City, N.Y., 1960.

274 LYND, Staughton. *Intellectual Origins of American Radicalism.* New York, 1968.

275 MALONE, Dumas. "The Relevance of Mr. Jefferson." *Va Q Rev,* 37 (1961), 332–349.

276 MARCUSE, Herbert, *et al. A Critique of Pure Tolerance.* Boston, 1966.

277 MARKMANN, Charles Lam. *The Noblest Cry: A History of the American Civil Liberties Union.* New York, 1965.

278 MASON, Alpheus T. *Free Government in the Making.* 3rd ed. New York, 1965.

279 MASON, Alpheus T. *Security Through Freedom.* Ithaca, N.Y., 1955.

280 MASON, Alpheus T., and Richard H. LEACH. *In Quest of Freedom: American Political Thought and Practice.* 2nd ed. New York, 1973.

281 MASON, Alpheus T., *et al. The Democratic Process: Lectures on the American Liberal Tradition.* New London, Conn., 1948.

282 MERRIAM, Charles E. *A History of American Political Theories.* New York, 1918.

283 MILL, J. S. *On Liberty.* Boston, 1921.

284 MILLER, Francis P., ed. *The Southern Press Considers the Constitution.* Chapel Hill, N.C., 1936.

285 MIRKIN, Harris G. "Judicial Review, Jury Review, and the Right of Revolution Against Despotism." *Polity,* 6 (1973), 36–70.

286 MITCHELL, William C. *The American Polity: A Social and Cultural Interpretation.* New York, 1962.

287 MORRIS, Clarence. "On Liberation and Liberty: Marcuse's and Mill's Essays Compared." *U Penn L Rev,* 118 (1970), 735–745.

288 PARRINGTON, Vernon L. *Main Currents in American Thought.* 3 vols. New York, 1927–1930.

289 PEKELIS, A. H. *Law and Social Action.* Ithaca, N.Y., 1950.

290 PETERSON, Merrill D. *The Jefferson Image in the American Mind.* New York, 1960.

291 POTTER, David M. *People of Plenty: Economic Abundance and American Character.* Chicago, 1954.

292 RHODES, James Ford. *History of the United States from the Compromise of 1850.* 8 vols. New York, 1886–1919.

293 ROBINSON, Donald L. *Slavery in the Structure of American Politics, 1765–1820.* New York, 1971.

294 ROSENBLUM, Victor. *Law as a Political Instrument.* Garden City, N.Y., 1955.

295 ROTTSCHAEFER, Henry. *The Constitution and Socio-Economic Change.* Ann Arbor, Mich., 1948.

296 RUMBLE, Wilfred E., Jr. *American Legal Realism: Skepticism, Reform, and the Judicial Process.* Ithaca, N.Y., 1968.

297 SCHLESINGER, Arthur M., Jr., and Morton G. WHITE, eds. *Paths of American Thought.* Boston, 1963.

298 SCHNEIDER, H. W. *A History of American Philosophy.* New York, 1946.

299 SPITZ, David. *Patterns of Anti-Democratic Thought.* New York, 1949.

300 STONE, Julius. *Legal Systems and Lawyers' Reasonings.* Stanford, Calif., 1964.

301 VAN RIPER, Paul P. *History of the United States Civil Service.* Evanston, Ill., 1958.

302 WALCUTT, Charles Child. "Thoreau in the Twentieth Century." *S Atl Q,* 39 (1940), 168–184.

303 WHITE, Morton G. *Social Thought in America.* New York, 1949.

304 WILSON, Francis G. "On Jeffersonian Tradition." *Rev Pol,* 5 (1943), 302–321.

305 WILTSE, Charles Maurice. *The Jeffersonian Tradition in American Democracy.* Chapel Hill, N.C., 1935.

306 WINDOLPH, Francis Lyman. *Leviathan and Natural Law.* Princeton, N.J., 1951.

307 WRIGHT, Benjamin F. "American Democracy and the Frontier." *Yale Rev,* 20 (1930), 349–365.

308 WRIGHT, Benjamin F. *American Interpretation of Natural Law.* Cambridge, Mass., 1931.

309 WRIGHT, Benjamin F., ed. *A Source Book of American Political Theory.* New York, 1929.

310 WRIGHT, Benjamin F. *Five Public Philosophies of Walter Lippmann.* Austin, Tex., 1973.

311 WRIGHT, Benjamin F. "The Philosopher of Jeffersonian Democracy." *Am Pol Sci Rev,* 22 (1928), 870–892.

312 YARMOLINSKY, Adam. *The Military Establishment: Its Impact on American Society.* New York, 1971.

313 YOUNG, Alfred M., ed. *Dissent: Explorations in the History of American Radicalism.* DeKalb, Ill., 1968.

B. 1607–1775

314 ADAMS, H. B. *Maryland's Influence upon Land Cessions to the United States.* Baltimore, 1877.

315 ANDREWS, Charles M. *The Colonial Period of American History.* 4 vols. New Haven, 1934–1938.

316 BASSETT, J. S. *The Constitutional Beginnings of North Carolina, 1663–1729.* Baltimore, 1894.

317 BILLAS, George A. *Law and Authority in Colonial America.* New York, 1965.

318 BREEN, Timothy H. *The Character of the Good Ruler: A Study of Puritan Political Ideas in New England, 1630–1730.* New Haven, 1970.

319 BREEN, Timothy H. "Who Governs: The Town Franchise in Seventeenth-Century Massachusetts." *Wm & M Q,* 27 (1970), 460–474.

320 BROWN, Robert E. *Middle-Class Democracy and the Revolution in Massachusetts, 1691–1780.* Ithaca, N.Y., 1955.

321 BROWN, Robert E., and Katherine BROWN. *Virginia: 1705–1788: Democracy or Aristocracy?* East Lansing, Mich., 1964.

322 CHAFEE, Zechariah, Jr. "Colonial Courts and the Common Law." *Proc Mass Hist Soc,* 68 (1944), 132–159.

323 CLARKE, Mary P. *Parliamentary Privilege in the American Colonies.* New Haven, 1943.

324 COTTON, John. *The Way of the Churches in New England.* London, 1645.

325 CRAVEN, Wesley Frank. *The Colonies in Transition, 1660–1713.* New York, 1967.

326 CRAVEN, Wesley Frank. *Dissolution of the Virginia Company; The Failure of a Colonial Experiment.* New York, 1932.

327 CRAVEN, Wesley Frank. *White, Red, and Black: The Seventeenth-Century Virginian.* Charlottesville, Va., 1971.

328 CUSHING, H. A. *History of the Transition from Provincial to Commonwealth Government in Massachusetts.* New York, 1896.

329 ERNST, James E. *The Political Thought of Roger Williams.* Seattle, Wash., 1929.

330 FLAHERTY, David H. *Essays in the History of Early American Law.* Chapel Hill, N.C., 1969.

331 FLAHERTY, David H. *Privacy in Colonial New England.* Charlottesville, Va., 1972.

332 FONER, Philip S. *The Life and Major Writings of Tom Paine.* New York, 1969.

333 GIPSON, L. H. *The British Empire before the American Revolution. Vol. XII: The Triumphant Empire: Britain Sails into the Storm.* New York, 1965.

334 GIPSON, L. H. *The British Empire before the American Revolution. Vol. XI: The Triumphant Empire: Rumblings of the Coming Storm.* New York, 1965.

335 GIPSON, L. H. *The British Empire before the American Revolution. Vol. X: The Triumphant Empire: Thunderclouds Gather in the West, 1763–1776.* New York, 1961.

336 GIPSON, L. H. *The Coming of the Revolution, 1763–1775.* New York, 1962.

337 HASKINS, George Lee. *Law and Authority in Early Massachusetts; A Study in Tradition and Design.* New York, 1960.

338 *Justices and Juries in Colonial America: Two Accounts, 1680–1722.* New York, 1972.

339 KELLOGG, Louise P. "The American Colonial Charter." *Rep Am Hist Assoc,* 1 (1903).

340 KNOLLENBERG, Bernard. *Origins of the American Revolution, 1759–1766.* New York, 1965.

341 LABAREE, L. W. *Royal Government in America.* New Haven, 1930.

342 LOKKEN, Roy N. "The Concept of Democracy in Colonial Political Thought." *Wm & M Q,* 16 (1959), 568–580.

343 MAIER, Pauline. "Popular Uprisings and Civil Authority in Eighteenth-Century America." *Wm & M Q,* 27 (1970), 3–35.

344 MERRITT, Richard L. *Symbols of American Community, 1736–1775.* New Haven, 1966.

345 MIDDLEKAUFF, Robert. *The Mathers: Three Generations of Puritan Intellectuals, 1596–1728.* New York, 1971.

346 MILLER, Perry. *The New England Mind: From Colony to Province.* Cambridge, Mass., 1953.

347 MILLER, Perry, and Thomas H. JOHNSON. *The Puritans.* New York, 1938.

348 MORGAN, Edmund S. *The Puritan Dilemma.* Boston, 1958.

349 MORGAN, Edmund S., and Helen M. MORGAN. *The Stamp Act Crisis: Prologue to Revolution.* Chapel Hill, N.C., 1953.

350 MORRIS, Lloyd R. *The Rebellious Puritan.* Boston, 1958.

351 MORRIS, Richard B. *Studies in the History of American Law, with Special Reference to the Seventeenth and Eighteenth Centuries.* New York, 1930.

352 MULLETT, C. F. *Fundamental Law and the American Revolution, 1760–1776.* New York, 1933.

353 OSGOOD, Herbert L. *The American Colonies in the Eighteenth Century.* 4 vols. New York, 1924.

354 OSGOOD, Herbert L. *The American Colonies in the Seventeenth Century.* 3 vols. New York, 1904–1907.

355 OSGOOD, Herbert L. "The Political Ideas of the Puritans." *Pol Sci Q,* 6 (1891), 1–28.

356 OTIS, James. "The Rights of the British Colonies (1764)." *U Mo Stud,* 4 (1929), 49–91.

357 PAINE, Thomas. *Complete Works.* 3 vols. Boston, 1859.

358 PERRY, Ralph Barton. *Puritanism and Democracy.* New York, 1944.

359 POLE, J. R. *Political Representation in England and the Origins of the American Revolution.* New York, 1966.

360 POMFRET, John E. *Founding the American Colonies, 1583–1660.* New York, 1970.

361 ROSENMEIER, Jesper. "The Teacher and the Witness: John Cotton and Roger Williams." *Wm & M Q,* 25 (1968), 408–431.

362 RUSSELL, Elmer B. *The Review of American Colonial Legislation by the King in Council.* New York, 1915.

363 SCHNEIDER, H. W. *The Puritan Mind.* New York, 1930.

364 SHEPHERD, William R. *History of Proprietary Government in Pennsylvania.* New York, 1896.

365 SYNDOR, Charles S. *Gentlemen Freeholders.* Chapel Hill, N.C., 1952.

366 TREVELYAN, George M. *England under the Stuarts.* 12th ed. London, 1925.

367 WASHBURNE, George A. *Imperial Control of the Administration of Justice in the Thirteen American Colonies, 1684–1776.* New York, 1923.

368 WERTENBAKER, T. J. *Give Me Liberty; The Struggle for Self-Government in Virginia.* Philadelphia, 1958.

369 WERTENBAKER, T. J. *The Puritan Oligarchy: The Founding of American Civilization.* New York, 1947.

370 WISE, John. *A Vindication of the Government of New England Churches.* Boston, 1777.

371 ZUCKERMAN, Michael. *Peaceable Kingdoms: New England Towns in the Eighteenth Century.* New York, 1970.

C. 1775–1790

372 ADAIR, Douglass. "The Authorship of the Disputed Federalist Papers." *Wm & M Q,* 1 (1944), 97–122, 235–264.

373 ADAIR, Douglass. "The Tenth Federalist Revisited." *Wm & M Q,* 8 (1951), 48–67.

374 ADAMS, John. *A Defense of the Constitutions of Government of the United States of America.* 3 vols. London, 1787–1788.

375 ADAMS, John. *Papers.* Eds. Lyman H. Butterfield *et al.* Cambridge, Mass., 1961–.

376 ADAMS, R. G. *Political Ideas of the American Revolution.* Durham, N.C., 1922.

377 ALDEN, John Richard. *The American Revolution, 1775–1783.* New York, 1954.

378 BAILYN, Bernard. *The Ideological Origins of the American Revolution.* Cambridge, Mass., 1967.

379 BALDWIN, Alice. *The New England Clergy and the American Revolution.* Durham, N.C., 1928.

380 BANCROFT, George. *History of the Formation of the Constitution of the United States.* 2 vols. New York, 1882.

381 BANNING, Lance. "Republican Ideology and the Triumph of the Constitution, 1789 to 1793." *Wm & M Q,* 31 (1974), 167–188.

382 BATES, F. G. *Rhode Island and the Formation of the Union.* New York, 1898.

383 BEARD, Charles A. *An Economic Interpretation of the Constitution of the United States.* New York, 1935 (reprint of 1913 ed.).

384 BECKER, Carl. *The Declaration of Independence.* New York, 1922.

385 BELOFF, Max, ed. *The Debate on the American Revolution, 1761–1783. A Sourcebook.* New York, 1960 (reprint of 1949 ed.).

386 BIRKBY, Robert H. "Politics of Accommodation: The Origin of the Supremacy Clause." *West Pol Q,* 19 (1966), 123–135.

387 BOWEN, Catherine Drinker. *Miracle at Philadelphia. Story of the Constitutional Convention, May to September 1787.* Boston, 1966.

388 BOYD, Julian P. *The Articles of Confederation and Perpetual Union.* Boston, 1960.

389 BOYD, Julian P. *The Declaration of Independence. The Evolution of the Text as Shown in Facsimiles of Various Drafts by Its Author, Thomas Jefferson.* Princeton, N.J., 1945.

390 BOYD, Julian P. "Thomas Jefferson's 'Empire of Liberty.' " *Va Q Rev,* 24 (1948), 538–555.

391 BRADLEY, Harold W. "The Political Thinking of George Washington." *J So Hist,* 11 (1945), 469–486.

392 BRODIE, Fawn M. *Thomas Jefferson: An Intimate History.* New York, 1974.

393 BROWN, Robert E. *Reinterpretation of the Formation of the American Constitution.* Boston, 1963.

394 BROWN, William G. *The Life of Oliver Ellsworth.* New York, 1970 (reprint of 1905 ed.).

395 BURNETT, E. C. *The Continental Congress.* New York, 1941.

396 BURNETT, E. C., ed. *Letters of Members of the Continental Congress.* 8 vols. Washington, D.C., 1921–1936.

397 BURNS, E. M. *James Madison, Philosopher of the Constitution.* New Brunswick, N.J., 1938.

398 CHAFEE, Zechariah, Jr. *Three Human Rights in the Constitution of 1787.* Lawrence, Kan., 1956.

399 CLARKSON, Paul S., and R. Samuel JETT. *Luther Martin of Maryland.* Baltimore, 1970.

400 CONNER, Paul. *Poor Richard's Politicks: Benjamin Franklin and His New American Order.* New York, 1965.

401 COOKE, Jacob E. "The Compromise of 1790." *Wm & M Q,* 27 (1970), 523–546.

402 COOLIDGE, A. C. *Theoretical and Foreign Elements in the Formation of the American Constitution.* Freiburg, Germany, 1892.

403 CORWIN, Edward S. "The Progress of Constitutional Theory between the Declaration of Independence and the Meeting of the Philadelphia Convention." *Am Hist Rev,* 30 (1925), 511–536.

404 CRARY, Catherine S., ed. *The Price of Loyalty; Tory Writings from the Revolutionary Era.* New York, 1973.

405 DANA, W. F. "The Declaration of Independence as Justification for Revolution." *Harv L Rev,* 13 (1900), 319–343.

406 DIAMOND, Martin. "Democracy and the Federalist: A Reconsideration of the Framers' Intent." *Am Pol Sci Rev,* 53 (1959), 52–68.

407 DICKERSON, O. M. "Writs of Assistance as a Cause of Revolution." *The Era of the American Revolution; Studies Subscribed to Evarts B. Greene.* Ed. Richard B. Morris. New York, 1939.

408 DICKINSON, John. *John Dickinson's Farmer's Letters.* Philadelphia, 1801.

409 DIETZE, Gottfried. *The Federalist: A Classic on Federalism and Free Government.* Baltimore, 1960.

410 DONAHOE, Bernard, and Marshall SMELSER. "The Congressional Power to Raise Armies: The Constitutional and Ratifying Conventions, 1787–1788." *Rev Pol,* 33 (1971), 202–211.

411 DOUGLASS, E. P. *Rebels and Democrats: The Struggle for Equal Political Rights and Majority Rule During the American Revolution.* Chapel Hill, N.C., 1955.

412 DUMBAULD, Edward. *The Declaration of Independence and What It Means Today.* Norman, Okla., 1950.

413 DUNBAR, Louise B. *A Study of "Monarchical" Tendencies in the United States from 1776 to 1801.* Urbana, Ill., 1922.

414 EIDELBERG, Paul. *The Philosophy of the American Constitution. A Reinterpretation of the Intentions of the Founding Fathers.* New York, 1968.

415 EISELEN, Malcolm Rogers. *Franklin's Political Theories.* Garden City, N.Y. 1928.

416 ELKINS, Stanley M., and Eric McKITRICK. "The Founding Fathers: Young Men of the Revolution." *Pol Sci Q,* 76 (1961), 181–216.

417 ELLIOTT, Jonathan, ed. *The Debates, Resolutions, and Other Proceedings in Convention on the Adoption of the Federal Constitution.* 5 vols. Washington, D.C., 1836.

418 FARRAND, Max. *The Framing of the Constitution.* New Haven, 1913.

419 FARRAND, Max, ed. *The Records of the Federal Convention of 1787.* 4 vols. New Haven, 1966.

420 FISKE, John. *The Critical Period of American History.* Boston, 1888.

421 FLEXNER, James Thomas. *George Washington.* 4 vols. Boston, 1965–1972. (One-vol. ed., Boston, 1974.)

422 FORD, Paul Leicester, ed. *Essays on the Constitution of the United States Published During Its Discussion by the People, 1787–1788.* New York, 1970 (reprint of 1892 ed.).

423 FORD, Paul Leicester, ed. *Pamphlets on the Constitution of the United States Published During Its Discussion by the People, 1787–1788.* New York, 1968 (reprint of 1888 ed.).

424 FRANKLIN, Benjamin. *Papers.* Eds. L. W. Labaree, *et al.* Vols. 1–14. New Haven, 1959–1970. Eds. W. B. Willcox, *et al.* Vols. 15–. New Haven, 1971–.

425 HAMILTON, Alexander. *Papers.* Eds. Harold C. Syrett and J. E. Cooke. New York, 1961–.

426 HAMILTON, Alexander, James MADISON, and John JAY. *The Federalist.* Ed. Max Beloff. New York, 1948.

427 HANDLIN, Oscar. *The Popular Sources of Political Authority: Documents on the Massachusetts Constitution of 1780.* Cambridge, Mass., 1966.

428 HARTZ, Louis. "American Political Thought and the American Revolution." *Am Pol Sci Rev,* 46 (1952), 321–342.

429 HENLINE, Ruth. "A Study of Notes on the State of Virginia as an Evidence of Jefferson's Reaction Against the Theories of the French Naturalists." *Va Mag Hist & Biog,* 55 (1947), 233–246.

430 HUNT, Gaillard. *The Life of James Madison.* New York, 1902.

431 JAMESON, J. Franklin, ed. *Essays in the Constitutional History of the United States in the Formative Period, 1775–1789.* Boston, 1889.

432 JENSEN, Merrill. *Articles of Confederation: An Interpretation of the Social-Constitutional History of the American Revolution.* Madison, Wis., 1963.

433 JENSEN, Merrill. *The Founding of a Nation: A History of the American Revolution, 1763–1776.* New York, 1968.

434 JENSEN, Merrill. *The New Nation: A History of the United States During the Confederation, 1781–1789.* New York, 1950.

435 JOHNSTON, Henry P., ed. *The Correspondence and Public Papers of John Jay.* New York, 1971 (reprint of 1890–1893 ed.).

436 KENYON, Cecelia M., ed. *The Anti-Federalists.* Indianapolis, 1966.

CONTEXT

437 KENYON, Cecelia M. "Men of Little Faith: The Anti-Federalists on the Nature of Representative Government." *Wm & M Q,* 12 (1955), 3–43.

438 KIMBALL, Marie. *Jefferson. War and Peace, 1776 to 1784.* New York, 1947.

439 KOCH, Adrienne. *Jefferson and Madison: The Great Collaboration.* New York, 1964 (reprint of 1950 ed.).

440 KOCH, Adrienne. *The Philosophy of Thomas Jefferson.* New York, 1943.

441 KOCH, Adrienne, and Harry AMMON. "The Virginia and Kentucky Resolutions: An Episode in Jefferson's and Madison's Defense of Civil Liberties." *Wm & M Q,* 5 (1948), 145–176.

442 LACY, Dan. *The Meaning of the American Revolution.* New York, 1966.

443 LEHMANN, Karl. *Thomas Jefferson, American Humanist.* New York, 1947.

444 McDONALD, Forrest. *E Pluribus Unum: The Formation of the American Republic, 1776–1790.* Boston, 1965.

445 McDONALD, Forrest. *We the People: The Economic Origins of the Constitution.* Chicago, 1958.

446 McILWAIN, Charles H. *The American Revolution: A Constitutional Interpretation.* New York, 1923.

447 McLAUGHLIN, Andrew C. *The Confederation and the Constitution.* New York, 1905.

448 McMASTER, J. B., and F. D. STONE. *Pennsylvania and the Federal Constitution, 1787–1788.* Philadelphia, 1888.

449 MADISON, James. *Notes of Debates in the Federal Convention of 1787.* Athens, Ohio, 1966.

450 MADISON, James. *Papers.* Ed. William T. Hutchinson. Vols. 1–7. Chicago, 1962–1971. Eds. Robert A. Rutland and William M. Rachal. Vols. 8–. Chicago, 1973–.

451 MAIN, Jackson Turner. *The Antifederalists: Critics of the Constitution, 1781–1788.* Chapel Hill, N.C., 1961.

452 MARKS, Frederick W., III. *Independence on Trial. Foreign Affairs and the Making of the Constitution.* Baton Rouge, La., 1973.

453 MARSHALL, John. *The Life of George Washington.* 5 vols. London, 1804–1807.

454 MARTIN, Luther. *The Genuine Information. . . .* Philadelphia, 1788.

455 MASON, Alpheus T. "The Federalist—A Split Personality." *Am Hist Rev,* 57 (1952), 625–643.

456 MASON, Alpheus T. *The States Rights Debate: Antifederalism and the Constitution.* 2nd ed. New York, 1972.

457 MILLER, John C. *Alexander Hamilton: Portrait in Paradox.* New York, 1959.

458 MILLER, John C. *Origins of the American Revolution.* Boston, 1943.

459 MITCHELL, Broadus. *Alexander Hamilton, Youth to Maturity, 1755–1788.* New York, 1957.

460 MITCHELL, Broadus. *Heritage from Hamilton.* New York, 1957.

461 MITCHELL, Broadus, and Louise P. MITCHELL. *Biography of the Constitution of the United States: Its Origins, Formation, Adoption, Interpretation.* New York, 1964.

462 MORISON, Samuel E. "Elbridge Gerry, Gentleman-Democrat." *N Eng Q,* 2 (1929), 6–33.

463 MORRIS, Richard B. *Alexander Hamilton and the Founding of the Nation.* New York, 1957.

464 MORRIS, Richard B., ed. *The Constitution Reconsidered.* New York, 1938.

465 MURPHY, William P. *The Triumph of Nationalism. State Sovereignty, the Founding Fathers, and the Making of the Constitution.* Chicago, 1967.

466 NELSON, William H. *The American Tory.* Oxford, 1961.

467 NEVINS, Allan. *The American States During and After the Revolution, 1775–1789.* New York, 1924.

468 NORTON, Mary Beth. "John Randolph's 'Plan of Accommodations.' " *Wm & M Q,* 28 (1971), 103–120.

469 OHLINE, Howard A. "Republicanism and Slavery: Origins of the Three-Fifths Clause in the United States Constitution." *Wm & M Q,* 28 (1971), 563–584.

470 OLIVER, Frederick Scott. *Alexander Hamilton, an Essay on American Union.* New York, 1907.

471 PIERCE, William L. "Notes on the Federal Convention of 1787." *Am Hist Rev,* 3 (1898), 310–334.

472 ROCHE, John P. "The Founding Fathers: A Reform Caucus in Action." *Am Pol Sci Rev,* 55 (1961), 799–816.

473 ROGOW, Arnold A. "The Federal Convention: Madison and Yates." *Am Hist Rev,* 60 (1955), 323–335.

474 ROSSITER, Clinton. *Alexander Hamilton and the Constitution.* New York, 1964.

475 ROSSITER, Clinton. *1787. The Grand Convention.* New York, 1968.

476 ROWLAND, Kate Mason. *The Life of George Mason.* 2 vols. New York, 1892.

477 RUTLAND, Robert A. *Birth of the Bill of Rights, 1776–1791.* Chapel Hill, N.C., 1955.

478 RUTLAND, Robert A. *The Ordeal of the Constitution: The Antifederalists and the Ratification Struggle of 1787–1788.* Norman, Okla., 1966.

479 RUTLAND, Robert A., ed. *The Papers of George Mason, 1725–1792.* 3 vols. Chapel Hill, N.C., 1970.

480 SCHACHNER, Nathan. *Alexander Hamilton.* New York, 1946.

481 SCHACHNER, Nathan. *The Founding Fathers.* New York, 1954.

482 SMITH, Edward P. "The Movement Toward a Second Constitutional Convention." *Essays in the Constitutional History of the United States.* Ed. J. F. Jameson. Boston, 1889.

483 SMYTH, Albert H., ed. *The Writings of Benjamin Franklin.* 10 vols. New York, 1905–1907.

484 STOURZH, Gerald. *Alexander Hamilton and the Idea of Republican Government.* Stanford, Calif., 1970.

485 STRAYER, Joseph R., ed. *The Delegate from New York, or, Proceedings of the Federal Convention of 1787, from the Notes of John Lansing, Jr.* Princeton, N.J., 1939.

486 TRENHOLME, L. I. *Ratification of the Federal Constitution in North Carolina.* New York, 1932.

487 TYLER, Moses Cort. *The Literary History of the American Revolution.* New York, 1897.

488 VAN DOREN, Carl. *The Great Rehearsal: The Story of the Making and Ratifying of the Constitution of the United States.* New York, 1948.

489 VAN TYNE, C. H. *History of the American Revolution, 1776–1783.* New York, 1905.

490 WALSH, C. M. *The Political Science of John Adams: A Study in the Theory of Mixed Government and Bicameral System.* New York, 1915.

491 WARREN, Charles. *The Making of the Constitution.* Cambridge, Mass., 1929.

492 WOOD, Gordon. *The Creation of the American Republic, 1776–1787.* Chapel Hill, N.C., 1969.

493 WRIGHT, Benjamin F. *Consensus and Continuity, 1776–1787.* Boston, 1958.

494 WRIGHT, Benjamin F. "*The Federalist* on the Nature of Political Man." *Ethics,* 59 (1949), 1–31.

495 ZAHNISER, M. R. *Charles Cotesworth Pinckney: Founding Father.* Chapel Hill, N.C., 1967.

D. 1790–1860

496 AARON, Daniel. *Men of Good Hope.* New York, 1951.

497 ABERNETHY, Thomas P. *The Burr Conspiracy.* New York, 1954.

498 ADAMS, Alice Dana. *The Neglected Period of Anti-Slavery in America, 1808–1831.* Boston, 1908.

499 ADAMS, Charles Francis, ed. *The Works of John Adams.* 10 vols. Boston, 1850–1856.

500 ADAMS, Henry. *History of the United States of America.* 9 vols. New York, 1909–1917.

501 ADAMS, John Quincy. *An Eulogy on the Life and Character of James Madison. Delivered in Boston, September 27, 1836.* Boston, 1836.

502 ADAMS, John Quincy. *The Jubilee of the Constitution. A Discourse Delivered April 30, 1839, Being the Fiftieth Anniversary of the Inauguration of General Washington.* New York, 1839.

503 AMMON, Harry. *James Monroe: The Quest for National Identity.* New York, 1971.

504 ANGLE, Paul M., ed. *Created Equal? The Complete Lincoln-Douglas Debates of 1858.* Chicago, 1958.

505 AUSTIN, James T. *The Life of Elbridge Gerry.* Boston, 1829.

506 BAKER, Gordon E. "Thomas Jefferson and Academic Freedom." *Am Assoc U Prof Bull,* 39 (1953), 377–387.

507 BASSETT, J. S. *The Federalist System, 1789–1801.* New York, 1907.

508 BASSETT, J. S. *Life of Andrew Jackson.* 2 vols. Garden City, N.Y., 1911.

CONTEXT

BEATTY, Richmond C. "Whitman's Political Thought." *S Atl Q,* 46 (1947), 72–83.

510 BERKHOFER, Robert F., Jr. "Jefferson, The Ordinance of 1784, and the Origins of the American Territorial System." *Wm & M Q,* 29 (1972), 231–262.

511 BERNS, Walter. "The Constitution and the Migration of Slaves." *Yale L J,* 78 (1968), 198–228.

512 BESTOR, Arthur. "State Sovereignty and Slavery." *J Ill State Hist Soc,* 59 (1961), 117–180.

513 BLAU, Joseph L., ed. *Social Theories of Jacksonian Democracy: Representative Writings of the Period 1825–1850.* New York, 1947.

514 BLEDSOE, Albert T. *An Essay on Liberty and Slavery.* Philadelphia, 1856.

515 BOUCHER, C. S. *The Nullification Controversy in South Carolina.* Chicago, 1916.

516 BOWERS, Claude G. *Jefferson and Hamilton: The Struggle for Democracy.* Boston, 1925.

517 BOWERS, Claude G. *Jefferson in Power: The Death Struggle of the Federalists.* Boston, 1936.

518 BOWLES, John B. *The Great Revival, 1787–1805: The Origins of the Southern Evangelical Mind.* Lexington, Ky., 1972.

519 BRANT, Irving. *James Madison.* 6 vols. Indianapolis, 1941–1961.

520 BROOKS, Van Wyck. *The Life of Emerson.* New York, 1932.

521 BROOKS, Van Wyck. *The Times of Melville and Whitman.* New York, 1947.

522 BROWN, Everett S. *The Constitutional History of the Louisiana Purchase, 1803–1812.* Clifton, N.J., 1970 (reprint of 1920 ed.).

523 BROWNSON, Orestes A. "The Laboring Classes." *Bos Q Rev,* 3 (1840), 358–395, 420–512.

524 BRUCE, W. C. *John Randolph of Roanoke, 1773–1823.* 2 vols. New York, 1922.

525 BRUCHEY, Stuart. "Alexander Hamilton and the State Banks, 1789 to 1795." *Wm & M Q,* 27 (1970), 347–378.

526 BUEL, Richard, Jr. *Securing the Revolution: Ideology in American Politics, 1789–1815.* Ithaca, N.Y., 1972.

527 CARPENTER, Jesse T. *The South as a Conscious Minority.* New York, 1930.

528 CATTERALL, R. C. H. *The Second Bank of the United States.* Chicago, 1903.

529 CHANNING, Edward. *The Jeffersonian System, 1801–1811.* New York, 1907.

530 CHAPMAN, John Jay. "Emerson, Sixty Years After." *Atl Month,* 79 (1897), 222–240.

531 CHASE, Salmon Portland, and Charles Dexter CLEVELAND. *Anti-Slavery Addresses of 1844 and 1845.* London, 1867.

532 CLARK, B. C. *John Quincy Adams: "Old Man Eloquent."* Boston, 1933.

533 COMMAGER, Henry Steele. *Theodore Parker.* Boston, 1936.

534 CRAVEN, Avery O. "The 1840's and the Democratic Process." *J So Hist,* 16 (1950), 161–176.

535 CRESSON, William P. *James Monroe.* Chapel Hill, N.C., 1946.

23

536 CROWE, Charles. *George Ripley: Transcendentalist and Utopian Socialist.* Athens, Ga., 1967.

537 CURRENT, Richard N. *Daniel Webster and the Rise of National Conservatism.* Boston, 1955.

538 CURRENT, Richard N. *John C. Calhoun.* New York, 1966.

539 DANGERFIELD, George. *The Awakening of American Nationalism, 1815–1828.* New York, 1965.

540 DANGERFIELD, George. *The Era of Good Feelings.* London, 1953.

541 DANIELS, Jonathan. *Ordeal of Ambition: Jefferson, Hamilton, Burr.* Garden City, N.Y., 1970.

542 DAUER, Manning J. *The Adams Federalists.* Baltimore, 1953.

543 DAUER, Manning J., and Hans HAMMOND. "John Taylor: Democrat or Aristocrat?" *J Pol,* 6 (1944), 381–403.

544 DEW, Thomas R. *An Assay on Slavery.* 2nd ed. Richmond, Va., 1849.

545 DICKENS, Charles. *American Notes, 1841.* New York, 1908.

546 DODD, W. E. "John Taylor of Caroline, Prophet of Secession." *John P. Branch Historical Papers of Randolph-Macon College,* 2 (1908), 214–252.

547 DORFMAN, Joseph. *The Economic Mind in American Civilization, 1800–1865.* New York, 1946.

548 DUBERMAN, Martin, ed. *The Anti-Slavery Vanguard: New Essays on the Abolitionists.* Princeton, N.J., 1965.

549 DUMOND, Dwight Lowell. *Anti-Slavery: The Crusade for Freedom in America.* Ann Arbor, Mich., 1961.

550 DUMOND, Dwight Lowell. *The Secession Movement, 1860–1861.* New York, 1931.

551 EATON, Clement. *The Mind of the Old South.* Baton Rouge, La., 1964.

552 ELLIOTT, E. N., ed. *Cotton Is King, and Pro-Slavery Arguments.* Augusta, Ga., 1860.

553 EMERSON, R. W. *Lectures and Biographical Sketches.* Cambridge, Mass., 1883.

554 FAULKNER, Robert K. "John Marshall and the Burr Trial." *J Am Hist,* 53 (1966), 247–258.

555 FILLER, Louis. *The Crusade Against Slavery, 1830–1860.* New York, 1960.

556 FISHER, G. P. "Jefferson and the Social Compact Theory." *Rep Am Hist Assoc* (1893), 165–177. *Yale Rev,* 2 (1894), 403–417.

557 FITZHUGH, George. *Cannibals All!* Richmond, Va., 1857.

558 FREEHLING, William W. *Prelude to Civil War: The Nullification Controversy in South Carolina, 1816–1836.* New York, 1966.

559 FUESS, C. M. *Daniel Webster.* 2 vols. Boston, 1930.

560 GOVAN, T. P. *Nicholas Biddle, Nationalist and Public Banker, 1786–1844.* Chicago, 1959.

561 GRAY, Henry David. *Emerson: A Statement of New England Transcendentalism as Expressed in the Philosophy of Its Chief Exponent.* Stanford, Calif., 1917.

562 HAMILTON, Holman. *Prologue to Conflict: The Crisis and Compromise of 1850.* Lexington, Ky., 1964.

563 HAMMOND, Bray. *Banks and Politics in America, from the Revolution to the Civil War.* Princeton, N.J., 1957.

564 HART, Albert Bushnell. *Slavery and Abolition.* New York, 1906.

565 HEMPHILL, W. Edwin, ed. *The Papers of John C. Calhoun.* Columbia, S.C., 1959–.

566 HENSHAW, David. *Remarks upon the Rights and Powers of Corporations.* Boston, 1837.

567 HODDER, Frank H. "Some Phases of the Dred Scott Case." *Miss Val Hist Rev,* 16 (1929), 3–22.

568 HORTON, John T. *James Kent: A Study in Conservatism.* New York, 1939.

569 HURD, John C. *The Law of Freedom and Bondage in the United States.* New York, 1862.

570 HURST, James Willard. *Law and the Conditions of Freedom in the Nineteenth Century.* Madison, Wis., 1956.

571 JENKINS, W. S. *Pro-Slavery Thought in the Old South.* Chapel Hill, N.C., 1935.

572 JOHNSTON, James Hugo. *Race Relations in Virginia and Miscegenation in the South 1776–1860.* Amherst, Mass., 1970.

573 "Judge Spencer Roane of Virginia: Champion of States' Rights—Foe of John Marshall." *Harv L Rev,* 66 (1953), 1242–1259.

574 KERBER, Linda K. *Federalists in Dissent: Imagery and Ideology in Jeffersonian America.* Ithaca, N.Y., 1970.

575 KNOX, J. Wendell. *Conspiracy in American Politics, 1787–1815.* Chapel Hill, N.C., 1964.

576 KRUTCH, Joseph Wood. *Henry David Thoreau.* New York, 1948.

577 LEAVELLE, Arnaud B., and Thomas I. COOK. "George Fitzhugh and the Theory of American Conservatism." *J Pol,* 7 (1945), 145–168.

578 LEGARÉ, Hugh Swinton. "Review of Kent's Commentaries on American Law." *So Rev,* 2 (1828), 72–113.

579 LEGARÉ, Hugh Swinton. *Writings.* 2 vols. Charleston, S.C., 1845.

580 LIEBER, Francis. *Essays on Property and Labor.* New York, 1847.

581 LUMPKIN, Wilson. *Removal of the Cherokee Indians from Georgia.* 2 vols. New York, 1907.

582 LYND, Staughton. *Class Conflict, Slavery and the United States Constitution: Ten Essays.* Indianapolis, 1968.

583 McKITRICK, Eric, ed. *Slavery Defended: The Views of the Old South.* Englewood Cliffs, N.J., 1963.

584 McWILLIAMS, John P. *Political Justice in a Republic. James Fenimore Cooper's America.* Berkeley, Calif., 1972.

585 MADDEN, Edward H. *Civil Disobedience and Moral Law in Nineteenth Century American Philosophy.* Seattle, Wash., 1968.

586 MADISON, James. *The Virginia Report of 1799–1800 Touching the Alien and Sedition Laws. . . .* Richmond, Va., 1850.

587 MALIN, James C. *The Nebraska Question, 1852–1854.* Lawrence, Kans., 1953.

588 MATTHIESSEN, F. O. *American Renaissance: Art and Expression in the Age of Emerson and Whitman.* New York, 1941.

589 MENDELSON, Jack. *Channing, the Reluctant Radical.* Boston, 1971.

590 MEYERS, Marvin. *The Jacksonian Persuasion.* Stanford, Calif., 1957.

591 MILLER, John C. *The Federalist Era, 1789–1801.* New York, 1960.

592 MILLER, Perry, ed. *The Legal Mind in America. From Independence to the Civil War.* Garden City, N.Y., 1962.

593 MONROE, Haskell, Jr., and James T. McINTOSH, eds. *The Papers of Jefferson Davis.* Baton Rouge, La., 1971–.

594 MONROE, James. *The People the Sovereign: Being a Comparison of the Government of the United States with Those of the Republics Which Have Existed Before, with the Causes of Their Decadence and Fall.* Philadelphia, 1867.

595 MOODY, Marjory M. "The Evolution of Emerson as an Abolitionist." *Am Lit,* 17 (1945–1946), 1–21.

596 MORISON, Samuel E. *The Life and Letters of Harrison Gray Otis.* 2 vols. Boston, 1913.

597 MUDGE, Eugene T. *The Social Philosophy of John Taylor of Caroline.* New York, 1939.

598 NELSON, William E. "The Impact of the Antislavery Movement upon Styles of Judicial Reasoning in Nineteenth Century America." *Harv L Rev,* 87 (1974), 513–566.

599 PETERSON, Merrill D., ed. *Democracy, Liberty and Property: The State Constitutional Conventions of the 1820's.* Indianapolis, 1966.

600 POAGE, George. *Henry Clay and the Whig Party.* Chapel Hill, N.C., 1936.

601 POTTER, David M. *The South and the Concurrent Majority.* Baton Rouge, La., 1972.

602 PRIEST, Josiah. *Bible Defense of Slavery; and Origin, Fortunes, and History of the Negro Race.* 5th ed. Glasgow, Ky., 1852.

603 PRINCE, Carl E. "The Passing of the Aristocracy: Jefferson's Removal of the Federalists, 1801–1805." *J Am Hist,* 57 (1970), 563–575.

604 ROSSITER, Clinton. *The American Quest, 1790–1860: An Emerging Nation in Search of Identity, Unity, and Modernity.* New York, 1971.

605 ROURKE, Constance Mayfield. *Trumpets of Jubilee.* New York, 1927.

606 RUSSEL, Robert R. "Constitutional Doctrine with Regard to Slavery in the Territories." *J So Hist,* 32 (1966), 466–486.

607 RUSSEL, Robert R. "The Issues in the Congressional Struggle over the Kansas-Nebraska Bill." *J So Hist,* 29 (1963), 187–210.

608 SCHLESINGER, Arthur M., Jr. *The Age of Jackson.* Boston, 1945.

609 SEARS, Louis M. *Jefferson and the Embargo.* Durham, N.C., 1927.

610 "The Security of Private Property." *Am L Mag,* 1 (1843), 318–347.

611 *Selections from the Writings and Speeches of William Lloyd Garrison.* Boston, 1852.

612 SHOEMAKER, F. C. *Missouri's Struggle for Statehood, 1804–1821.* Jefferson City, Mo., 1916.

613 SIEBERT, W. H. *The Underground Railroad from Slavery to Freedom.* New York, 1898.

614 SKIDMORE, Thomas. *The Rights of Man to Property.* New York, 1829.

615 SMELSER, Marshall. *The Democratic Republic, 1801–1815.* New York, 1968.

616 SMITH, James Morton. "The Grass Roots Origins of the Kentucky Resolutions." *Wm & M Q,* 27 (1970), 221–245.

617 SMITH, T. C. *Parties and Slavery, 1850–1859.* New York and London, 1906.

618 SPAIN, August O. *The Political Theory of John C. Calhoun.* New York, 1951.

619 SPRAGUE, Marshall. *So Vast So Beautiful a Land; Louisiana and the Purchase.* Boston, 1974.

620 STARKEY, Marion L. *The Cherokee Nation.* New York, 1946.

621 STILL, Bayrd. "An Interpretation of the Statehood Process, 1800 to 1850." *Miss Val Hist Rev,* 23 (1936), 189–204.

622 SYNDOR, Charles S. *The Development of Southern Sectionalism, 1819–1848.* Baton Rouge, La., 1948.

623 TAYLOR, John. *Construction Construed and Constitutions Vindicated.* Richmond, Va., 1820.

624 TAYLOR, John. *New Views of the Constitution of the United States.* Washington, D.C., 1823.

625 THOMAS, John L. "Romantic Reform in America, 1815–1865." *Am Q,* 17 (1965), 656–681.

626 DE TOCQUEVILLE, Alexis. *Democracy in America.* (Henry Reeve, tr.) 2 vols. Boston, 1882.

627 TURNER, Kathryn. "Federalist Policy and the Judiciary Act of 1801." *Wm & M Q,* 22 (1965), 3–32.

628 UPSHUR, Abel P. *A Brief Inquiry into the True Nature and Character of Our Federal Government; Being a Review of Judge Story's Commentaries on the Constitution of the United States.* Petersburg, Va., 1840.

629 VAN DEUSEN, Glyndon G. *The Jacksonian Era, 1828–1848.* New York, 1959.

630 VAN DEUSEN, Glyndon G. *The Life of Henry Clay.* Boston, 1937.

631 WAINWRIGHT, Jonathan Mayhew. *Inequality of Individual Wealth, the Ordinance of Providence, and Essential to Civilization.* Boston, 1835.

632 WARD, J. W. *Andrew Jackson: Symbol for an Age.* New York, 1955.

633 WARFIELD, Ethelbert D. *The Kentucky Resolutions of 1798. An Historical Study.* New York, 1887.

634 WAYLAND, Francis. *The Elements of Moral Science.* New York, 1835.

635 WHARTON, Francis. *State Trials of the United States During the Administrations of Washington and Adams.* New York, 1970 (reprint of 1849 ed.).

636 WHITE, Leonard D. *The Federalists: A Study in Administration.* New York, 1948.

637 WHITE, Leonard D. *The Jacksonians: A Study in Administrative History.* New York, 1954.

638 WHITE, Leonard D. *The Jeffersonians: A Study in Administrative History, 1801–1829.* New York, 1951.

639 WILBURN, Jean Alexander. *Biddle's Bank; the Crucial Years.* New York, 1967.

640 WILSON, Major L. " 'Liberty and Union.' An Analysis of Three Concepts Involved in the Nullification Controversy." *J So Hist,* 33 (1967), 331–355.

641 WILTSE, Charles Maurice. *John C. Calhoun.* 3 vols. Indianapolis, 1944–1951.

642 WISH, Harvey. *George Fitzhugh: Propagandist of the Old South.* Baton Rouge, La., 1943.

643 WOOSTER, R. A. *The Secession Conventions of the South.* Princeton, N.J., 1962.

644 WRIGHT, Benjamin F. "Political Institutions and the Frontier." Ed. D. R. Fox. *Sources of Culture in the Middle West.* New York and London, 1934.

645 WROTH, L. K., and H. B. ZOBEL, eds. *Legal Papers of John Adams.* 3 vols. Cambridge, Mass., 1965.

646 YOUNG, J. S. *A Political and Constitutional Study of the Cumberland Road.* Chicago, 1904.

E. 1860–1877

647 BESTOR, Arthur. "The American Civil War as a Constitutional Crisis." *Am Hist Rev,* 69 (1964), 327–352.

648 BROCK, W. R. *An American Crisis: Congress and Reconstruction, 1865–1867.* New York, 1963.

649 BUCK, Paul H. *The Road to Reunion.* Boston, 1937.

650 BURGESS, John W. *Civil War and the Constitution, 1859–1865.* 2 vols. New York, 1901.

651 BURGESS, John W. *Reconstruction and the Constitution, 1866–1872.* New York, 1902.

652 COLE, A. C. "Lincoln's Election an Immediate Menace to Slavery in the States." *Am Hist Rev,* 36 (1931), 740–767.

653 CONKLING, A. R. *The Life and Letters of Roscoe Conkling.* New York, 1889.

654 "The Correspondence of Robert Toombs, Alexander H. Stephens, and Howell Cobb." *Rep Am Hist Assoc,* 2 (1911).

655 COULTER, E. Merton. *The Confederate States of America, 1861–1865.* Baton Rouge, La., 1951.

656 COULTER, E. Merton. *The South During Reconstruction, 1865–1877.* Baton Rouge, La., 1947.

657 CRAVEN, Avery O. *The Coming of the Civil War.* New York, 1942.

658 CRAVEN, Avery O. *Reconstruction: The Ending of the Civil War.* New York, 1969.

659 DAVIS, Jefferson. *The Rise and Fall of the Confederate Government.* 2 vols. New York, 1881.

660 DONALD, David. *An Excess of Democracy: The American Civil War and the Social Process.* Oxford, 1960.

661 DONALD, David. *Charles Sumner and the Rights of Man*. New York, 1970.

662 DONALD, David. *Lincoln Reconsidered: Essays on the Civil War Era*. New York, 1956.

663 DORRIS, J. T. *Pardon and Amnesty under Lincoln and Johnson: The Restoration of the Confederates to Their Rights and Privileges, 1861–1898*. Chapel Hill, N.C., 1953.

664 FLEMING, W. A. *Documentary History of Reconstruction*. 2 vols. Cleveland, Ohio, 1905–1907.

665 HARRIS, William C. *Presidential Reconstruction in Mississippi*. Baton Rouge, La., 1967.

666 HAWORTH, P. L. *The Hayes-Tilden Disputed Election of 1876*. Cleveland, Ohio, 1906.

667 HELPER, Hinton R. *The Impending Crisis of the South: How to Meet It*. New York, 1860.

668 HUME, Richard L. "The Arkansas Constitutional Convention of 1868: A Case Study in the Politics of Reconstruction." *J So Hist*, 39 (1973), 183–206.

669 HURD, John C. *The Theory of Our National Existence, as Shown by the Government of the United States Since 1861*. Boston, 1881.

670 HYMAN, Harold M. *A More Perfect Union. The Impact of the Civil War and Reconstruction on the Constitution*. New York, 1973.

671 HYMAN, Harold M. *The Era of the Oath: Northern Loyalty Tests during the Civil War and Reconstruction*. Philadelphia, 1954.

672 KENDRICK, Benjamin B. *The Journal of the Joint Committee of Fifteen on Reconstruction*. New York, 1914.

673 LEE, Charles Robert. *The Confederate Constitutions*. Chapel Hill, N.C., 1963.

674 LIEBER, Francis. *Two Lectures on the Constitution of the United States*. New York, 1861.

675 McKITRICK, Eric. *Andrew Johnson and Reconstruction*. Chicago, 1960.

676 McPHERSON, James H. *The Struggle for Equality: Abolitionists and the Negro in the Civil War and Reconstruction*. Princeton, N.J., 1964.

677 MILTON, George F. *Abraham Lincoln and the Fifth Column*. New York, 1942.

678 NEVINS, Allan. *The Emergence of Lincoln*. 2 vols. New York, 1950.

679 NEVINS, Allan. *The Emergence of Modern America, 1865–1878*. New York, 1928.

680 NEVINS, Allan. *Hamilton Fish: The Inner History of the Grant Administration*. New York, 1936.

681 NEVINS, Allan. *Ordeal of the Union*. 2 vols. New York, 1947.

682 PALUDAN, Phillip S. "The American Civil War Considered as a Crisis in Law and Order." *Am Hist Rev*, 77 (1972), 1013–1034.

683 PARKS, J. H. "State's Rights in a Crisis: Governor Joseph E. Brown versus President Jefferson Davis." *J So Hist*, 32 (1966), 3–24.

684 PATRICK, Rembert W. *The Reconstruction of the Nation*. New York, 1967.

685 POORE, B. P., ed. *The Conspiracy Trial for the Murder of the President, and the Attempt to Overthrow the Government by the Assassination of Its Principal Officers.* 3 vols. Boston, 1865–1866.

686 POTTER, David M. *Lincoln and His Party in the Secession Crisis.* New Haven, 1942.

687 RANDALL, J. G., and David DONALD. *The Civil War and Reconstruction.* 2nd ed. Lexington, Mass., 1969.

688 SANDBURG, Carl. *Abraham Lincoln: The War Years.* 4 vols. New York, 1939.

689 SMITH, George P. "Republican Reconstruction and Section Two of the Fourteenth Amendment." *West Pol Q.* (1970), 829–853.

690 STAMPP, Kenneth M. *The Era of Reconstruction, 1865–1877.* New York, 1965.

691 STEPHENS, Alexander H. *A Constitutional View of the Late War Between the States.* 2 vols. Philadelphia, 1868–1870.

692 STRODE, Hudson. *Jefferson Davis.* 3 vols. New York, 1955–1964.

693 TREFOUSSE, Hans L. *The Radical Republicans: Lincoln's Vanguard for Racial Justice.* New York, 1969.

694 WIECEK, William M. "The Great Writ and Reconstruction: The Habeas Corpus Act of 1867." *J So Hist,* 36 (1970), 530–548.

695 WILSON, Woodrow. "State Rights." *The Cambridge Modern History.* Eds. A. W. Ward, *et al.* Vol. VII. New York, 1907.

696 WOODWARD, C. Vann. *Reunion and Reaction: The Compromise of 1877 and the End of Reconstruction.* Boston, 1951.

F. 1877–1929

697 ADAMS, Brooks. *The Law of Civilization and Decay.* New York, 1896.

698 ADAMS, Brooks. *The Theory of Social Revolutions.* New York, 1913.

699 ALLEN, Frederick Lewis. *Only Yesterday: An Informal History of the Nineteen Twenties.* New York, 1931.

700 ANDERSON, Oscar E. "The Pure Food Issue: A Republican Dilemma, 1906–1912." *Am Hist Rev,* 61 (1956), 550–573.

701 BAKER, Ray Stannard. *Woodrow Wilson: Life and Letters.* 8 vols. Garden City, N.Y., 1927–1939.

702 BARNARD, Harry. *Rutherford B. Hayes and His America.* Indianapolis, 1954.

703 BELLAMY, Edward. *Looking Backward, 2000–1887.* New York, 1889.

704 BENSON, Lee. *Merchants, Farmers, and Railroads: Railroad Regulation and New York Politics, 1850–1887.* Cambridge, Mass., 1957.

705 BERMAN, Edward. *Labor and the Sherman Act.* New York, 1930.

706 BLUM, John M. *The Republican Roosevelt.* Boston, 1954.

707 BLUMBERG, Dorothy Rose. *Florence Kelley: The Making of a Social Pioneer.* New York, 1966.

708 BOURNE, Randolph. *Untimely Papers.* New York, 1947.

CONTEXT

709 BOWERS, Claude G. *Beveridge and the Progressive Era.* Boston, 1932.

710 BRAEMAN, John. *Albert J. Beveridge: American Nationalist.* Chicago, 1971.

711 BUCK, S. J. *The Granger Movement.* Cambridge, Mass., 1913.

712 CARNEGIE, Andrew. *The Gospel of Wealth and Other Timely Essays.* Ed. E. C. Kirkland. Cambridge, Mass., 1962.

713 CARNEGIE, Andrew. "Wealth." *N Am Rev,* 148 (1889), 654–664.

714 CHAMBERLAIN, John. *Farewell to Reform: Being a History of the Rise, Life and Decay of the Progressive Mind in America.* New York, 1932.

715 CLARK, John B. "Feudalism or Commonwealth." *Ind,* 54 (1902), 1275–1279.

716 COBEN, Stanley. *A. Mitchell Palmer: Politician.* New York, 1963.

717 COCHRAN, Thomas C., and William MILLER. *The Age of Enterprise.* New York, 1942.

718 COMMONS, John R., and John B. ANDREWS. *Principles of Labor Legislation.* New York, 1916.

719 CONWELL, Russell H. *Acres of Diamonds.* New York, 1915.

720 CROLY, Herbert. *Marcus Alonzo Hanna.* New York, 1912.

721 CROLY, Herbert. *Progressive Democracy.* New York, 1914.

722 CROLY, Herbert. *The Promise of American Life.* New York, 1909.

723 DAVIDSON, John Wells, ed. *A Crossroads of Freedom: The 1912 Campaign Speeches of Woodrow Wilson.* New Haven, 1956.

724 DESTLER, Chester McArthur. *American Radicalism, 1865–1901.* New London, Conn., 1946.

725 DILLON, John F. "Address of the President." *Rep Am Bar Assoc* (1892), 167–211.

726 DOS PASSOS, John. *U.S.A., The Big Money.* New York, 1930.

727 DUNNE, Finley Peter. *Dissertations by Mr. Dooley.* New York, 1906.

728 FAULKNER, Harold U. *Politics, Reform and Expansion, 1890–1900.* New York, 1959.

729 FAULKNER, Harold U. *The Quest for Social Justice, 1898–1914.* New York, 1931.

730 FAY, Charles N. *Business in Politics.* Cambridge, Mass., 1926.

731 FINE, Sidney. *Laissez-Faire and the General Welfare State: A Study of Conflict in American Thought, 1865–1901.* Ann Arbor, Mich., 1956.

732 FRAENKEL, O. K., ed. *The Curse of Bigness; Miscellaneous Papers of Louis D. Brandeis.* New York, 1934.

733 FULLER, R. G. *Child Labor and the Constitution.* New York, 1929.

734 GARRATY, John A. *The New Commonwealth, 1877–1890.* New York, 1968.

735 GEIGER, George Raymond. *The Philosophy of Henry George.* New York, 1933.

736 GEORGE, Henry. *Progress and Poverty.* New York, 1880.

737 GHENT, William J. "Benevolent Feudalism." *Ind,* 54 (1902), 781–788.

738 GHENT, William J. *Mass and Class: A Survey of Social Divisions.* New York, 1903.

739 GITLOW, Benjamin. *I Confess: The Truth about American Communism*. New York, 1940.

740 HARLAN, Louis R., and John W. BLASSINGAME, eds. *The Booker T. Washington Papers*. Urbana, Ill., 1972–.

741 HICKS, John D. *The Populist Revolt*. Minneapolis, 1931.

742 HICKS, John D. *Republican Ascendancy, 1921–1933*. New York, 1960.

743 HOFSTADTER, Richard. *The Age of Reform*. New York, 1955.

744 HOFSTADTER, Richard. *Social Darwinism in American Thought, 1860–1915*. Philadelphia, 1945.

745 HOOVER, Herbert. *American Individualism*. Garden City, N.Y., 1922.

746 JACOBS, Clyde E. *Law Writers and the Courts: The Influence of Thomas P. Cooley, Christopher G. Tiedeman, and John F. Dillon upon American Constitutional Law*. Berkeley, Calif., 1954.

747 JAMES, William. *Pragmatism: A New Name for Some Old Ways of Thinking*. New York, 1907.

748 JOHNSON, Donald O. *The Challenge to American Freedoms: World War I and the Rise of the American Civil Liberties Union*. Lexington, Ky., 1963.

749 JONES, Alan. "Thomas M. Cooley and Laissez-Faire Constitutionalism: A Reconsideration." *J Am Hist*, 53 (1967), 751–771.

750 JOSEPHSON, Matthew. *The Politicos*. New York, 1938.

751 JOSEPHSON, Matthew. *The Robber Barons*. New York, 1934.

752 KOLKO, Gabriel. *Railroads and Regulation, 1877–1916*. Princeton, N.J., 1965.

753 LASLETT, John H. M. *Labor and the Left: A Study of Socialist and Radical Influences on the American Labor Movement, 1881–1924*. New York, 1970.

754 LEUCHTENBURG, William E. *The Perils of Prosperity, 1914–1932*. Chicago, 1958.

755 LEWIS, E. R. *A History of American Political Thought from the Civil War to the World War*. New York, 1937.

756 LEWIS, Sinclair. *Babbitt*. New York, 1922.

757 LINK, Arthur S. *Woodrow Wilson and the Progressive Era, 1900–1917*. New York, 1954.

758 LIPPMANN, Walter. *Drift and Mastery*. New York, 1914.

759 LLOYD, Henry Demarest. *Wealth Against Commonwealth*. New York, 1894.

760 McCLOSKEY, Robert G. *American Conservatism in the Age of Enterprise, 1865–1910*. Cambridge, Mass., 1951.

761 MENCKEN, H. L. *Notes on Democracy*. New York, 1926.

762 MILLER, George H. *Railroads and the Granger Laws*. Madison, Wis., 1971.

763 MOODY, John. *The Truth about the Trusts*. New York, 1904.

764 MORE, Paul Elmer. "Property Is the Basis of Civilization." *Shelbourne Essays*, ninth series, *Aristocracy and Justice*. Boston, 1915.

765 MURRAY, Robert K. *Red Scare: A Study in National Hysteria, 1919–1920*. Minneapolis, 1955.

766 MUZZEY, D. S. *James G. Blaine*. New York, 1934.

767 NATHAN, Maud. *The Story of an Epoch-Making Movement.* Garden City, N.Y., 1926.

768 ODEGARD, Peter H. *Pressure Politics: The Story of the Anti-Saloon League.* New York, 1928.

769 PARKMAN, Francis. "The Woman Question." *N Am Rev,* 129 (1879), 303–321.

770 PATTEN, Simon N. *The New Basis of Civilization.* New York, 1907.

771 PATTEN, Simon N. *The Theory of Prosperity.* New York, 1902.

772 PAXSON, Frederick L. *America at War, 1917–1918.* Boston, 1939.

773 PAXSON, Frederick L. *The Post-War Years; Normalcy, 1918–1923.* Boston, 1948.

774 POLLACK, Norman. *The Populist Response to Industrial America.* New York, 1962.

775 POST, Louis F. *The Deportations Delirium of Nineteen-Twenty: A Personal Narrative of an Historical Official Experience.* Chicago, 1923.

776 POUND, Roscoe. "The Scope and Purpose of Sociological Jurisprudence." *Harv L Rev,* 24 (1911), 591–619; 25 (1911), 140–168; 25 (1912), 489–516.

777 PROTHRO, James W. *The Dollar Decade: Business Ideas in the 1920's.* Baton Rouge, La., 1954.

778 PURCELL, Edward A., Jr. "Ideas and Interests: Businessmen and the Interstate Commerce Act." *J Am Hist,* 54 (1967), 561–578.

779 QUEENY, Edgar M. *The Spirit of Enterprise.* New York, 1943.

780 RAUSCHENBUSCH, Walter. *Christianity and Social Crisis.* New York, 1907.

781 REED, Louis S. *The Labor Philosophy of Samuel Gompers.* New York, 1930.

782 REGIER, C. C. *The Era of the Muckrakers.* Chapel Hill, N.C., 1932.

783 ROCHE, John P. "Civil Liberty in the Age of Enterprise." *U Chi L Rev,* 31 (1963), 103–135.

784 RUDWICK, Elliott M. "The Niagara Movement." *J Neg Hist,* 42 (1957), 177–200.

785 SOULE, George. *Prosperity Decade: A Chapter from American Economic History, 1917–1929.* London, 1947.

786 SUMNER, William Graham. *What Social Classes Owe to Each Other.* New York, 1883.

787 TIMBERLAKE, James H. *Prohibition and the Progressive Movement, 1900–1920.* Cambridge, Mass., 1953.

788 TURNER, F. J. *The Frontier in American History.* New York, 1920.

789 VEBLEN, Thorstein. *The Theory of Business Enterprise.* New York, 1904.

790 WARD, Lester F. "Plutocracy and Paternalism." *The Forum,* 20 (1895), 300–310.

791 WARNER, John Dewitt. "Consolidation of Wealth: Political Aspects." *Ind,* 54 (1902), 1045–1049.

792 WASHINGTON, Booker T. *Up from Slavery.* New York, 1900.

793 WEINSTEIN, James. *The Decline of Socialism in America, 1912–1925.* New York, 1967.

794 WEYL, Walter. *The New Democracy.* New York, 1914.

795 WHITE, Leonard D. *The Republican Era: 1869–1901.* New York, 1958.

796 WIEBE, R. H. *The Search for Order, 1877–1920.* New York, 1965.

797 WILLOUGHBY, William F. *Government Organization in War Time and After.* New York, 1919.

798 WILSON, Charles Morrow. *Commoner, William Jennings Bryan.* Garden City, N.Y., 1970.

799 WILSON, Woodrow. "The Character of Democracy in the United States." *An Old Master and Other Essays.* New York, 1893.

800 WILSON, Woodrow. *The New Freedom.* New York, 1913.

801 WOOD, Stephen B. *Constitutional Politics in the Progressive Era: Child Labor and the Law.* Chicago, 1968.

802 WOODDY, Carroll H. *The Growth of the Federal Government, 1915–1932.* New York, 1934.

803 WOODWARD, C. Vann. *Tom Watson, Agrarian Rebel.* New York, 1955.

G. *1929–1941*

804 ARNOLD, Thurman W. *The Folklore of Capitalism.* New Haven, 1937.

805 ARNOLD, Thurman W. *The Symbols of Government.* New York, 1935.

806 ARNOLD, Thurman W. "Trial by Combat and the New Deal." *Harv L Rev,* 47 (1934), 913–947.

807 AUERBACH, Jerold D. *Labor and Liberty: The La Follette Committee and the New Deal.* Indianapolis, 1966.

808 BERLE, Adolf A., and Gardiner C. MEANS. *The Modern Corporation and Private Property.* New York, 1932.

809 BROGAN, Denis W. *The Era of Franklin D. Roosevelt; A Chronicle of the New Deal and Global War.* New Haven, 1950.

810 BURNS, James M. *Roosevelt: The Lion and the Fox.* New York, 1956.

811 CONKIN, Paul. *FDR and the Origins of the Welfare State.* New York, 1967.

812 DEWEY, John. *Liberalism and Social Action.* Boston, 1935.

813 DIXON, Wecter. *Age of Great Depression.* New York, 1948.

814 DOUGLAS, Paul H. *Social Security in the United States: Analysis and Appraisal of the Federal Social Security Act.* New York, 1936.

815 EINAUDI, Mario. *The Roosevelt Revolution.* New York, 1959.

816 FUSFELD, Daniel R. *The Economic Thought of Franklin D. Roosevelt, and the Origins of the New Deal.* New York, 1956.

817 GREER, Thomas H. *What Roosevelt Thought: The Social and Political Ideas of Franklin D. Roosevelt.* East Lansing, Mich., 1958.

818 HOOVER, Herbert. *Addresses upon the American Road.* New York, 1938.

819 HOOVER, Herbert. *The Challenge to Liberty.* New York, 1934.

820 JENKIN, Thomas Paul. *Reactions of Major Groups to Positive Government in the United States, 1930–1940; A Study in Contemporary Political Thought.* Berkeley, Calif., 1945.

821 KEMLER, Edgar. *The Deflation of American Ideals: An Ethical Guide for New Dealers.* Washington, D.C. 1941.

822 LERNER, Max. *Ideas for the Ice Age.* New York, 1941.

823 LEUCHTENBURG, William E. *Franklin D. Roosevelt and the New Deal, 1932–1940.* New York, 1963.

824 LINDLEY, Ernest K. *The Roosevelt Revolution.* New York, 1933.

825 LIPPMANN, Walter. *The New Imperative.* New York, 1935.

826 McBAIN, Howard L. "The Constitution and the New Deal." *Yale Rev,* 25 (1935), 114–130.

827 MASON, Alpheus T. "The Dilemma of Liberalism." *J Soc Phil,* 3 (1938), 223–234.

828 MILLS, Ogden L. *Liberalism Fights On.* New York, 1936.

829 MILLS, Ogden L. *What of Tomorrow?* New York, 1935.

830 MOLEY, Raymond. *After Seven Years.* New York, 1939.

831 MOONEY, Booth. *Roosevelt and Rayburn.* Philadelphia, 1971.

832 NOURSE, Edwin G., *et al. Three Years of the Agricultural Adjustment Administration.* Washington, D.C., 1937.

833 PARIS, J. D. *Monetary Policies of the United States, 1932–1938.* New York, 1938.

834 PHELPS, Orme W. *The Legislative Background of the Fair Labor Standards Act: A Study of the Growth of National Sentiment in Favor of Government Regulation of Wages, Hours and Child Labor.* Chicago, 1939.

835 President's Research Committee. *Recent Social Trends in the United States.* Washington, D.C., 1933.

836 ROOSEVELT, F. D. *Looking Forward.* New York, 1933.

837 SCHLESINGER, Arthur M., Jr. *The Age of Roosevelt.* Boston, 1957–.

838 TUGWELL, Rexford Guy. *The Democratic Roosevelt.* Garden City, N.Y., 1957.

839 WALLACE, Henry. *New Frontiers.* New York, 1935.

840 WOLFSKILL, George. *The Revolt of the Conservatives: A History of the American Liberty League, 1934–1940.* Boston, 1962.

H. 1941–1961

841 AARON, Daniel. *Writers on the Left: Episodes in American Literary Communism.* New York, 1961.

842 ACHESON, Dean. *Present at the Creation.* New York, 1969.

843 ANTHONY, J. Garner. *Hawaii under Army Rule.* Stanford, Calif., 1955.

844 BARTLEY, Numan V. *The Rise of Massive Resistance: Race and Politics in the South During the 1950's.* Baton Rouge, La., 1969.

845 BELL, Daniel. *The End of Ideology.* New York, 1960.

CONTEXT

846 BELL, Daniel. *The New American Right.* New York, 1955.

847 BELZ, Herman. "Changing Conceptions of Constitutionalism in the Era of World War II and the Cold War." *J Am Hist,* 59 (1972), 640–669.

848 BERLE, Adolf A. *The Emerging Common Law of Free Enterprise: Antidote to the Omnipotent State.* Philadelphia, 1951.

849 BERLE, Adolf A. *The 20th Century Capitalist Revolution.* New York, 1954.

850 BERNSTEIN, Cyrus. "The Saboteur Trial: A Case History." *Geo Wash L Rev,* 11 (1943), 131–190.

851 BIDDLE, Francis. *In Brief Authority.* Garden City, N.Y., 1962.

852 BOSCH, William J. *Judgment on Nuremberg: American Attitudes Toward the Major German War-Crime Trials.* Chapel Hill, N.C., 1970.

853 BOWLES, Chester. "Do Controls Endanger Democracy?" *NY Times Mag* (Dec. 21, 1947), 12, 29–32.

854 BUCHANAN, A. Russell. *The United States and World War II.* 2 vols. New York, 1964.

855 COOKE, Alistair. *Generation on Trial: U.S.A. v. Alger Hiss.* New York, 1950.

856 DIVINE, Robert A. *Foreign Policy and U.S. Presidential Elections, 1940–1960.* 2 vols. New York, 1974.

857 DULLES, Foster Rhea. *America's Rise to World Power, 1898–1954.* New York, 1954.

858 FAIRMAN, Charles. "Some New Problems of the Constitution Following the Flag." *Stan L Rev,* 1 (1949), 585–645.

859 GALBRAITH, J. K. *The Affluent Society.* Boston, 1958.

860 GALBRAITH, J. K. *American Capitalism: Concept of Countervailing Power.* Boston, 1952.

861 GATES, Robbins L. *The Making of Massive Resistance: Virginia's Politics of Public School Desegregation, 1954–1956.* Chapel Hill, N.C., 1964.

862 GREEN, Sedgwick N. "Applicability of American Laws to Overseas Areas Controlled by the United States." *Harv L Rev,* 68 (1955), 781–812.

863 GRODZINS, Morton. *Americans Betrayed: Politics and the Japanese Evacuation.* Chicago, 1949.

864 HACKER, Andrew. *The Corporation Take-Over.* New York, 1964.

865 HOOVER, Herbert. *Addresses upon the American Road: World War II, 1941–1945.* Princeton, N.J., 1946.

866 KING, Martin Luther, Jr. *Stride Toward Freedom: The Montgomery Story.* New York, 1958.

867 LATHAM, Earl. *The Communist Controversy in Washington: From the New Deal to McCarthy.* Cambridge, Mass., 1966.

868 LILIENTHAL, David. *Big Business: A New Era.* New York, 1952.

869 LIPPMANN, Walter. *The Public Philosophy.* Boston, 1955.

870 MILLS, C. Wright. *The Power Elite.* New York, 1956.

871 MURPHY, Walter F. "The South Counter-Attacks: The Anti-NAACP Laws." *West Pol Q,* 12 (1959), 371–390.

872 NIEBUHR, Reinhold. *The Children of Light and the Children of Darkness.* New York, 1944.

873 NIZER, Louis. *The Implosion Conspiracy.* Garden City, N.Y., 1973.

874 NOLTE, Ernst. *Three Faces of Fascism.* New York, 1966.

875 NOSSITER, Bernard D. *The Mythmakers: An Essay on Power and Wealth.* Boston, 1964.

876 PREUSS, Lawrence. "Some Aspects of the Human Rights Provisions of the Charter and Their Execution in the United States." *Am J Int L,* 46 (1952), 289–296.

877 QUINN, Theodore K. *I Quit Monster Business.* New York, 1948.

878 RIESMAN, David. *The Lonely Crowd.* New Haven, 1950.

879 SCHNEIR, Walter, and Miriam SCHNEIR. *Invitation to an Inquest: Reopening the Rosenberg "Atom Spy" Case.* Baltimore, 1973.

880 STERN, Philip M., and Harold P. GREEN. *Oppenheimer Case: Security on Trial.* New York, 1969.

881 STONE, I. F. *The Haunted Fifties.* New York, 1963.

882 TEN BROEK, Jacobus, *et al. Prejudice, War and the Constitution: Causes and Consequences of the Evacuation of the Japanese Americans in World War II.* Berkeley, Calif., 1958.

883 THOMAS, Dorothy, *et al. Japanese American Evacuation and Resettlement.* 3 vols. Berkeley, Calif., 1946–1954.

884 WARREN, Robert Penn. *Segregation: The Inner Conflict in the South.* New York, 1956.

885 WHYTE, W. H. *The Organization Man.* New York, 1956.

886 WIENER, Norbert. *Cybernetics.* Cambridge, Mass., 1948.

887 WITTNER, Lawrence. *Rebels Against War: The American Peace Movement 1941–1960.* New York, 1969.

I. 1961–

888 ADELSON, Alan. *SDS: A Profile.* New York, 1972.

889 ALTBACH, Philip G. *Student Politics in America.* New York, 1974.

890 "Anatomy of a Riot: An Analytical Symposium of the Causes and Effects of Riots." *J Urb L,* 45 (1968), 499–901.

891 ARENDT, Hannah. *Crises of the Republic.* New York, 1972.

892 ARENDT, Hannah. *On Violence.* New York, 1970.

893 *Autobiography of Malcolm X.* New York, 1965.

894 BACCIOCCO, Edward J., Jr. *The New Left in America; Reform to Revolution; 1956 to 1970.* Stanford, Calif., 1974.

895 BERLE, Adolf A. *The American Economic Republic.* New York, 1963.

896 BERMAN, Ronald. *America in the Sixties. An Intellectual History.* New York, 1968.

897 BROWN, Claude. *Manchild in the Promised Land.* New York, 1965.

898 BURNHAM, Walter Dean. "The Changing Shape of the American Political Universe." *Am Pol Sci Rev,* 59 (1965), 7–28.

899 CLECAK, Peter. *Radical Paradoxes; Dilemmas of the American Left: 1945–1970.* New York, 1973.

900 COHEN, Carl. *Civil Disobedience: Conscience, Tactics and the Law.* New York, 1971.

901 COHEN, Mitchell, and Dennis HALE, eds. *The New Student Left.* Boston, 1966.

902 CONANT, Ralph W. *Prospects for Revolution: A Study of Riots, Civil Disobedience, and Insurrection in Contemporary America.* New York, 1971.

903 DOUGLAS, William O. *Points of Rebellion.* New York, 1970.

904 EPSTEIN, Jason. *The Great Conspiracy Trial.* New York, 1970.

905 FERBER, Michael, and Staughton LYND. *The Resistance.* Boston, 1971.

906 FLACKS, Richard. *Youth and Social Change.* Chicago, 1972.

907 FORD, Thomas R., ed. *The Revolutionary Theme in Contemporary America.* Lexington, Ky., 1965.

908 FRANK, John P. *American Law, the Case for Radical Reform.* New York, 1969.

909 FULBRIGHT, J. William. "The Strain of Violence." *University: A Princeton Quarterly,* no. 20 (spring 1964), 9–13.

910 GALBRAITH, John Kenneth. *Economics and the Public Purpose.* Boston, 1973.

911 GALBRAITH, John Kenneth. *The New Industrial State.* 2nd ed., rev. Boston, 1971.

912 GILLAM, Richard. "White Racism and the Civil Rights Movement." *Yale Rev,* 62 (1973), 520–543.

913 GOODELL, Charles. *Political Prisoners in America.* New York, 1973.

914 GOODMAN, Paul. *Utopian Essays and Practical Proposals.* New York, 1964.

915 HAKMAN, Nathan. "Old and New Left Activity in the Legal Order: An Interpretation." *J Soc Iss,* 27 (1971), 105–121.

916 HAKMAN, Nathan. "Political Trials in the Legal Order." *J Pub L,* 21 (1972), 73–126.

917 HARRINGTON, Michael. *The Other America: Poverty in the United States.* New York, 1962.

918 HICKEL, Walter J. *Who Owns America?* Englewood Cliffs, N.J., 1971.

919 HOOK, Sidney. *Academic Freedom and Academic Anarchy.* New York, 1970.

920 JACOBS, Paul, and Saul LANDAU. *The New Radicals.* New York, 1966.

921 KELMAN, Steven. *Push Comes to Shove.* Boston, 1970.

922 KING, Martin Luther, Jr. "Letter from Birmingham City Jail." *Free Government in the Making.* Ed. Alpheus T. Mason. 3rd ed. New York, 1965.

923 LASCH, Christopher. *The New Radicalism in America.* New York, 1965.

924 LIPSET, Seymour Martin, and Sheldon WOLIN, eds. *The Berkeley Student Revolt.* Garden City, N.Y., 1965.

925 LOWI, Theodore J. *Politics of Disorder.* New York, 1971.

926 McCONNELL, Grant. *Private Power and American Democracy.* New York, 1966.

927 McGEE, John S. *In Defense of Industrial Concentration.* New York, 1971.

928 McKAY, Robert B., *et al. Attica: The Official Report of the New York State Special Commission on Attica.* New York, 1972.

929 MUSE, Benjamin. *The American Negro Revolution: From Non-Violence to Black Power.* Bloomington, Ind., 1968.

930 National Commission on the Causes and Prevention of Violence. *To Establish Justice, to Insure Domestic Tranquility: Final Report.* Washington, D.C., 1970.

931 National Advisory Commission on Civil Disorders. *Report.* Washington, D.C., 1968.

932 National Advisory Commission on Civil Disorders. *Supplemental Studies.* Washington, D.C., 1968.

933 NELSON, Jack, and Ronald J. OSTROW. *The FBI and the Berrigans: The Making of a Conspiracy.* New York, 1972.

934 NEWFIELD, Jack. *A Prophetic Minority.* New York, 1966.

935 O'NEILL, William. *Coming Apart: An Informal History of the Sixties.* Chicago, 1971.

936 President's Commission on Campus Unrest. *Report.* Washington, D.C., 1970.

937 President's Commission on Law Enforcement and Administration of Justice. *The Challenge of Crime in a Free Society: A Report.* Washington, D.C., 1967.

938 RAINES, John C., ed. *Conspiracy; The Implications of the Harrisburg Trial for the Democratic Tradition.* New York, 1974.

939 RAWLS, John. *A Theory of Justice.* Cambridge, Mass., 1971.

940 RIESMAN, David. *Abundance for What?* New York, 1964.

941 ROBINSON, Donald L. "The Routinization of Crisis Government." *Yale Rev,* 63 (1973), 161–174.

942 RUSZAK, Theodore. *The Making of a Counter Culture.* Garden City, N.Y., 1970.

943 SILBERMAN, Charles. *Crisis in Black and White.* New York, 1964.

944 SKINNER, B. F. *Beyond Freedom and Dignity.* New York, 1971.

945 SKOLNICK, Jerome H. *Politics of Protest. Violent Aspects of Protest and Confrontation.* New York, 1969.

946 TAYLOR, Telford. *Nuremberg and Vietnam: An American Tragedy.* New York, 1970.

947 TEODORI, Massimo. *The New Left: A Documentary History.* Indianapolis, 1969.

948 U.S. Commission on Marihuana and Drug Abuse. *Marihuana: A Signal of Misunderstanding. First Report.* Washington, D.C., 1972.

949 U.S. Senate. Select Committee on Presidential Campaign Activities. *Final Report.* 3 vols. 93rd Cong., 2nd session, 1974. Washington, D.C., 1974.

950 VELVEL, Lawrence R. *Undeclared War and Civil Disobedience: The American System in Crisis.* New York, 1970.

951 VERNON, Raymond. *Sovereignty at Bay: The Multinational Spread of U.S. Enterprises.* New York, 1971.

952 WALKER, Daniel. *Rights in Conflict: Convention Week in Chicago, August 25–29, 1968: A Report.* New York, 1969.

953 WALZER, Michael. *Obligations: Essays on Disobedience, War and Citizenship.* New York, 1970.

954 WESTIN, Alan F., ed. *Freedom Now! The Civil Rights Struggle in America.* New York, 1964.

955 WIRT, Frederick M. *Politics of Southern Equality: Law and Social Change in a Mississippi County.* Chicago, 1970.

956 WOLFE, Alan. *The Seamy Side of Democracy. Repression in America.* New York, 1973.

IV. Political Institutions

A. The Congress

957 The Association of the Bar of the City of New York. *Congress and the Public Trust.* New York, 1970.

958 ATKINSON, Charles R. *The Committee on Rules and the Overthrow of Speaker Cannon.* New York, 1911.

959 BROWN, Douglas W. "The Proposal to Give Congress the Power to Nullify the Constitution." *Am L Rev,* 57 (1923), 161–181.

960 CARR, Robert K. *The House Committee on Un-American Activities, 1945–1950.* Ithaca, N.Y., 1952.

961 CASSELL, Frank A. *Merchant Congressman in the Young Republic: Samuel Smith of Maryland, 1752–1839.* Madison, Wis., 1971.

962 CHIU, Chang-Wei. *The Speakers of the House of Representatives Since 1896.* New York, 1928.

963 CLEVELAND, Frederick N., *et al. Congress and Urban Problems.* Washington, D.C., 1969.

964 COOK, Fred J. *Nightmare Decade: The Life and Times of Senator Joe McCarthy.* New York, 1971.

965 FOLLETT, Mary Parker. *The Speaker of the House of Representatives.* New York, 1896.

966 FURLONG, P. J. "The Origins of the House Committee on Ways and Means." *Wm & M Q,* 25 (1968), 587–604.

967 GALLOWAY, George B. *History of the House of Representatives.* New York, 1961. Rev. ed. by Sidney Wise. New York, 1976.

968 GARRATY, John A. *Henry Cabot Lodge.* New York, 1953.

969 GOODMAN, Walter. *The Committee: The Extraordinary Career of the House Committee on Un-American Activities.* New York, 1968.

970 GWINN, William R. *Uncle Joe Cannon, Archfoe of Insurgency.* New York, 1957.

971 HAMILTON, Walton H., and Douglass ADAIR. *The Power to Govern.* New York, 1937.

972 HAYNES, G. B. *The Senate of the United States: Its History and Practice.* 2 vols. Boston, 1938.

973 JEWELL, Malcolm E., and Samuel C. PATTERSON. *The Legislative Process in the United States.* New York, 1966.

974 LANG, L. J., ed. *Autobiography of Thomas Collier Platt.* New York, 1910.

975 LUCE, Robert. *Congress—an Explanation.* Cambridge, Mass., 1926.

976 LUCE, Robert. *Legislative Assemblies.* Boston, 1924.

977 LUCE, Robert. *Legislative Procedure.* Boston, 1922.

978 MANLEY, John F. *The Politics of Finance: The House Committee on Ways and Means.* Boston, 1970.

979 MIKVA, Abner J., and Joseph R. LUNDY. "The 91st Congress and the Constitution." *U Chi L Rev,* 38 (1971), 449–499.

980 MORGAN, Donald G. *Congress and the Constitution: A Study of Responsibility.* Cambridge, Mass., 1966.

981 OGDEN, August R. *The Dies Committee: A Study of the Special House Committee for the Investigation of Un-American Activities.* Washington, D.C., 1945.

982 PATTERSON, James T. *Congressional Conservatism and the New Deal: The Growth of the Conservative Coalition in Congress, 1933–1939.* Lexington, Ky., 1967.

983 PATTERSON, James T. *Mr. Republican, a Biography of Robert A. Taft.* Boston, 1972.

984 POLSBY, Nelson W. "Strengthening Congress in National Policy-Making." *Yale Rev,* 59 (1970), 481–497.

985 ROBINSON, W. A. *Thomas B. Reed.* New York, 1930.

986 ROTHMAN, David J. *Politics and Power: The United States Senate, 1869–1901.* Cambridge, Mass., 1966.

987 SHERMAN, John. *Recollections of Forty Years in the House, Senate, and Cabinet.* Chicago, 1895.

988 SWANSTROM, Ray. *The United States Senate, 1789–1801.* Washington, D.C., 1962.

989 TREFOUSSE, Hans L. *Benjamin Franklin Wade: Radical Republican from Ohio.* New York, 1963.

990 WHITE, William S. *Citadel: The Story of the U.S. Senate.* New York, 1956.

991 WILLOUGHBY, William F. *Principles of Legislative Organization and Administration.* Washington, D.C., 1934.

992 WILSON, Woodrow. *Congressional Government.* Boston, 1885.

B. The Presidency

993 American Bar Association. Committee on Electoral College Reform. *Electing the President.* Chicago, 1967.

994 BERNSTEIN, Carl, and Bob WOODWARD. *All the President's Men.* New York, 1974.

995 BURNS, James M. *Presidential Government; The Crucible of Leadership.* Boston, 1966.

996 CALDWELL, Robert G. *James A. Garfield, Party Chieftain.* Hamden, Conn., 1965.

997 CHAMBERLAIN, Joseph P. *The Judicial Function in Federal Administrative Agencies.* New York, 1942.

998 CHAMBERS, Reid Peyton, and Ronald D. ROTUNDA. "Reform of Presidential Nominating Conventions." *Va L Rev,* 56 (1970), 179–214.

999 COCHRAN, Bert. *Harry Truman and the Crisis Presidency.* New York, 1973.

1000 CORWIN, Edward S. *The President. Office and Powers, 1787–1957.* 4th ed. New York, 1957.

1001 CUMMINGS, Homer, and Carl McFARLAND. *Federal Justice. Chapters in the History of Justice and the Federal Executive.* New York, 1937.

1002 CURTIS, Benjamin R. *Executive Prower.* Boston, 1862.

1003 DAVID, Paul. "The Vice-Presidency: Its Institutional Evolution and Contemporary Status." *J Pol,* 29 (1967), 721–748.

1004 EISENHOWER, Dwight D. *The White House Years.* 2 vols. Garden City, N.Y., 1963–1965.

1005 ELLIFF, John T. *Crime, Dissent, and the Attorney-General: The Justice Department in the 1960's.* Beverly Hills, Calif., 1971.

1006 FEERICK, John D. *From Failing Hands. The Story of Presidential Succession.* New York, 1965.

1007 FENNO, Richard F., Jr. *The President's Cabinet.* Cambridge, Mass., 1954.

1008 HARRIS, Richard. *Justice: The Crisis of Law, Order and Freedom in America.* New York, 1970.

1009 HART, James. *The American Presidency in Action, 1789: A Study in Constitutional History.* New York, 1948.

1010 HESSELTINE, William B. *Lincoln and the War Governors.* New York, 1948.

1011 HOUSE, Lolabel. *A Study of the Twelfth Amendment of the Constitution of the United States.* Philadelphia, 1901.

1012 HOWE, G. F. *Chester A. Arthur.* New York, 1934.

1013 HUGHES, Emmet John. *The Living Presidency.* New York, 1973.

1014 HUSTON, Luther A. *The Department of Justice.* New York, 1967.

1015 HUSTON, Luther A., *et al. Roles of the Attorney General of the United States.* Washington, D.C., 1968.

1016 HYMAN, Sidney, ed. "The Office of the American Presidency." *Ann Am Acad Pol Soc Sci,* 307 (1956), 1–155.

1017 JACKSON, Carlton. *Presidential Vetos, 1792–1945.* Athens, Ga., 1967.

1018 JAMES, Marquis. *Andrew Jackson: Portrait of a President.* Indianapolis, 1937.

1019 JOHNSON, Lyndon B. *The Vantage Point; Perspectives of the Presidency, 1963–1969.* New York, 1971.

1020 KALLENBACH, Joseph E. *The American Chief Executive.* New York, 1966.

1021 KALLENBACH, Joseph E. "The New Presidential Succession Act." *Am Pol Sci Rev,* 41 (1947), 931–941.

1022 KALLENBACH, Joseph E. "Our Electoral College Gerrymander." *Midw J Pol Sci,* 4 (1960), 162–191.

1023 KOENIG, Louis W. *The Chief Executive.* Rev. ed. New York, 1968.

1024 KOENIG, Louis W. *The Presidency and the Crisis. Powers of the Office from the Invasion of Poland to Pearl Harbor.* New York, 1944.

1025 KURTZ, Stephen G. *The Presidency of John Adams; The Collapse of Federalism, 1795–1800.* Philadelphia, 1957.

1026 LASKI, Harold J. *The American Presidency. An Interpretation.* New York, 1940.

1027 LATHAM, Earl, ed. *The Philosophy and Policies of Woodrow Wilson.* Chicago, 1958.

1028 LINK, Arthur S. *Wilson.* Princeton, N.J., 1947–.

1029 LONGAKER, Richard P. *The Presidency and Civil Liberties.* Ithaca, N.Y., 1961.

1030 McCOY, Donald R., and Richard T. RUETTEN. *Quest and Response; Minority Rights and the Truman Administration.* Lawrence, Kan., 1973.

1031 MALONE, Dumas. *Jefferson and His Time.* Boston, 1948–.

1032 MILES, Rufus E., Jr. *The Department of Health, Education and Welfare.* New York, 1974.

1033 MORGAN, H. Wayne. *William McKinley and His America.* Syracuse, N.Y., 1963.

1034 MORGAN, Ruth P. *The President and Civil Rights. Policy-Making by Executive Order.* New York, 1970.

1035 MORISON, E. E., and John M. BLUM, eds. *The Letters of Theodore Roosevelt.* 8 vols. Cambridge, Mass., 1951–1954.

1036 MOWRY, George E. *The Era of Theodore Roosevelt, 1900–1912.* New York, 1958.

1037 NAVASKY, Victor S. *Kennedy Justice.* New York, 1971.

1038 NEUSTADT, Richard E. *Presidential Power: The Politics of Leadership.* New York, 1960.

1039 NEVINS, Allan. *Grover Cleveland.* New York, 1932.

1040 NICOLAY, John, and John HAY. *Abraham Lincoln: A History.* 10 vols. New York, 1890.

1041 PATTERSON, C. Perry. *Presidential Government in the United States. The Unwritten Constitution.* Chapel Hill, N.C., 1947.

1042 POLSBY, Nelson W., and Aaron B. WILDAVSKY. *Presidential Elections: Strategies of American Electoral Politics.* 3rd ed. New York, 1971.

1043 "The Presidential Office." *L & Cont Prob,* 21 (1956), 607–752.

1044 PRINGLE, Henry F. *Theodore Roosevelt.* New York, 1931.

1045 *The Public Papers and Addresses of Franklin D. Roosevelt.* 13 vols. New York, 1938–1950.

POLITICAL INSTITUTIONS

1046 RANDALL, J. G. *Constitutional Problems under Lincoln.* Rev. ed. Urbana, Ill., 1951.

1047 RANDALL, J. G. *Lincoln the President.* 4 vols. New York, 1945–1952.

1048 REEDY, George E. *The Twilight of the Presidency.* New York, 1970.

1049 SANDERS, Jennings B. *Evolution of Executive Departments of the Continental Congress, 1774–1789.* Chapel Hill, N.C., 1935.

1050 SCHLESINGER, Arthur M., Jr. *A Thousand Days; John F. Kennedy in the White House.* Boston, 1965.

1051 SCHLESINGER, Arthur M., Jr., ed. *History of American Presidential Elections, 1789–1968.* 4 vols. New York, 1971.

1052 SCHLESINGER, Arthur M., Jr. *The Imperial Presidency.* Boston, 1973.

1053 SHERWOOD, Robert. *Roosevelt and Hopkins.* New York, 1948.

1054 SHORT, Lloyd M. *The Development of National Administrative Organization in the United States.* Baltimore, 1923.

1055 SMALL, Norman J. *Some Presidential Interpretations of the Presidency.* Baltimore, 1932.

1056 STANWOOD, Edward. *A History of the Presidency.* Boston, 1900.

1057 SWISHER, Carl B., ed. *Selected Papers of Homer Cummings, Attorney General of the United States, 1933–1939.* New York, 1939.

1058 "Symposium: The Presidency in Transition." *J Pol,* 11 (1949), 5–256.

1059 TAFT, William Howard. *Our Chief Magistrate and His Powers.* New York, 1916.

1060 TAFT, William H. *The Presidency: Its Duties, Its Powers, Its Opportunities and Its Limitations.* New York, 1916.

1061 THACH, Charles C., Jr. *The Creation of the American Presidency, 1775–1789. A Study in Constitutional History.* Baltimore, 1922.

1062 THOMAS, Benjamin Platt. *Abraham Lincoln: A Biography.* New York, 1952.

1063 THOMAS, C. M. *American Neutrality in 1793: A Study in Cabinet Government.* New York, 1931.

1064 TOURTELLOT, Arthur Bernon, ed. *The Presidents on the Presidency.* Garden City, N.Y., 1964.

1065 TRUMAN, Harry S. *Memoirs.* 2 vols. Garden City, N.Y., 1955–1956.

1066 TUGWELL, Rexford Guy. *The Democratic Roosevelt* (see 838).

1067 TUGWELL, Rexford Guy. *The Enlargement of the American Presidency.* Garden City, N.Y., 1960.

1068 TUGWELL, Rexford Guy, and Thomas E. CRONIN. *The Presidency Reappraised.* New York, 1974.

1069 U.S. Commission on the Organization of the Executive Branch. *Final Reports.* Washington, D.C., 1949.

1070 U.S. Senate. Committee on Judiciary. Subcommittee on Constitutional Amendments. *Hearings on Presidential Inability and Vacancies in the Office of Vice-President.* 88th Cong., 2nd sess., 1964. Washington, D.C., 1964.

1071 U.S. Senate. Committee on Judiciary. Subcommittee on Constitutional Amendments. *The Electoral College.* 87th Cong., 1st sess., 1961. Washington, D.C., 1961.

1072 WILLIAMS, Irving G. *Rise of the Vice-Presidency.* Washington, D.C., 1956.

1073 WILMERDING, Lucius, Jr. *The Electoral College.* New Brunswick, N.J., 1958.

1074 WILSON, Woodrow. *Papers.* Eds. Arthur S. Link, *et al.* Princeton, N.J., 1966–.

1075 WINTER, Ralph K., Jr. *Watergate and the Law; Political Campaigns and Presidential Power.* Washington, D.C., 1974.

1076 YOUNG, Donald. *American Roulette: The History and Dilemma of the Vice-Presidency.* New York, 1965.

C. The Federal Judiciary

General

1077 ADAMANY, David. "Legitimacy, Realigning Elections, and the Supreme Court." *Wis L Rev,* 1973 (1973), 790–846.

1078 BEARD, Charles A. *The Supreme Court and the Constitution.* Englewood Cliffs, N.J., 1962 (reprint of 1912 ed.).

1079 CARSON, Hampton L. *The Supreme Court of the United States: Its History.* 2 vols. Philadelphia, 1892.

1080 CUSHMAN, Robert E. "The History of the Supreme Court in Resume." *Minn L Rev,* 7 (1923), 275–305.

1081 DUNHAM, Allison, and Philip B. KURLAND, eds. *Mr. Justice. Biographical Studies of Twelve Supreme Court Justices.* Chicago, 1956.

1082 FREUND, Paul A., ed. *The Oliver Wendell Holmes Devise History of the Supreme Court of the United States.* 11 vols. New York, 1971–.

1083 JAMESON, J. Franklin. "The Predecessor of the Supreme Court." *Essays in the Constitutional History of the United States.* Boston, 1889.

1084 LATHAM, Earl. "The Supreme Court and the Supreme People." *J Pol,* 16 (1954), 207–235.

1085 McCLOSKEY, Robert G. *The American Supreme Court.* Chicago, 1960.

1086 McGOWAN, Carl. "The Supreme Court in the American Constitutional System: The Problem in Historical Perspective." *Not Dame Law,* 33 (1958), 527–547.

1087 MASON, Alpheus T. *The Supreme Court from Taft to Warren.* Rev. ed. Baton Rouge, La., 1968.

1088 MENDELSON, Wallace. *Capitalism, Democracy, and the Supreme Court.* New York, 1960.

1089 MYERS, Gustavus. *History of the Supreme Court of the United States.* Chicago, 1925.

1090 PARKER, John J. "The Judicial Office of the United States." *N Y U L Q Rev,* 23 (1948), 225–238.

1091 PAUL, Julius. *The Legal Realism of Jerome N. Frank: A Study of Fact-Skepticism and the Judicial Process.* The Hague, 1959.

1092 PFEFFER, Leo. *This Honorable Court: A History of the United States Supreme Court.* Boston, 1965.

1093 PHILLIPS, Harlan B., ed. *Felix Frankfurter Reminisces.* New York, 1960.

1094 RODELL, Fred. *Nine Men: A History of the Supreme Court from 1790 to 1955.* New York, 1955.

1095 ROSENBERG, J. Mitchell. *Jerome Frank: Jurist and Philosopher.* New York, 1970.

1096 SCHICK, Marvin. *Learned Hand's Court.* Baltimore, 1970.

1097 STEAMER, Robert J. *The Supreme Court in Crisis: A History of Conflict.* Amherst, Mass., 1971.

1098 "Studies in Judicial Biography." *Vand L Rev,* 10 (1957), 167–413; 18 (1965), 367–716.

1099 SWINDLER, William F. "The Chief Justice and Law Reform, 1921–1971." *S Ct Rev* (1971), 241–264.

1100 SWISHER, Carl B. *The Growth of Constitutional Power in the United States.* Chicago, 1946.

1101 WAITE, Morrison R. "The Supreme Court of the United States." *Alb L J,* 36 (1887), 318.

1102 WARREN, Charles. *The Supreme Court in United States History.* 2 vols. Boston, 1932.

1103 WESTIN, Alan F., ed. *An Autobiography of the Supreme Court. Off-the-Bench Commentaries by the Justices.* New York, 1963.

1104 WILLOUGHBY, Westel Woodbury. *The Supreme Court of the United States; Its History and Influence in Our Constitutional System.* Baltimore, 1890.

1790–1864

1105 ADAMS, John S., ed. *An Autobiographical Sketch by John Marshall.* Ann Arbor, Mich., 1937.

1106 BAKER, Leonard. *John Marshall: A Life in Law.* New York, 1974.

1107 BAXTER, Maurice G. *Daniel Webster and the Supreme Court.* Amherst, Mass., 1966.

1108 BEVERIDGE, Albert J. *The Life of John Marshall.* 4 vols. Boston, 1916–1919.

1109 BURKE, Joseph C. "The Cherokee Cases: A Study in Law, Politics, and Morality." *Stan L Rev,* 21 (1969), 500–531.

1110 BURNETTE, Lawrence, Jr. "Peter V. Daniel: Agrarian Justice." *Va Mag Hist & Biog,* 62 (1954), 289–305.

1111 CATTERALL, H. T. "Some Antecedents of the Dred Scott Case." *Am Hist Rev,* 30 (1924), 56–71.

1112 "Chief Justice John Marshall: A Symposium." *U Penn L Rev,* 104 (1955), 1–68.

1113 CONNOR, Henry G. *John Archibald Campbell, Associate Justice of the U.S. Supreme Court 1853–1861.* Boston, 1920.

1114 CORWIN, Edward S. "The Dred Scott Decision in the Light of Contemporary Legal Doctrines." *Am Hist Rev,* 17 (1911), 52–69.

1115 CORWIN, Edward S. *John Marshall and the Constitution. A Chronicle of the Supreme Court.* New Haven, 1921.

POLITICAL INSTITUTIONS

1116 CROSSKEY, William W. "John Marshall and the Constitution." *U Chi L Rev,* 23 (1956), 377–397.

1117 CURTIS, Benjamin R., Jr. *A Memoir of Benjamin Robbins Curtis.* Boston, 1879.

1118 DAVIS, J. C. Brancroft. "Federal Courts Prior to the Adoption of the Constitution." 131 U.S. Appendix.

1119 DEWEY, Donald O. *Marshall Versus Madison: The Political Background of Marbury vs. Madison.* New York, 1970.

1120 DODD, W. E. "Chief Justice Marshall and Virginia, 1813–1821." *Am Hist Rev,* 12 (1907), 776–787.

1121 DUNCAN, George W. "John Archibald Campbell." *Trans Ala Hist Soc* 5 (1904), 107–151.

1122 DUNNE, Gerald T. *Justice Joseph Story and the Rise of the Supreme Court.* New York, 1970.

1123 ELLIS, Richard E. *The Jeffersonian Crisis: Courts and Politics in the Young Republic.* New York, 1971.

1124 FARRAND, Max. "The Judiciary Act of 1801." *Am Hist Rev,* 5 (1900), 682–686.

1125 FAULKNER, Robert K. *The Jurisprudence of John Marshall.* Princeton, N.J., 1968.

1126 FRANK, John P. *Justice Daniel Dissenting: A Biography of Peter V. Daniel, 1784–1860.* Cambridge, Mass., 1964.

1127 FRANKFURTER, Felix. "John Marshall and the Judicial Function." *Harv L Rev,* 69 (1955), 217–238.

1128 GARVEY, Gerald. "The Constitutional Revolution of 1837 and the Myth of Marshall's Monolith." *West Pol Q,* 18 (1965), 27–34.

1129 GOEBEL, Julius, Jr. *The Oliver Wendell Holmes Devise History of the Supreme Court of the United States. Volume I: Antecedents and Beginnings to 1801.* New York, 1971.

1130 GUNTHER, Gerald, ed. *John Marshall's Defense of McCulloch Versus Maryland.* Stanford, Calif., 1969.

1131 HAINES, Charles G. "Political Theories of the Supreme Court from 1789 to 1835." *Am Pol Sci Rev,* 2 (1908), 221–244.

1132 HAINES, Charles G. *The Role of the Supreme Court in American Government and Politics: 1789–1835.* Berkeley, Calif., 1944.

1133 HAINES, Charles G., and Foster H. SHERWOOD. *The Role of the Supreme Court in American Government and Politics, 1835–1864.* Berkeley, Calif., 1957.

1134 HENDERSON, Dwight F. *Courts for a New Nation.* Washington, D.C., 1971.

1135 HOPKINS, Vincent C. *Dred Scott's Case.* New York, 1951.

1136 HUGHES, Charles E. "Roger Brooke Taney." *Am Bar Assoc J,* 17 (1931), 785–790.

1137 JONES, W. Melville, ed. *Chief Justice John Marshall: A Reappraisal.* Ithaca, N.Y., 1956.

1138 KNUDSON, Jerry W. "The Jeffersonian Assault on the Federalist Judiciary, 1802–1805; Political Forces and Press Reaction." *Am J Leg Hist,* 14 (1970), 55–75.

1139 KONEFSKY, Samuel J. *John Marshall and Alexander Hamilton: Architects of the American Constitution.* New York, 1964.

1140 KUTLER, Stanley I., ed. *John Marshall.* Englewood Cliffs, N.J., 1972.

1141 LAWRENCE, Alexander A. *James Moore Wayne: Southern Unionist.* Chapel Hill, N.C., 1943.

1142 LEACH, Richard H. "Benjamin Robbins Curtis: Judicial Misfit." *N Eng Q,* 25 (1952), 507–523.

1143 LERNER, Max. "John Marshall and the Campaign of History." *Colum L Rev,* 39 (1939), 396–431.

1144 LEVIN, A. J. "Mr. Justice William Johnson. . . ." *Mich L Rev,* 42 (1944), 803–830; 43 (1944), 497–548; 46 (1947), 131–186; 46 (1948), 481–520; 47 (1949), 477–536.

1145 LEWIS, Walker. *Without Fear or Favor. A Biography of Chief Justice Roger Brooke Taney.* Boston, 1965.

1146 LONGAKER, Richard P. "Andrew Jackson and the Judiciary." *Pol Sci Q,* 71 (1956), 341–364.

1147 LOTH, David Goldsmith. *Chief Justice: John Marshall and the Growth of the Republic.* New York, 1949.

1148 McCLELLAN, J. *Joseph Story and the American Constitution: A Study in Political and Legal Thought.* Norman, Okla., 1971.

1149 McCLOSKEY, Robert G., ed. *The Works of James Wilson.* 2 vols. Cambridge, Mass., 1967.

1150 MARSHALL, John. *Papers.* Ed. H. A. Johnson. Chapel Hill, N.C., 1974–.

1151 MENDELSON, Wallace. "Sectional Politics and the Rise of Judicial Supremacy." *J Pol,* 9 (1947), 255–272.

1152 MILES, Edwin A. "After John Marshall's Decision: *Worcester v. Georgia* and the Nullification Crisis." *J So Hist,* 39 (1973), 519–544.

1153 MONAGHAN, Frank. *John Jay.* New York, 1935.

1154 MORGAN, Donald G. *Justice William Johnson, the First Dissenter: The Career and Constitutional Philosophy of a Jeffersonian Judge.* Columbia, S.C., 1971.

1155 MORRIS, Richard B. *John Jay: The Nation and the Court.* Boston, 1967.

1156 NETTELS, Curtis. "The Mississippi Valley and the Federal Judiciary, 1807–1837." *Miss Val Hist Rev,* 12 (1925), 202–226.

1157 NEWMYER, R. Kent. "Justice Joseph Story, the Charles River Bridge Case and the Crisis of Republicanism." *Am J Leg Hist,* 17 (1973), 232–245.

1158 NEWMYER, R. Kent. *The Supreme Court under Marshall and Taney.* New York, 1968.

1159 PALMER, Ben W. *Marshall and Taney. Statesmen of the Law.* Minneapolis, 1939.

1160 RANSOM, William L., *et al.* "Roger Brooke Taney: Chief Justice of the Supreme Court of the United States (1836–1864)." *Geo L J,* 24 (1936), 809–909.

1161 ROPER, Donald M. "In Quest of Judicial Objectivity: The Marshall Court and the Legitimation of Slavery." *Stan L Rev,* 21 (1969), 532–547.

1162 SAYLOR, J. R. "Creation of the Federal Judiciary." *Bay L Rev,* 8 (1956), 257–282.

1163 SCHMIDHAUSER, John R. "Judicial Behavior and the Sectional Crisis of 1837–1860." *J Pol,* 23 (1961), 615–640.

1164 SCHUCHMAN, John S. "The Political Background of the Political-Question Doctrine: The Judges and the Dorr War." *Am J Leg Hist,* 16 (1972), 111–125.

1165 SCHWARTZ, Mortimer D., and John C. HOGAN, eds. *Joseph Story.* New York, 1959.

1166 *Scott v. Sandford.* 19 Howard. (60 U.S.) 393 (1857).

1167 SHRINER, Charles A. *William Paterson.* Paterson, N.J., 1940.

1168 SMITH, C. P. *James Wilson, Founding Father: 1742–1798.* Chapel Hill, N.C., 1956.

1169 SMITH, Charles W., Jr. *Roger B. Taney: Jacksonian Jurist.* Chapel Hill, N.C., 1936.

1170 SPECTOR, Robert M. "Lincoln and Taney: A Study in Constitutional Polarization." *Am J Leg Hist,* 15 (1971), 199–214.

1171 STORY, William W., ed. *The Miscellaneous Writings of Joseph Story.* Boston, 1852.

1172 SURRENCY, Erwin C. "The Judiciary Act of 1801." *Am J Leg Hist,* 2 (1958), 53–65.

1173 SWISHER, Carl B. "Dred Scott One Hundred Years After." *J Pol,* 19 (1957), 167–183.

1174 SWISHER, Carl B. *The Oliver Wendell Holmes Devise History of the Supreme Court of the United States. Volume V: The Taney Period 1836–1864.* New York, 1974.

1175 SWISHER, Carl B. *Roger B. Taney.* New York, 1935.

1176 TEISER, Sidney. "The Genesis of the Supreme Court." *Va L Rev,* 25 (1939), 398–421.

1177 THAYER, James Bradley. *John Marshall.* Boston, 1901.

1178 THOMAS, C. S. "Jefferson and the Judiciary." *Const Rev,* 10 (1926), 67–76.

1179 WARREN, Charles. "The Early History of the Supreme Court of the United States in Connection with Modern Attacks on the Judiciary." *Mass L Q,* 8 (1922), 1–23.

1180 WARREN, Charles. "The First Decade of the Supreme Court of the United States." *U Chi L Rev,* 7 (1940), 631–645.

1181 WARREN, Charles. "New Light on the History of the Federal Judiciary Act of 1789." *Harv L Rev,* 37 (1923), 49–132.

1182 WEISENBURGER, Francis P. *The Life of John McLean: A Politician on the United States Supreme Court.* Columbus, Ohio, 1937.

1183 WOODBURY, Levi. *Writings of Levi Woodbury, Political, Judicial and Literary.* Boston, 1852.

1864–1941

1184 ABRAHAM, Henry J. "John Marshall Harlan: A Justice Neglected." *Va L Rev,* 41 (1955), 871–891.

1185 ALSOP, Joseph, and Turner CATLEDGE. *The 168 Days.* Garden City, N.Y., 1938.

1186 ATKINSON, David N. "Mr. Justice Cardozo and the New Deal: An Appraisal." *Vill L Rev,* 15 (1969), 68–82.

1187 BAKER, Leonard. *Back to Back. The Duel Between FDR and the Supreme Court.* New York, 1967.

1188 BICKEL, Alexander M. "Mr. Taft Rehabilitates the Court." *Yale L J,* 79 (1969), 1–45.

1189 BICKEL, Alexander M. *The Unpublished Opinions of Mr. Justice Brandeis.* Cambridge, Mass., 1957.

1190 BIDDLE, Francis. *Justice Holmes, Natural Law and the Supreme Court.* New York, 1961.

1191 BOWEN, Catherine Drinker. *Yankee from Olympus. Justice Holmes and His Family.* Boston, 1944.

1192 BRABNER-SMITH, John W. "Congress vs. Supreme Court—A Constitutional Amendment?" *Va L Rev,* 22 (1936), 665–675.

1193 BRADLEY, C., ed. *Miscellaneous Writings of the Late Hon. Joseph P. Bradley.* Newark, N.J., 1902.

1194 BRANT, Irving. *Storm over the Constitution.* Indianapolis, 1936.

1195 BREWER, David J. "The Nation's Anchor." *Alb L J,* 57 (1898), 166–170.

1196 BREWER, David J. "The Nation's Safeguard." *Rep N Y State Bar Assoc,* 16 (1893), 37–47.

1197 BREWER, David J. "Protection to Private Property from Public Attachment." *Ry & Corp L J,* 10 (1891), 281–283.

1198 CATE, Wirt A. *Lucius Q. C. Lamar. . . .* Chapel Hill, N.C., 1935.

1199 CHAMBERS, John W. "The Big Switch: Justice Roberts and the Minimum-Wage Cases." *Lab Hist,* 10 (1969), 44–73.

1200 CLARK, Floyd B. *Constitutional Doctrines of Justice Harlan.* New York, 1969 (reprint of 1915 ed.).

1201 CLARK, Grenville. "The Supreme Court Issue." *Yale Rev,* 26 (1937), 669–688.

1202 CLARKE, John H. "The Naked Question of the Constitutionality of the Court Proposal." *Vit Speeches,* 3 (1937), 369–370.

1203 CLIFFORD, Philip G. *Nathan Clifford, Democrat.* New York, 1922.

1204 CORWIN, Edward S. *Constitutional Revolution, Ltd.* Claremont, Calif., 1941.

1205 CORWIN, Edward S. "Curbing the Court." *Ann Am Acad Pol Soc Sci,* 185 (1936), 45–55.

1206 CORWIN, Edward S. *Twilight of the Supreme Court.* New Haven, 1934.

1207 DANELSKI, David J. "A Supreme Court Justice Steps Down." *Yale Rev,* 54 (1965), 411–425.

1208 DANELSKI, David J., and Joseph S. TULCHIN, eds. *The Autobiographical Notes of Charles Evans Hughes.* Cambridge, Mass., 1973.

1209 DISHMAN, Robert B. "Mr. Justice White and the Rule of Reason." *Rev Pol,* 13 (1951), 229–243.

1210 DORO, Marion E. "The Brandeis Brief." *Vand L Rev,* 11 (1958), 783–799.

1211 EARLY, Stephen T. "James Clark McReynolds and the Judicial Process." Ph.D. dissertation, University of Virginia, 1954.

1212 ERIKSSON, Erik McKinley. *The Supreme Court and the New Deal. A Study of Recent Constitutional Interpretation.* Rosemead, Calif., 1940.

1213 FAIRMAN, Charles. "The Education of a Justice: Justice Bradley and Some of His Colleagues." *Stan L Rev,* 1 (1949), 217–255.

1214 FAIRMAN, Charles. "Justice Samuel Miller: A Study of a Judicial Statesman." *Pol Sci Q,* 50 (1935), 15–44.

1215 FAIRMAN, Charles. "Mr. Justice Bradley's Appointment to the Supreme Court and the Legal Tender Cases." *Harv L Rev,* 54 (1941), 977–1134, 1128–1155.

1216 FAIRMAN, Charles. *Mr. Justice Miller and the Supreme Court, 1862–1890.* Cambridge, Mass., 1939.

1217 FAIRMAN, Charles. *The Oliver Wendell Holmes Devise History of the Supreme Court of the United States. Volume VI: Reconstruction and Reunion, 1864–1888.* New York, 1971.

1218 FAIRMAN, Charles. "What Makes a Great Justice? Mr. Justice Bradley and the Supreme Court, 1870–1892." *Bos U L Rev,* 30 (1950), 49–102.

1219 FEGAN, Hugh J. "Edward Douglass White, Jurist and Statesman." *Geo L J,* 14 (1925), 1–21, 148–168; 15 (1926), 1–23.

1220 FITE, Katherine B., and Louis B. RUBENSTEIN. "Curbing the Supreme Court: State Experiences and Federal Proposals." *Mich L Rev,* 35 (1937), 762–787.

1221 FRAENKEL, O. K. "What Can Be Done about the Constitution and the Supreme Court." *Colum L Rev,* 37 (1937), 212–226.

1222 FRANKFURTER, Felix, ed. *Mr. Justice Brandeis.* New Haven, 1932.

1223 FRANKFURTER, Felix. *Mr. Justice Holmes and the Supreme Court.* Cambridge, Mass., 1939.

1224 FREUND, Paul A. "Charles Evans Hughes as Chief Justice." *Harv L Rev,* 81 (1967), 4–43.

1225 FREUND, Paul A. "Mr. Justice Brandeis." *Harv L Rev,* 70 (1957), 769–792.

1226 GRAHAM, James M. "Law's Labor Lost: Judicial Politics in the Progressive Era." *Wis L Rev,* 1972 (1972), 447–476.

1227 HART, Albert Bushnell. *Salmon Portland Chase.* Boston, 1899.

1228 HECKMAN, Richard Allen, and Betty Jean HALL. "Berea College and the Day Law." *Reg Ky Hist Soc,* 66 (1968), 35–52.

1229 HELLMAN, George S. *Benjamin N. Cardozo, American Judge.* New York, 1940.

1230 HENDEL, Samuel. *Charles Evans Hughes and the Supreme Court.* New York, 1951.

1231 HICKMAN, Martin B. "Mr. Justice Holmes: A Reappraisal." *West Pol Q,* 5 (1952), 66–83.

1232 HOLMES, Oliver Wendell, Jr. *Collected Legal Papers.* New York, 1920.

1233 HOLMES, Oliver Wendell, Jr. *Speeches.* Boston, 1913.

1234 HOWE, Mark A. DeWolfe, ed. *The Holmes-Laski Letters.* 2 vols. Cambridge, Mass., 1953.

1235 HOWE, Mark A. DeWolfe, ed. *The Holmes-Pollock Letters.* 2 vols. Cambridge, Mass., 1941.

1236 HOWE, Mark A. DeWolfe. *Justice Oliver Wendell Holmes.* 2 vols. Cambridge, Mass., 1957–1962.

1237 HOWE, Mark A. DeWolfe, ed. *The Occasional Speeches of Oliver Wendell Holmes.* Cambridge, Mass., 1962.

1238 HUGHES, David F. "Salmon P. Chase: Chief Justice." Ph.D. dissertation, Princeton University, 1963.

1239 HUNTER, Robert M. "Shall the Supreme Court Have New Blood?" *O State L J,* 3 (1937), 125–141.

1240 JACKSON, Robert H. *The Struggle for Judicial Supremacy. A Study of a Crisis in American Power Politics.* New York, 1941.

1241 "John Marshall Harlan, 1833–1911." *Ky L J,* 46 (1958), 321–474.

1242 KENT, Charles A. *Memoir of Henry Billings Brown.* New York, 1915.

1243 KERR, Charles. "The Thirty Years' War on the Supreme Court." *Va L Rev,* 17 (1931), 629–652.

1244 KING, Willard L. *Melville Weston Fuller.* New York, 1950.

1245 KLINKHAMER, Sister Marie Carolyn. *Edward Douglas White, Chief Justice of the United States.* Washington, D.C., 1943.

1246 KONEFSKY, Samuel J. *The Legacy of Holmes and Brandeis.* New York, 1956.

1247 KUTLER, Stanley I. *Judicial Power and Reconstruction Politics.* Chicago, 1968.

1248 LAMAR, Clarinda P. *The Life of Joseph Rucker Lamar, 1857–1916.* New York, 1926.

1249 LASKI, Harold J. "The Political Philosophy of Mr. Justice Holmes." *Yale L J,* 40 (1931), 683–695.

1250 LATHAM, Frank B. *Great Dissenter: Supreme Court Justice John Marshall Harlan (1833–1911).* New York, 1970.

1251 LEONARD, Charles A. *A Search for a Judicial Philosophy. Mr. Justice Roberts and the Constitutional Revolution of 1937.* Port Washington, N.Y., 1971.

1252 LERNER, Max, ed. *The Mind and Faith of Justice Holmes. His Speeches, Essays, Letters, and Judicial Opinions.* New York, 1943.

1253 LEVY, Beryl Harold. *Cardozo and the Frontiers of Legal Thinking.* Cleveland, Ohio, 1969.

1254 McDEVITT, Matthew. *Joseph McKenna, Associate Justice of the United States.* Washington, D.C., 1946.

1255 McELWAIN, Edwin. "The Business of the Supreme Court as Conducted by Chief Justice Hughes." *Harv L Rev,* 63 (1949), 5–26.

1256 McGOVNEY, D. O. "Reorganization of the Supreme Court." *Calif L Rev,* 25 (1937), 389–412.

1257 McLEAN, Joseph E. *William Rufus Day: Supreme Court Justice from Ohio.* Baltimore, 1947.

1258 MAGRATH, C. Peter. *Morrison R. Waite: The Triumph of Character.* New York, 1963.

1259 MASON, Alpheus T. *Brandeis: A Free Man's Life.* New York, 1946.

1260 MASON, Alpheus T. *Brandeis: Lawyer and Judge in the Modern State.* Princeton, N.J., 1933.

1261 MASON, Alpheus T. *The Brandeis Way.* Princeton, N.J., 1938.

1262 MASON, Alpheus T. "Charles Evans Hughes: An Appeal to the Bar of History." *Vand L Rev,* 6 (1952), 1–19.

1263 MASON, Alpheus T. "The Conservative World of Mr. Justice Sutherland." *Am Pol Sci Rev,* 32 (1938), 443–477.

1264 MASON, Alpheus T. "Has the Supreme Court Abdicated?" *N Am Rev,* 238 (1934), 353–360.

1265 MASON, Alpheus T. *The Supreme Court: Vehicle of Revealed Truth or Power Group, 1930–1937.* Boston, 1953.

1266 MASON, Alpheus T. *William Howard Taft: Chief Justice.* New York, 1965.

1267 MENDELSON, Wallace. "Mr. Justice Field and Laissez-Faire." *Va L Rev,* 36 (1950), 45–58.

1268 "Mr. Justice Cardozo." *Harv L Rev,* 52 (1939), 353–489.

1269 MURPHY, James B. *L. Q. C. Lamar: Pragmatic Patriot.* Baton Rouge, La., 1973.

1270 NOBLITT, Harding Coolidge. "The Supreme Court and the Progressive Era, 1902–1921." Ph.D. dissertation, University of Chicago, 1955.

1271 O'BRIEN, Kenneth B., Jr. "Education, Americanization and the Supreme Court in the 1920's." *Am Q,* 13 (1961), 161–171.

1272 PASCHAL, Joel Francis. *Mr. Justice Sutherland. A Man Against the State.* Princeton, N.J., 1951.

1273 PAUL, A. M. *Conservative Crisis and the Rule of Law: Attitudes of Bar and Bench, 1887–1895.* Ithaca, N.Y., 1960.

1274 PEABODY, James Bishop, ed. *The Holmes-Einstein Letters.* New York, 1964.

1275 PERKINS, Dexter. *Charles Evans Hughes and American Democratic Statesmanship.* Boston, 1956.

1276 PERRIGO, Lynn I. "The Federal Judiciary: An Analysis of Proposed Revisions." *Minn L Rev,* 21 (1937), 481–511.

1277 POLLARD, Joseph P. *Mr. Justice Cardozo. A Liberal Mind in Action.* New York, 1935.

1278 PRINGLE, Henry F. *Life and Times of William Howard Taft.* 2 vols. New York, 1939.

1279 PRITCHETT, C. Herman. "Justice Holmes and a Liberal Court." *Va Q Rev,* 24 (1948), 43–58.

1280 PUSEY, Merlo J. *Charles Evans Hughes.* 2 vols. New York, 1951.

1281 PUSEY, Merlo J. *The Supreme Court Crisis.* New York, 1937.

1282 RAGAN, Allen E. *Chief Justice Taft.* Columbus, Ohio, 1938.

POLITICAL INSTITUTIONS

1283 RATNER, Sidney. "Was the Supreme Court Packed by President Grant?" *Pol Sci Q,* 50 (1935), 342–356.

1284 RIBBLE, F. D. G. "The Constitutional Doctrines of Chief Justice Hughes." *Colum L Rev,* 41 (1941), 1190–1215.

1285 ROELOFS, Vernon William. "William R. Day: A Study in Constitutional History." Ph.D. dissertation, University of Michigan, 1942.

1286 ROOSEVELT, Theodore. "Judges and Progress." *Outlook,* 100 (1912), 40–48.

1287 SHIRAS, Winfield, ed. *Justice George Shiras, Jr. of Pittsburgh . . ., 1892–1903.* Pittsburgh, 1953.

1288 SILVER, David M. *Lincoln's Supreme Court.* Urbana, Ill., 1956.

1289 STEPHENSON, D. Grier, Jr. "The Chief Justice as Leader: The Case of Morrison Remick Waite." *Wm & M L Rev,* 14 (1973), 899–927.

1290 STONE, Harlan Fiske. "Fifty Years' Work of the United States Supreme Court." *Am Bar Assoc J,* 14 (1928), 428–436.

1291 SUTHERLAND, George. "Principle or Expedient?" *Proc N Y State Bar Assoc,* 44 (1921), 263–282.

1292 SWINDLER, William F. *Court and Constitution in the Twentieth Century: The Old Legality, 1889–1932.* Indianapolis, 1969.

1293 SWISHER, Carl B. *Stephen J. Field: Craftsman of the Law.* Chicago, 1969 (reprint of 1930 ed.).

1294 TRIMBLE, Bruce R. *Chief Justice Waite: Defender of the Public Interest.* Princeton, N.J., 1938.

1295 TWISS, Benjamin R. *Lawyers and the Constitution: How Laissez-Faire Came to the Supreme Court.* Princeton, N.J., 1942.

1296 UROFSKY, Melvin I. *Mind of One Piece: Brandeis and American Reform.* New York, 1971.

1297 UROFSKY, Melvin I., and David W. LEVY, eds. *Letters of Louis D. Brandeis.* Albany, N.Y., 1971–.

1298 U.S. Senate. Committee on the Judiciary. *Reorganization of the Federal Judiciary.* Hearings on S. 1392, March 10–April 23, 1937, 6 pts. 75th Cong., 1st sess., 1937. Washington, D.C., 1937.

1299 WARNER, H. Landon. *The Life of Mr. Justice Clarke: A Testament to the Power of Liberal Dissent in America.* Cleveland, Ohio, 1959.

1300 WARREN, Earl. "Chief Justice William Howard Taft." *Yale L J,* 67 (1958), 353–362.

1301 WESTIN, Alan F. "John Marshall Harlan and the Constitutional Rights of Negroes." *Yale L J,* 66 (1957), 637–710.

1302 WESTIN, Alan F. "Stephen J. Field and the Headnote to O'Neil v. Vermont: A Snapshot of the Fuller Court." *Yale L J,* 67 (1958), 363–383.

1303 WESTIN, Alan F. "The Supreme Court, the Populist Movement and the Campaign of 1896." *J Pol,* 15 (1953), 3–41.

1304 WHITE, Edward D. *Legal Traditions and Other Papers.* St. Louis, Mo., 1927.

1305 WHITE, Edward D. "The Supreme Court of the United States." *Am Bar Assoc J,* 7 (1921), 341–343.

1306 WHITE, G. Edward. "The Rise and Fall of Justice Holmes." *U Chi L Rev,* 39 (1971), 51–77.

1307 WIECEK, William M. "The Reconstruction of Federal Judicial Power, 1863–1875." *Am J Leg Hist,* 13 (1969), 333–359.

1308 WYZANSKI, Charles E., Jr. "The Democracy of Justice Oliver Wendell Holmes." *Vand L Rev,* 7 (1954), 311–324.

1941–

1309 BAKER, Liva. *Felix Frankfurter.* New York, 1969.

1310 BICKEL, Alexander M. "The New Supreme Court: Prospects and Problems." *Tul L Rev,* 45 (1971), 229–244.

1311 BICKEL, Alexander M. *Politics and the Warren Court.* New York, 1965.

1312 BICKEL, Alexander M. *The Supreme Court and the Idea of Progress.* New York, 1970.

1313 BLAND, Randall W. *Private Pressure on Public Law: The Legal Career of Justice Thurgood Marshall.* Port Washington, N.Y., 1973.

1314 BOLNER, James J. "Mr. Chief Justice Vinson." Ph.D. dissertation, University of Virginia, 1962.

1315 BYRNES, James F. "The South Respects the Written Constitution: Supreme Court Has No Power to Amend the Constitution." *Vit Speeches,* 23 (1957), 331–335.

1316 BYRNES, James F. "The Supreme Court Must Be Curbed." *U S News & World Rep,* 40 (May 18, 1956), 50–54.

1317 "Chief Justice Stone." *Colum L Rev,* 46 (1946), 693–800.

1318 CHRISTMAN, Henry M., ed. *The Public Papers of Chief Justice Earl Warren.* New York, 1959.

1319 COUNTRYMAN, Vern, ed. *Douglas of the Supreme Court.* Garden City, N.Y., 1959.

1320 COX, Archibald. *The Warren Court: Constitutional Decision as an Instrument of Social Reform.* Cambridge, Mass., 1968.

1321 DECKER, Raymond G. "Justice Hugo L. Black: The Balancer of Absolutes." *Calif L Rev,* 59 (1971), 1335–1355.

1322 DORSEN, Norman. "The Second Mr. Justice Harlan: A Constitutional Conservative." *N Y U L Rev,* 44 (1969), 249–271.

1323 DOUGLAS, William O. *Go East, Young Man; The Autobiography of William O. Douglas.* New York, 1974.

1324 ELMAN, Philip, ed. *Of Law and Men. Papers and Addresses of Felix Frankfurter.* New York, 1956.

1325 FAIRMAN, Charles. "The Attack on the Segregation Cases." *Harv L Rev,* 70 (1956), 83–94.

1326 FITZGERALD, Mark J. "Justice Reed: A Study of a Center Judge." Ph.D. dissertation, University of Chicago, 1950.

1327 FRANK, John P. "Fred Vinson and the Chief Justiceship." *U Chi L Rev,* 21 (1954), 212–246.

1328 FRANK, John P. "Justice Murphy: The Goals Attempted." *Yale L J,* 59 (1949), 1–26.

1329 FRANK, John P. *Mr. Justice Black: The Man and His Opinions.* New York, 1949.

1330 FRANKFURTER, Felix. "Mr. Justice Roberts." *U Penn L Rev,* 104 (1955), 311–317.

1331 FREUND, Paul A. "Storm over the American Supreme Court." *Mod L Rev,* 21 (1958), 345–358.

1332 GERHART, Eugene. *America's Advocate: Robert H. Jackson.* Indianapolis, 1958.

1333 GOLDBERG, Arthur J. *Equal Justice: The Supreme Court in the Warren Era.* Evanston, Ill., 1971.

1334 GRAHAM, Fred P. *The Self-Inflicted Wound.* New York, 1970.

1335 GRESSMAN, Eugene. "The Controversial Image of Mr. Justice Murphy." *Geo L J,* 47 (1959), 631–654.

1336 GUNTHER, Gerald. "In Search of Judicial Quality on a Changing Court: The Case of Justice Powell." *Stan L Rev,* 24 (1972), 1001–1035.

1337 HAMILTON, Virginia Van Der Veer. *Hugo Black: The Alabama Years.* Baton Rouge, La., 1972.

1338 HARPER, Fowler, V. *Justice Rutledge and the Bright Constellation.* Indianapolis, 1957.

1339 HOWARD, J. Woodford. *Mr. Justice Murphy: A Political Biography.* Princeton, N.J., 1968.

1340 "In Memoriam: Fred M. Vinson." *Northw U L Rev,* 49 (1954), 1–75.

1341 JAFFE, Louis L. "The Judicial Universe of Mr. Justice Frankfurter." *Harv L Rev,* 62 (1949), 357–412.

1342 JAFFE, Louis L. "Mr. Justice Jackson." *Harv L Rev,* 68 (1955), 940–998.

1343 KATCHER, Leo. *Earl Warren: A Political Biography.* New York, 1967.

1344 KOHLMEIER, Louis M., Jr. *God Save This Honorable Court; The Supreme Court Crisis.* New York, 1972.

1345 KONEFSKY, Samuel J. *Chief Justice Stone and the Supreme Court.* New York, 1946.

1346 KONEFSKY, Samuel J. *The Constitutional World of Mr. Justice Frankfurter.* New York, 1949.

1347 KURLAND, Philip B., ed. *Felix Frankfurter and the Supreme Court; Extrajudicial Essays on the Court and the Constitution.* Chicago, 1970.

1348 KURLAND, Philip B. *Politics, the Constitution, and the Warren Court.* Chicago, 1969.

1349 KURLAND, Philip B. "Toward a Political Supreme Court." *U Chi L Rev,* 37 (1969), 19–46.

1350 LEVITAN, David M. "Mr. Justice Rutledge." *Va L Rev,* 34 (1948), 393–416, 526–552.

1351 LEVY, Leonard W., ed. *The Supreme Court under Earl Warren.* New York, 1972.

1352 LYTLE, Clifford M. *The Warren Court and Its Critics.* Tucson, Ariz., 1968.

1353 McCLOSKEY, Robert G. *The Modern Supreme Court.* Cambridge, Mass., 1972.

1354 MASON, Alpheus T. "The Burger Court in Historical Perspective." *Pol Sci Q,* 89 (1974), 27–45.

1355 MASON, Alpheus T. *Harlan Fiske Stone: Pillar of the Law.* New York, 1956.

1356 MENDELSON, Wallace. "The Court Must Not Be Curbed; A Reply to Mr. Byrnes." *J Pol,* 19 (1957), 81–86.

1357 MENDELSON, Wallace. "Hugo Black and Judicial Discretion." *Pol Sci Q,* 85 (1970), 17–39.

1358 MENDELSON, Wallace. *Justices Black and Frankfurter: Conflict in the Court.* Chicago, 1961.

1359 MITAU, G. Theodore. *Decade of Decision: The Supreme Court and the Constitutional Revolution, 1954–1964.* New York, 1967.

1360 "Mr. Justice Black: Thirty Years in Retrospect." *UCLA L Rev,* 14 (1967), 397–552.

1361 "Mr. Justice Jackson—A Symposium." *Stan L Rev,* 8 (1955), 3–76.

1362 O'BRIEN, F. William. "Mr. Justice Reed and Democratic Pluralism." *Geo L J,* 45 (1957), 364–387.

1363 PRITCHETT, C. Herman. *The Roosevelt Court. A Study in Judicial Politics and Values, 1937–1947.* New York, 1948.

1364 REHNQUIST, William H. "Memorandum on Motion to Recuse." 409 U.S. 824 (1972).

1365 "Robert H. Jackson: 1892–1954." *Colum L Rev,* 55 (1955), 435–525.

1366 ROCHE, John P. "The Utopian Pilgrimage of Mr. Justice Murphy." *Vand L Rev,* 10 (1957), 369–394.

1367 RUTLEDGE, Wiley B. *A Declaration of Legal Faith.* Lawrence, Kan., 1947.

1368 SAYLER, Richard H., *et al.,* eds. *The Warren Court. A Critical Analysis.* New York, 1969.

1369 SCANLAN, Alfred L. "The Roosevelt Court Becomes the Truman Court." *Not Dame Law,* 26 (1951), 214–267.

1370 SCHUBERT, Glendon A. *Dispassionate Justice: A Synthesis of the Judicial Opinions of Robert H. Jackson.* Indianapolis, 1969.

1371 SCHUBERT, Glendon A. *The Future of the Nixon Court.* Honolulu, 1972.

1372 SCHWARTZ, Bernard. *The Supreme Court: Constitutional Revolution in Retrospect.* New York, 1957.

1373 SHOGAN, Robert. *A Question of Judgment: The Fortas Case and the Struggle for the Supreme Court.* Indianapolis, 1972.

1374 SIMON, James F. *In His Own Image; The Supreme Court in Richard Nixon's America.* New York, 1973.

1375 SIMPSON, Dwight J. "Robert H. Jackson and the Doctrine of Judicial Restraint." *UCLA L Rev,* 3 (1956), 325–359.

1376 STRICKLAND, Stephen, ed. *Hugo Black and the Supreme Court: A Symposium.* Indianapolis, 1967.

1377 SWINDLER, William F. *Court and Constitution in the 20th Century. The New Legality, 1932–1968.* Indianapolis, 1972.

1378 SWINDLER, William F. "The Court, the Constitution and Chief Justice Burger." *Vand L Rev,* 27 (1974), 443–474.

1379 SWINDLER, William F. "The Warren Court: Completion of a Constitutional Revolution." *Vand L Rev,* 23 (1970), 205–250.

1380 "Symposium on Justice Felix Frankfurter." *Yale L J,* 67 (1957), 179–323.

1381 "Symposium: The Warren Court." *Mich L Rev,* 67 (1968), 219–358.

1382 THOMAS, Helen Shirley. *Felix Frankfurter, Scholar on the Bench.* Baltimore, 1960.

1383 U.S. House of Representatives. Committee on the Judiciary. *Associate Justice William O. Douglas.* Final report by the Special Subcommittee on H. Res. 920, pursuant to H. Res. 93, a resolution authorizing the committee on the judiciary to conduct studies and investigations relating to certain matters within its jurisdiction. 91st Cong., 2nd sess., 1970. Washington, D.C., 1970.

1384 VINSON, Fred M. "Our Enduring Constitution." *Wash & Lee L Rev,* 6 (1949), 1–11.

1385 WARREN, Earl. *A Republic, If You Can Keep It.* New York, 1972.

1386 WEAVER, John D. *Warren: The Man, the Court, the Era.* Boston, 1967.

1387 WECHSLER, Herbert. "Stone and the Constitution." *Colum L Rev,* 46 (1946), 764–800.

1388 WEIDNER, Paul A. "Justice Jackson and the Judicial Function." *Mich L Rev,* 53 (1955), 567–594.

1389 WILLIAMS, Charlotte. *Hugo L. Black.* Baltimore, 1950.

D. Political Parties

1390 AGAR, Herbert. *The Price of Union.* Boston, 1950.

1391 American Political Science Association. *Toward a More Responsible Two-Party System.* New York, 1950.

1392 BANNER, James M. *To the Hartford Convention: The Federalists and the Origins of Party Politics in Massachusetts, 1789–1815.* New York, 1970.

1393 CHAMBERS, Nisbet, and Walter Dean BURNHAM. *The American Party Systems: Stages of Political Development.* New York, 1967.

1394 CUNNINGHAM, Noble E., Jr. *The Jeffersonian Republicans in Power: Party Operations, 1801–1809.* Chapel Hill, N.C., 1963.

1395 CUNNINGHAM, Noble E., Jr. *The Jeffersonian Republicans: The Formation of Party Organization, 1789–1801.* Chapel Hill, N.C., 1957.

1396 FORMISANO, Ronald P. "Deferential-Participant Politics: The Early Republic's Political Culture, 1789–1840." *Am Pol Sci Rev,* 68 (1974), 473–487.

1397 GINSBERG, Benjamin. "Critical Elections and the Substance of Party Conflict: 1844–1968." *Midw J Pol Sci,* 16 (1972), 603–625.

1398 HASBROUK, P. D. *Party Government in the House of Representatives.* New York, 1927.

1399 HESSELTINE, William B. *The Rise and Fall of Third Parties, from Anti-Masonry to Wallace.* Washington, D.C., 1948.

1400 HOFSTADTER, Richard. *The Idea of a Party System: The Rise of Legitimate Opposition in the United States, 1780–1840.* Berkeley, Calif., 1969.

1401 KEY, V. O., Jr. "A Theory of Critical Elections." *J Pol,* 17 (1955), 3–18.

1402 KEY, V. O., Jr. *Politics, Parties and Pressure Groups.* 5th ed. New York, 1964.

1403 LINK, Eugene P. *Democratic Republican Societies, 1790–1800.* New York, 1942.

1404 LIVERMORE, Shaw. *The Twilight of Federalism: The Disintegration of the Federalist Party, 1815–1830.* Princeton, N.J., 1962.

1405 MAIN, Jackson Turner. *Political Parties Before the Constitution.* Chapel Hill, N.C., 1973.

1406 MERRIAM, Charles E., and Louise OVERACKER. *Primary Elections.* Chicago, 1928.

1407 OBERHOLTZER, E. P. *The Referendum in America.* New York, 1911.

1408 OSTROGORSKI, M. *Democracy and the Organization of Political Parties.* Vol. II: *The United States.* Chicago, 1964.

1409 PORTER, Kirk H., and Donald Bruce JOHNSON. *National Party Platforms, 1840–1956.* Urbana, Ill., 1956.

1410 POULSHOCK, S. Walter. *The Two Parties and the Tariff in the 1880's.* Syracuse, N.Y., 1965.

1411 RYAN, Mary P. "Party Formation in the United States Congress, 1789 to 1796: A Quantitative Analysis." *Wm & M Q,* 28 (1971), 523–542.

1412 SCHLESINGER, Arthur M., Jr., ed. *History of U.S. Political Parties.* 4 vols. New York, 1973.

1413 SUNDQUIST, James L. "Whither the American Party System?" *Pol Sci Q,* 88 (1973), 559–581.

1414 TURNER, John J., Jr. "The Twelfth Amendment and the First American Party System." *Hist,* 35 (1973), 221–237.

E. State and Local Institutions

1415 ABRAHAM, Henry J., and Robert R. BENEDETTI. "The State Attorney General: A Friend of the Court?" *U Penn L Rev,* 117 (1969), 795–828.

1416 BAKKEN, Gordon Morris. "Judicial Review in the Rocky Mountain Territorial Courts." *Am J Leg Hist,* 15 (1971), 56–65.

1417 BANFIELD, Edward C., and James Q. WILSON. *City Politics.* Cambridge, Mass., 1965.

1418 CAMPBELL, Alan, ed. *The States and the Urban Crisis.* Englewood Cliffs, N.J., 1970.

1419 DODD, W. F. "The First State Constitutional Conventions, 1776–1783." *Am Pol Sci Rev,* 2 (1908), 545–562.

1420 DOWNS, Anthony. *Opening Up the Suburbs.* New Haven, 1973.

1421 GREEN, Fletcher M. *Constitutional Development in the South Atlantic States, 1776–1860.* Chapel Hill, N.C., 1930.

1422 GREENE, Jack P. *The Quest for Power: The Lower House of Assembly in the Southern Royal Colonies, 1689–1776.* Chapel Hill, N.C., 1963.

1423 GRIFFITH, Lucille. *The Virginia House of Burgesses, 1750–1774.* Northport, Ala., 1963.

1424 HAMLIN, Paul M., and Charles BAKER. *The Supreme Court of Judicature of the Province of New York, 1691–1704.* 3 vols. New York, 1959.

1425 HOLCOMBE, Arthur N. *State Government in the United States.* New York, 1916.

1426 HOWARD, A. E. Dick. "State Constitutions and the Environment." *Va L Rev,* 58 (1972), 193–229.

1427 "The Impact of Voter Equality on the Representational Structures of Local Government." *U Chi L Rev,* 39 (1972), 639–657.

1428 *Journal of Debates and Proceedings in the Convention of Delegates Chosen to Revise the Constitution of Massachusetts (1820).* New ed., rev. & corrected. Boston, 1853.

1429 KEY, V. O., Jr. *American State Politics.* New York, 1965.

1430 KING, Rufus. *Ohio; The First Fruits of the Ordinance of 1787.* Boston, 1891.

1431 KRISLOV, Samuel. "Constituency Versus Constitutionalism: The Desegregation Issue and Tensions and Aspirations of Southern Attorneys General." *Midw J Pol Sci,* 3 (1959), 75–92.

1432 LEVY, Leonard W. *The Law of the Commonwealth and Chief Justice Shaw.* Cambridge, Mass., 1957.

1433 LIPSON, Leslie. *The American Governor from Figurehead to Leader.* Chicago, 1939.

1434 LOCKARD, Duane. *The Politics of State and Local Government.* New York, 1963.

1435 McCAIN, Paul M. *The County Court in North Carolina Before 1750.* Durham, N.C., 1954.

1436 MAIN, Jackson Turner. *The Sovereign States, 1775–1783.* New York, 1973.

1437 MAIN, Jackson Turner. *The Upper House in Revolutionary America, 1763–1788.* Madison, Wisc., 1967.

1438 MICHELMAN, Frank I., and Terrence SANDALOW. *Materials on Government in Urban Areas.* St. Paul, Minn., 1970.

1439 MURPHY, Thomas P. *Metropolitics and the Urban County.* Washington, D.C., 1970.

1440 NELSON, Margaret V. *A Study of Judicial Review in Virginia, 1789–1928.* New York, 1947.

1441 NELSON, William E. "Changing Conceptions of Judicial Review: The Evolution of Constitutional Theory in the States, 1790–1860." *U Penn L Rev,* 120 (1972), 1166–1185.

1442 NIEDHOFFER, Arthur. *Behind the Shield: The Police in Urban Society.* Garden City, N.Y., 1967.

1443 PESSEN, Edward. "Who Governed the Nation's Cities in the 'Era of the Common Man'?" *Pol Sci Q,* 87 (1972), 591–614.

1444 *Proceedings and Debates of the Virginia State Convention of 1829–1830.* Richmond, Va., 1830.

1445 REID, John Philip. *Chief Justice: The Judicial World of Charles Doe.* Cambridge, Mass., 1967.

1446 *Reports of the Proceedings and Debates of the Convention of 1821, Assembled for the Purpose of Amending the Constitution of the State of New York.* Albany, N.Y., 1821.

1447 SAYRE, Wallace S., and Herbert KAUFMAN. *Governing New York City; Politics in the Metropolis.* New York, 1960.

1448 SCHLESINGER, Arthur M. *The Rise of the City, 1878–1898.* New York, 1933.

1449 SMITH, Franklin A. *Judicial Review of Legislation in New York, 1906–1936.* New York, 1952.

1450 STEFFENS, Lincoln. *The Shame of the Cities.* New York, 1904.

1451 STEWART, Frank Mann. *A Half Century of Municipal Reform: The History of the National Municipal League.* Berkeley, Calif., 1950.

1452 STURM, Albert L. *Thirty Years of State Constitution-Making: 1938–1968.* New York, 1970.

1453 SYED, Anwar H. *The Political Theory of American Local Government.* New York, 1966.

1454 TEAFORD, Jon. "City Versus State: The Struggle for Legal Ascendancy." *Am J Leg Hist,* 17 (1973), 51–65.

1455 WOLFINGER, Raymond E. "Why Political Machines Have Not Withered Away and Other Revisionist Thoughts." *J Pol,* 34 (1972), 365–398.

V. Doctrines and Politics

A. Separation and Sharing of Powers

General

1456 BINKLEY, Wilfred E. *President and Congress.* New York, 1962.

1457 BLACK, Henry Campbell. *The Relation of the Executive Power to Legislation.* Princeton, N.J., 1919.

1458 GINNANE, Robert W. "The Control of Federal Administration by Congressional Resolutions and Committees." *Harv L Rev,* 66 (1953), 569–611.

1459 GREEN, Frederick. "Separation of Governmental Powers." *Yale L J,* 29 (1920), 369–393.

1460 HARRIS, Joseph P. *Congressional Control of Administration.* Washington, D.C., 1964.

1461 JOHANNES, John R. "Where Does the Buck Stop?—Congress, President, and the Responsibility for Legislative Initiation." *West Pol Q,* 25 (1972), 396–415.

1462 KRAINES, Oscar. "The President Versus Congress: The Keep Commission, 1905–1909: First Comprehensive Presidential Inquiry into Administration." *West Pol Q,* 23 (1970), 5–54.

1463 MacMAHON, Arthur W. "Congressional Oversight of Administration: The Power of the Purse." *Pol Sci Q,* 58 (1943), 161–190, 380–414.

1464 MILLER, Arthur S. "Congressional Power to Define the Presidential Pocket Veto Power." *Vand L Rev,* 25 (1972), 557–572.

1465 MILLETT, John D., and Lindsay ROGERS. "The Legislative Veto and the Reorganization Act of 1939." *Pub Ad Rev,* 1 (1941), 176–189.

1466 PARKER, Reginald. "The Historic Basis of Administrative Law: Separation of Powers and Judicial Supremacy." *Rut L Rev,* 12 (1958), 449–481.

1467 PARKER, Reginald. "Separation of Powers Revisited." *Mich L Rev,* 49 (1951), 1009–1038.

1468 REINSTEIN, Robert J., and Harvey A. SILVERGLATE. "Legislative Privilege and the Separation of Powers." *Harv L Rev,* 86 (1973), 1113–1182.

1469 ROSENTHAL, Albert J. "The Constitution, Congress, and Presidential Elections." *Mich L Rev,* 67 (1968), 1–38.

1470 "Separation of Powers and Executive Privilege: The Watergate Briefs." *Pol Sci Q,* 88 (1973), 582–654.

1471 SHARP, Malcolm P. "The Classical American Doctrine of the Separation of Powers." *U Chi L Rev,* 2 (1935), 385–436.

1472 VANDERBILT, Arthur T. *The Doctrine of Separation of Powers and Its Present-day Significance.* Lincoln, Neb., 1963.

1473 VILE, M. J. C. *Constitutionalism and the Separation of Powers.* Oxford, 1967.

1474 WARP, George. "Independent Regulatory Commissions and the Separation of Powers Doctrine." *Not Dame Law,* 16 (1941), 181–193.

1475 WRIGHT, Benjamin F. "The Origins of the Separation of Powers in America." *Origins of American Political Thought.* Ed. John P. Roche. New York, 1967.

The Congress

Membership, Apportionment, and Privileges

1476 AUERBACH, Carl A. "The Reapportionment Cases: One Person, One Vote—One Vote, One Value." *S Ct Rev* (1964), 1–87.

1477 BAKER, Gordon E. *The Reapportionment Revolution: Representation, Political Power, and the Supreme Court.* New York, 1966.

1478 *Baker v. Carr.* 369 U.S. 186 (1962).

1479 BALL, Howard. *The Warren Court's Conceptions of Democracy: An Evaluation of the Supreme Court's Apportionment Opinions.* Rutherford, N.J., 1971.

1480 *Bond v. Floyd.* 385 U.S. 116 (1966).

1481 CARPENETI, Walter L. "Legislative Apportionment: Multimember Districts and Fair Representation." *U Penn L Rev,* 120 (1972), 666–700.

1482 *Colgrove v. Green.* 328 U.S. 549 (1946).

1483 CORTNER, Richard C. *The Apportionment Cases.* Knoxville, Tenn., 1970.

1484 DIXON, Robert G., Jr. *Democratic Representation: Reapportionment in Law and Politics.* New York, 1968.

1485 *Dombrowski v. Eastland.* 387 U.S. 82 (1967).

1486 EDWARDS, James M. "The Gerrymander and 'One Man, One Vote.' " *N Y U L Rev,* 46 (1971), 879–899.

1487 FRIEDELBAUM, S. H. "Baker v. Carr: The New Doctrine of Judicial Intervention and Its Implications for American Federalism." *U Chi L Rev,* 29 (1962), 673–704.

1488 GAZELL, James A. "One Man, One Vote: Its Long Germination." *West Pol Q,* 23 (1970), 445–462.

1489 *Gravel v. United States.* 408 U.S. 606 (1972).

1490 HACKER, Andrew. *Congressional Districting: The Issue of Equal Representation.* Rev. ed. Washington, D.C., 1964.

1491 HANSON, Royce. *The Political Thicket: Reapportionment and Constitutional Democracy.* Englewood Cliffs, N.J., 1966.

1492 "Immunity under the Speech or Debate Clause for Republication and from Questioning about Sources." *Mich L Rev,* 71 (1973) 1251–1274.

1493 IRWIN, William P. "Representation and Election: The Reapportionment Cases in Retrospect." *Mich L Rev,* 67 (1969), 729–754.

1494 KINDREGAN, C. P. "The Cases of Adam Clayton Powell, Jr., and Julian Bond: The Right of Legislative Bodies to Exclude Members-Elect." *Suf U L Rev,* 2 (1968), 58–80.

1495 LEE, Calvin B. T. *One Man, One Vote: WMCA and the Struggle for Equal Representation.* New York, 1967.

1496 "Legislative Exclusion: Julian Bond and Adam Clayton Powell." *U Chi L Rev,* 35 (1968), 151–172.

1497 McKAY, Robert B. *Reapportionment: The Law and Politics of Equal Representation.* New York, 1965.

1498 *Mahan v. Howell.* 410 U.S. 315 (1973).

1499 NEAL, Phil C. "Baker v. Carr: Politics in Search of Law." *S Ct Rev* (1962), 252–327.

1500 POLSBY, Nelson W., ed. *Reapportionment in the 1970's.* Berkeley, Calif., 1971.

1501 *Powell v. McCormack.* 395 U.S. 486 (1969).

1502 *Reynolds v. Sims.* 377 U.S. 533 (1964).

1503 SCHUBERT, Glendon A. *Reapportionment.* New York, 1965.

1504 WEEKS, Kent M. *Adam Clayton Powell and the Supreme Court.* New York, 1971.

1505 YANKWICH, Leon R. "The Immunity of Congressional Speech—Its Origin, Meaning and Scope." *U Penn L Rev,* 99 (1951), 960–977.

Legislative Power

1506 BAKER, Ralph H. *The National Bituminous Coal Commission.* Baltimore, 1941.

1507 BURNS, James M. *Congress on Trial; The Legislative Process and the Administrative State.* New York, 1949.

1508 CORWIN, Edward S. "The Schechter Case—Landmark or What?" *N Y U L Q Rev,* 13 (1936), 151–190.

1509 CUSHMAN, Robert E. *The Independent Regulatory Commission.* New York, 1941.

1510 FISHER, Louis. "Delegating Power to the President." *J Pub L,* 19 (1970), 251–282.

1511 *J. W. Hampton, Jr., & Co. v. United States.* 276 U.S. 394 (1928)

1512 HYMAN, Jacob D., and Nathaniel L. NATHANSON. "Judicial Review of Price Control: The Battle of the Meat Regulations." *Ill L Rev,* 42 (1947), 584–634.

1513 JAFFE, Louis L. "An Essay on Delegation of Legislative Power." *Colum L Rev,* 47 (1947), 359–376, 561–593.

1514 MacAVOY, Paul W., ed. *Crisis of the Regulatory Commissions: An Introduction to a Current Issue of Public Policy.* New York, 1970.

1515 MacCALLUM, Gerald C., Jr. "Legislative Intent." *Yale L J,* 75 (1966), 754–787.

1516 *McCulloch v. Maryland.* 4 Wheaton (17 U.S.) 316 (1819).

1517 *Schechter Poultry Corp. v. United States.* 259 U.S. 495 (1935).

1518 *Wayman v. Southard.* 10 Wheaton (23 U.S.) 1 (1825).

1519 *Yakus v. United States.* 321 U.S. 414 (1944).

Regulation of Commerce

1520 ASCH, Peter. *Economic Theory and the Antitrust Dilemma.* New York, 1970.

1521 BARNARD, Robert C., and Sergeai S. ZLINKOFF. "Patents, Procedure and the Sherman Act; The Supreme Court and a Competitive Economy." *Geo Wash L Rev,* 17 (1948), 1–58.

1522 BARRETT, Edward L., Jr. "State Taxation of Interstate Commerce: 'Direct Burden,' 'Multiple Burdens' or What Have You?" *Vand L Rev,* 4 (1951), 496–532.

1523 BENSON, Paul R., Jr. *The Supreme Court and the Commerce Clause, 1937–1970.* New York, 1970.

1524 BROWN, Ray A. "The Constitution, the Supreme Court and the N.I.R.A." *Ore L Rev,* 13 (1934), 102–121.

1525 *Brown v. Maryland.* 12 Wheaton (25 U.S.) 419 (1827).

1526 *Carter v. Carter Coal Co.* 298 U.S. 238 (1936).

1527 *Champion v. Ames.* 188 U.S. 321 (1903).

1528 *Cooley v. Board of Wardens of the Port of Philadelphia.* 12 Howard (53 U.S.) 299 (1852).

1529 CORTNER, Richard C. *The Arizona Train Limit Case: Southern Pacific v. Arizona.* Tucson, Ariz., 1970.

1530 CORTNER, Richard C. *The Wagner Act Cases.* Knoxville, Tenn., 1964.

1531 CORWIN, Edward S. *Commerce Power Versus States Rights.* Princeton, N.J., 1936.

1532 CORWIN, Edward S. "Congress' Power to Prohibit Commerce, a Crucial Constitutional Issue." *Corn L Q,* 18 (1933), 477–506.

1533 CUSHMAN, Robert E. "National Police Power under the Commerce Clause." *Minn L Rev,* 4 (1920), 247–281.

1534 DOWLING, Noel T. "Interstate Commerce and the State Power." *Colum L Rev,* 47 (1947), 547–560.

1535 DOWLING, Noel T. "Interstate Commerce and the State Power." *Va L Rev,* 27 (1940), 1–28.

1536 DUNHAM, Allison. "Congress, the States and Commerce." *J Pub L,* 8 (1959), 47–65.

1537 FELLMAN, David. "Federalism and the Commerce Clause, 1937–1947." *J Pol,* 10 (1948), 155–167.

1538 FRANKFURTER, Felix. *The Commerce Clause under Marshall, Taney, and Waite.* Chapel Hill, N.C., 1937.

1539 GANOE, John I. "The Roosevelt Court and the Commerce Clause." *Ore L Rev,* 24 (1945), 71–147.

1540 GAVIT, Bernard C. *The Commerce Clause of the United States Constitution.* Bloomington, Ind., 1932.

1541 *Gibbons v. Ogden.* 9 Wheaton (22 U.S.) 1 (1824).

1542 GRANT, J. A. C. "Commerce, Production, and the Fiscal Power of Congress." *Yale L J,* 45 (1936), 751–778, 991–1021.

1543 *Hammer v. Dagenhart.* 247 U.S. 251 (1918).

1544 *Heart of Atlanta Motel, Inc. v. United States.* 379 U.S. 241 (1964).

1545 KALLENBACH, Joseph E. *Federal Cooperation with the States under the Commerce Clause.* Ann Arbor, Mich., 1942.

1546 KRAMER, Victor H. "The Antitrust Division and the Supreme Court, 1890–1953." *Va L Rev,* 40 (1954), 433–463.

1547 KUTLER, Stanley I. "Chief Justice Taft, National Regulation and the Commerce Clause." *J Am Hist,* 51 (1965), 651–668.

1548 *The License Cases.* 5 Howard (46 U.S.) 504 (1847).

1549 MARTELL, Helen. "Legal Aspects of the Tennessee Valley Authority." *Geo Wash L Rev,* 7 (1939), 983–1012.

1550 MEYER, B. H. *History of the Northern Securities Case.* New York, 1972 (reprint of 1906 ed.).

1551 MOSHER, Lester E. "Mr. Justice Rutledge's Philosophy of the Commerce Clause." *N Y U L Rev,* 27 (1952), 218–247.

1552 *National Labor Relations Board v. Jones & Laughlin Corp.* 301 U.S. 1 (1937).

1553 *The Passenger Cases.* 7 Howard (48 U.S.) 283 (1849).

1554 POWELL, Thomas Reed. "Insurance as Commerce." *Harv L Rev,* 57 (1944), 937–1008.

1555 RAMASWAWY, M. *The Commerce Clause in the Constitution of the United States.* New York, 1948.

1556 RIBBLE, F. D. G. *State and National Power over Commerce.* New York, 1937.

1557 SHARFMAN, I. L. *The Interstate Commerce Commission.* 5 vols. New York, 1931–1937.

1558 SHOLLEY, John B. "The Negative Implications of the Commerce Clause." *U Chi L Rev,* 3 (1936), 556–596.

1559 *Southern Pacific Co. v. Arizona.* 325 U.S. 761 (1945).

1560 *Stafford v. Wallace.* 258 U.S. 495 (1922).

1561 STERN, Robert L. "The Commerce Clause and the National Economy, 1933–1946." *Harv L Rev,* 59 (1946), 645–693, 883–947.

1562 STERN, Robert L. "The Problems of Yesteryear—Commerce and Due Process." *Vand L Rev,* 4 (1951), 446–468.

1563 STERN, Robert L. "That Commerce Which Concerns More States Than One." *Harv L Rev,* 47 (1934), 1335–1366.

1564 *Swift & Co. v. United States.* 196 U.S. 375 (1905).

1565 TAFT, William Howard. *The Anti-Trust Act and the Supreme Court.* New York, 1914.

1566 THORELLI, Hans B. *The Federal Anti-Trust Policy: Origination of an American Tradition.* Baltimore, 1955.

1567 *United States v. E. C. Knight Co.* 156 U.S. 1 (1895).

1568 VAN CISE, Jerrold G. *Understanding the Antitrust Laws.* 6th ed. New York, 1973.

1569 *Wabash Railway Co. v. Illinois.* 118 U.S. 557 (1886).

1570 *Wickard v. Filburn.* 317 U.S. 111 (1942).

1571 *Willson v. Black-Bird Creek Marsh Co.* 2 Peters (27 U.S.) 245 (1829).

Monetary Powers

1572 *Bailey v. Drexel Furniture Co.* 259 U.S. 20 (1922).

1573 COLLIER, Charles S. "Judicial Bootstraps and the General Welfare Clause: The AAA Opinion." *Geo Wash L Rev,* 4 (1936), 211–242.

1574 CORWIN, Edward S. "The Spending Power of Congress—Apropos the Maternity Act." *Harv L Rev,* 36 (1923), 548–582.

1575 CUSHMAN, Robert E. "Social and Economic Controls Through Federal Taxation." *Minn L Rev,* 18 (1934), 759–783.

1576 DAWSON, John P. "The Gold-Clause Decisions." *Mich L Rev,* 33 (1935), 647–684.

1577 EGGERT, Gerald G. "Richard Olney and the Income Tax Cases." *Miss Val Hist Rev,* 48 (1961), 24–41.

1578 FARRELLY, David G. "Justice Harlan's Dissent in the Pollock Case." *So Calif L Rev,* 24 (1951), 175–182.

1579 *Gold Clause Cases.* 294 U.S. 240 (1935).

1580 HOLMES, John W. "Federal Spending Power and States Rights." *Mich L Rev,* 34 (1936), 637–649.

1581 *Hylton v. United States.* 3 Dallas (3 U.S.) 171 (1796).

1582 LAWSON, James F. *The General Welfare Clause; A Study of the Power of Congress under the Constitution of the United States.* Washington, D.C., 1934.

1583 *Legal Tender Cases.* 12 Wallace (79 U.S.) 457 (1871).

1584 *McRay v. United States.* 195 U.S. 27 (1904).

1585 *Pollock v. Farmers' Loan & Trust Co.* 157 U.S. 429 (1895).

1586 POST, Russell L. "Constitutionality of Government Spending for General Welfare." *Va L Rev,* 22 (1935), 1–38.

1587 POWELL, Thomas Reed. "The Waning of Intergovernmental Tax Immunities." *Harv L Rev,* 58 (1945), 633–674.

1588 RATNER, Sidney. *Taxation and Democracy in America.* New York, 1967.

1589 *South Carolina v. United States.* 199 U.S. 437 (1905).

1590 *Springer v. United States.* 102 U.S. 586 (1881).

1591 *Steward Machine Co. v. Davis.* 301 U.S. 548 (1937).

1592 *United States v. Butler.* 297 U.S. 1 (1936).

1593 WARREN, Charles. *Congress as Santa Claus or National Donations and the General Welfare Clause of the Constitution.* Charlottesville, Va., 1932.

Investigatory and Contempt Powers

1594 *Anderson v. Dunn.* 6 Wheaton (19 U.S.) 204 (1821).

1595 *Barenblatt v. United States.* 360 U.S. 109 (1959).

1596 BECK, Carl. *Contempt of Congress: A Study of the Prosecutions Initiated by the Committee on Un-American Activities, 1945–1957.* New Orleans, La., 1959.

1597 *In re Chapman.* 166 U.S. 661 (1897).

1598 CHASE, Harold W. "Improving Congressional Investigations: A No-Progress Report." *Tem L Q,* 30 (1957), 126–155.

1599 "Congressional Investigations, a Symposium." *U Chi L Rev,* 18 (1951), 421–661.

1600 *Kilbourn v. Thompson.* 103 U.S. 168 (1881).

1601 LANDIS, James M. "Constitutional Limitations on the Congressional Power of Investigation." *Harv L Rev,* 40 (1926), 153–221.

1602 McGEARY, M. Nelson. *The Development of Congressional Investigative Power.* New York, 1940.

1603 McKAY, Robert B. "Congressional Investigations and the Supreme Court." *Calif L Rev,* 51 (1963), 267–295.

1604 *Russell v. United States.* 369 U.S. 749 (1962).

1605 SLATNICK, Michael. "The Congressional Investigatory Power: Ramifications of the Watkins-Barenblatt Enigma." *U Miami L Rev,* 14 (1960), 381–411.

1606 *Sweezy v. New Hampshire.* 354 U.S. 234 (1957).

1607 TAYLOR, Telford. *Grand Inquest: The Story of Congressional Investigations.* New York, 1955.

1608 *United States v. Rumely.* 345 U.S. 41 (1953).

1609 *Watkins v. United States.* 354 U.S. 178 (1957).

Impeachment

1610 BENEDICT, Michael Les. *The Impeachment and Trial of Andrew Johnson.* New York, 1973.

1611 BERGER, Raoul. *Impeachment.* Cambridge, Mass., 1973.

1612 BRANT, Irving. *Impeachment: Trials and Errors.* New York, 1972.

1613 CARRINGTON, R. W. "The Impeachment Trial of Samuel Chase." *Va L Rev,* 9 (1923), 485–500.

1614 DeWITT, D. M. *The Impeachment and Trial of Andrew Johnson, Seventeenth President of the United States.* New York, 1903.

1615 HUGHES, David F. "Chief Justice Chase at the Impeachment Trial of Andrew Johnson." *N Y State Bar J,* 41 (1969), 218–233.

1616 LILLICH, Richard B. "The Chase Impeachment." *Am J Leg Hist,* 4 (1960), 49–72.

1617 LOMASK, Milton. *Andrew Johnson: President on Trial.* New York, 1960.

1618 PINE, Norman. "The Impeachment Dilemma: Crisis in Constitutional Government." *Yale Rev L & Soc Act,* 3 (1973), 99–143.

1619 STANSBURY, Arthur J. *Report of the Trial of James H. Peck.* Boston, 1833.

1620 TURNER, Lynn W. "The Impeachment of John Pickering." *Am Hist Rev,* 54 (1949), 485–507.

1621 U.S. House of Representatives. Committee on the Judiciary. *Impeachment: Selected Materials.* 93rd Cong., 1st sess., 1973. Washington, D.C., 1973.

1622 U.S. House of Representatives. Committee on the Judiciary. *President Richard M. Nixon.* Report by the Committee on H. Res. 803. 93rd Cong., 2nd sess., 1974. Washington, D.C., 1974.

Statutory Protection of Civil Rights

1623 ANTIEAU, Chester. *Federal Civil Rights Acts; Civil Practice.* Rochester, N.Y., 1971.

1624 BERGER, Morroe. *Equality by Statute: The Revolution in Civil Rights.* Rev. ed. New York, 1968.

1625 BREST, Paul A. "The Federal Government's Power to Protect Negroes and Civil Rights Workers Against Privately Inflicted Harm." *Harv Civ R.—Civ Lib L Rev,* 1 (1966), 2–59; 2 (1966), 1–51.

1626 CARR, Robert K. *Federal Protection of Civil Rights: Quest for a Sword.* Ithaca, N.Y., 1947.

1627 *Civil Rights Cases.* 109 U.S. 3 (1883).

1628 FEUERSTEIN, Howard M. "Civil Rights Crimes and the Federal Power to Punish Private Individuals for Interference with Federally Secured Rights." *Vand L Rev,* 19 (1966), 641–682.

1629 FRANTZ, Laurent B. "Congressional Power to Enforce the Fourteenth Amendment Against Private Acts." *Yale L J,* 73 (1964), 1353–1384.

1630 HOWARD, J. Woodford, and Cornelius BUSHOVEN. "The Screws Case Revisited." *J Pol,* 29 (1967), 617–636.

1631 MALICK, Clay P. "Terry v. Adams: Governmental Responsibility for the Protection of Civil Rights." *West Pol Q,* 7 (1954), 51–64.

1632 *Screws v. United States.* 325 U.S. 91 (1945).

1633 *United States v. Price.* 383 U.S. 787 (1966).

1634 *Ex parte Yarbrough.* 110 U.S. 651 (1884).

The Presidency

General

1635 BERGER, Raoul. *Executive Privilege: A Constitutional Myth.* Cambridge, Mass., 1974.

1636 BERGER, Raoul. "Executive Privilege and Congressional Inquiry." *UCLA L Rev,* 12 (1965), 1044–1118.

1637 BERMAN, Edward. *Labor Disputes and the President.* New York, 1924.

1638 BRECKENRIDGE, Adam C. *The Executive Privilege: Presidential Control over Information.* Lincoln, Neb., 1974.

1639 CHURCH, Frank. "Impoundment of Appropriated Funds: The Decline of Congressional Control over Executive Discretion." *Stan L Rev,* 22 (1970), 1240–1253.

1640 CORWIN, Edward S. *The President; Office and Powers, 1787–1957.* (See 1000.)

1641 "Executive Impounding of Funds: The Judicial Response." *U Chi L Rev,* 40 (1973), 328–357.

1642 "Executive Orders and the Development of Presidential Power." *Vill L Rev,* 17 (1972), 688–712.

1643 "Government Litigation in the Supreme Court: The Roles of the Solicitor General." *Yale L J,* 78 (1969), 1442–1481.

1644 GRUNDSTEIN, Nathan D. "Presidential Subdelegation of Administrative Authority in Wartime." *Geo Wash L Rev,* 15 (1947), 247–283; 16 (1948), 301–341, 478–507.

1645 HART, James. *The Ordinance Making Powers of the President of the United States.* New York, 1970.

1646 HIRSCHFIELD, Robert S., ed. *The Power of the Presidency.* New York, 1973.

1647 "The Presidential Veto Power: A Shallow Pocket." *Mich L Rev,* 70 (1971), 148–170.

1648 "The Philadelphia Plan: A Study in the Dynamics of Executive Power." *U Chi L Rev,* 39 (1972), 723–760.

1649 REDFORD, Emmette S. "The President and the Regulatory Commission." *Tex L Rev,* 44 (1965), 288–321.

1650 U.S. Senate. Committee on the Judiciary. Subcommittee on Separation of Powers. *Executive Privilege: The Withholding of Information by the Executive.* 92nd Cong., 1st sess., 1971. Washington, D.C., 1971.

1651 *United States v. Nixon.* 418 U.S. 683 (1974).

Appointments and Nominations

1652 ABRAHAM, Henry J. *Justices and Presidents: A Political History of Appointments to the Supreme Court.* New York, 1974.

1653 BEISER, Edward N. "The Haynsworth Affair Reconsidered: The Significance of Conflicting Perceptions of the Judicial Role." *Vand L Rev,* 23 (1970), 263–292.

1654 BLACK, Charles L., Jr. "A Note on Senatorial Consideration of Supreme Court Nominees." *Yale L J,* 79 (1970), 657–664.

DOCTRINES AND POLITICS

1655 BLACK, Forrest R. "The Role of the United States Senate in Passing on the Nominations to Membership in the Supreme Court of the United States." *Ky L J,* 19 (1931), 226–238.

1656 CARMEN, Ira H. "The President, Politics and the Power of Appointment: Hoover's Nomination of Mr. Justice Cardozo." *Va L Rev,* 55 (1969), 616–659.

1657 CHASE, Harold W. *Federal Judges: The Appointing Process.* Minneapolis, 1972.

1658 COLE, Kenneth C. "The Role of the Senate in the Confirmation of Judicial Nominations." *Am Pol Sci Rev,* 28 (1934), 875–894.

1659 CORWIN, Edward S. "Tenure of Office and the Removal Power under the Constitution." *Colum L Rev,* 27 (1927), 353–399.

1660 DANELSKI, David J. *A Supreme Court Justice Is Appointed.* New York, 1964.

1661 FRANK, John P. "The Appointment of Supreme Court Justices." *Wis L Rev,* 1941 (1941), 172–210, 343–379, 461–512.

1662 GARRATY, John A. "Holmes' Appointment to the U.S. Supreme Court." *N Eng Q,* 22 (1949), 291–303.

1663 GOLDMAN, Sheldon. "Johnson and Nixon Appointees to the Lower Federal Courts." *J Pol,* 34 (1972), 934–942.

1664 GROSSMAN, Joel B., and Stephen L. WASBY. "Haynsworth and Parker: History Does Live Again." *S C L Rev,* 23 (1971), 345–359.

1665 GROSSMAN, Joel B., and Stephen L. WASBY. "The Senate and Supreme Court Nominations: Some Reflections." *Duke L J,* 1972 (1972), 557–591.

1666 HALSELL, Willie D. "The Appointment of L. Q. C. Lamar to the Supreme Court." *Miss Val Hist Rev,* 28 (1941), 399–412.

1667 HARRIS, Richard. *Decision.* New York, 1971.

1668 HART, James. *Tenure of Office under the Constitution.* Baltimore, 1930.

1669 HOOGENBOOM, Ari. *Outlawing the Spoils. A History of the Civil Service Reform Movement, 1865–1883.* Urbana, Ill., 1961.

1670 *Humphrey's Executor v. United States.* 295 U.S. 602 (1935).

1671 KURLAND, Philip B. "The Appointment and Disappointment of Supreme Court Justices." *L & Soc Ord,* 1972 (1972), 183–237.

1672 LEUCHTENBURG, William E. "A Klansman Joins the Court: The Appointment of Hugo L. Black." *U Chi L Rev,* 41 (1973), 1–31.

1673 LEUCHTENBURG, William E. "The Case of the Contentious Commissioner: Humphrey's Executor v. U.S." *Freedom and Reform: Essays in Honor of Henry Steele Commager.* Eds. Harold M. Hyman and Leonard W. Levy. New York, 1967.

1674 LEUCHTENBURG, William E. "Franklin D. Roosevelt's Supreme Court 'Packing' Plan." *Essays on the New Deal.* Eds. W. H. Droze, *et al.* Austin, Tex., 1969.

1675 McCONNELL, A. Mitchell, Jr. "Haynsworth and Carswell: A New Senate Standard of Excellence." *Ky L J,* 59 (1970), 7–34.

1676 McHARGUE, Daniel S. "President Taft's Appointments to the Supreme Court." *J Pol,* 12 (1950), 478–510.

1677 MURPHY, Walter F. "In His Own Image: Mr. Chief Justice Taft and Supreme Court Appointments." *S Ct Rev* (1961), 159–193.

1678 *Myers v. United States.* 272 U.S. 52 (1926).

1679 ROGERS, William P. "Judicial Appointments in the Eisenhower Administration." *J Am Jud Soc,* 41 (1957), 38–42.

1680 "Temporary Appointment Power of the President." *U Chi L Rev,* 41 (1973), 146–163.

1681 TODD, A. L. *Justice on Trial: The Case of Louis D. Brandeis.* New York, 1964.

1682 WALSH, Lawrence E. "Selection of Supreme Court Justices." *Am Bar Assoc J,* 56 (1970), 555–560.

Foreign Affairs and the Military Power

1683 ALFORD, Neill H. "The Legality of American Military Involvement in Vietnam: A Broader Perspective." *Yale L J,* 75 (1966), 1109–1121.

1684 BERDAHL, Clarence A. *War Powers of the Executive in the United States.* Urbana, Ill., 1921.

1685 BERGER, Raoul. "The Presidential Monopoly of Foreign Relations." *Mich L Rev,* 71 (1972), 1–58.

1686 BERGER, Raoul. "War-Making by the President." *U Penn L Rev,* 121 (1972), 29–86.

1687 BLACKMAN, John L., Jr. *Presidential Seizure in Labor Disputes.* Cambridge, Mass., 1967.

1688 BORCHARD, Edwin. "The Charter and the Constitution." *Am J Int L,* 39 (1945), 97–101.

1689 BYRD, Elbert M., Jr. *Treaties and Executive Agreements in the United States. Their Separate Roles and Limitations.* The Hague, 1960.

1690 CHAFEE, Zechariah, Jr. "Amending the Constitution to Cripple Treaties." *La L Rev,* 12 (1952), 345–382.

1691 CHEEVER, Daniel S., and H. Field HAVILAND, Jr. *American Foreign Policy and the Separation of Powers.* Cambridge, Mass., 1952.

1692 "Congress, the President, and the Power to Commit Forces to Combat." *Harv L Rev,* 81 (1968), 1771–1805.

1693 CORTNER, Richard C. *The Jones & Laughlin Case.* New York, 1970.

1694 CORWIN, Edward S. *The Constitution and World Organization.* Princeton, N.J., 1944.

1695 CORWIN, Edward S. *The President's Control of Foreign Relations.* Princeton, N.J., 1917.

1696 CORWIN, Edward S. "The Steel Seizure Case—A Judicial Brick Without Straw." *Colum L Rev,* 53 (1953), 53–66.

1697 CORWIN, Edward S. *Total War and the Constitution.* New York, 1947.

1698 *In re Debs.* 158 U.S. 564 (1895).

1699 FAIRMAN, Charles. *The Law of Martial Rule.* Chicago, 1930.

1700 FALK, Richard A. *Legal Order in a Violent World.* Princeton, N.J., 1968.

1701 FALK, Richard A. *The Six Legal Dimensions of the Vietnam War.* Princeton, N.J., 1968.

1702 FRIEDMAN, Leon. "Conscription and the Constitution: The Original Understanding." *Mich L Rev,* 67 (1969), 1493–1552.

1703 FRIEDMAN, Leon, and Burt NEUBORNE. *Unquestioning Obedience to the President: The ACLU Case Against the Legality of the War in Vietnam.* New York, 1972.

1704 FULBRIGHT, J. William. "American Foreign Policy in the 20th Century under an 18th Century Constitution." *Corn L Q,* 47 (1961), 1–13.

1705 GRUNDSTEIN, Nathan D. "Presidential Subdelegation of Administrative Authority in War-time." *Geo Wash L Rev,* 16 (1948), 301–341, 478–507.

1706 HENDRY, James McLeod. *Treaties and Federal Constitutions.* Washington, D.C., 1955.

1707 HENKIN, Louis. *Foreign Affairs and the Constitution.* Mineola, N.Y., 1972.

1708 HOLMAN, F. E. "Treaty Law Making: A Blank Check for Writing a New Constitution." *Am Bar Assoc J,* 36 (1950), 707–710.

1709 HULL, Roger C., and John C. NOVOGRAD. *Law and Vietnam.* New York, 1968.

1710 HUNTINGTON, Samuel P. "Civilian Control and the Constitution." *Am Pol Sci Rev,* 50 (1956), 676–699.

1711 HYMAN, Jacob D. "Constitutional Aspects of the Covenant." *L & Cont Prob,* 14 (1949), 451–478.

1712 JACKSON, Robert H. "A Presidential Legal Opinion." *Harv L Rev,* 66 (1953), 1353–1361.

1713 JAVITS, Jacob, and Don KELLERMAN. *Who Makes War; The President Versus Congress.* New York, 1973.

1714 *The Insular Cases.* 182 U.S. 1 (1901).

1715 KAUPER, Paul G. "The Steel Seizure Case: Congress, the President and the Supreme Court." *Mich L Rev,* 51 (1952), 141–182.

1716 *Korematsu v. United States.* 323 U.S. 214 (1944).

1717 LOFGREN, Charles A. *"United States v. Curtiss-Wright Export Corporation:* An Historical Reassessment." *Yale L J,* 83 (1973), 1–32.

1718 LOFGREN, Charles A. "War-Making under the Constitution: The Original Understanding." *Yale L J,* 81 (1972), 672–702.

1719 LOVELL, John P., and Philip S. KRONENBERG, eds. *New Civil-Military Relations. The Agonies of Adjustment to Post-Vietnam Realities.* New Brunswick, N.J., 1974.

1720 LUSKY, Louis. "Congressional Amnesty for War Resisters: Policy Considerations and Constitutional Problems." *Vand L Rev,* 25 (1972), 525–556.

1721 McCLURE, Wallace. *International Executive Agreements: Democratic Procedure under the Constitution of the United States.* New York, 1941.

1722 McCONNELL, Grant. *The President Seizes the Steel Mills.* Montgomery, Ala., 1960.

1723 McDOUGAL, Myers S., and Asher LANS. "Treaties and Congressional-Executive or Presidential Agreements: Interchangeable Instruments of National Policy." *Yale L J,* 54 (1945), 181–351.

1724 MALAWER, Stuart S. "The Vietnam War under the Constitution: Legal Issues Involved in the United States Military Involvement in Vietnam." *U Pitt L Rev,* 31 (1969), 205–241.

1725 MATTHEWS, Craig. "The Constitutional Power of the President to Conclude International Agreements." *Yale L J,* 64 (1955), 345–389.

1726 MAY, Ernest R., ed. *The Ultimate Decision: The President as Commander in Chief.* New York, 1960.

1727 MILLETT, Stephen M. "The Constitutionality of Executive Agreen.ents: An Analysis of *United States v. Belmont."* Ph.D. dissertation. Ohio State University, 1972.

1728 MILLIS, Walter. *The Constitution and the Common Defense.* New York, 1959.

1729 *Missouri V. Holland.* 252 U.S. 416 (1920).

1730 MOORE, John Norton. *Law and the Indo-China War.* Princeton, N.J., 1971.

1731 *Prize Cases.* 2 Black (67 U.S.) 635 (1863).

1732 PUSEY, Merlo J. *The Way We Go to War.* Boston, 1969.

1733 RANKIN, Robert S. *When Civil Law Fails: Martial Law and Its Legal Basis in the United States.* Durham, N.C., 1939.

1734 RANKIN, Robert S., and Winfried R. DALLMAYER. *Freedom and Emergency Powers in the Cold War.* New York, 1964.

1735 *Reid v. Covert.* 351 U.S. 487 (1957).

1736 REVELEY, W. T., III. "Presidential War-Making: Constitutional Prerogative or Usurpation." *Va L Rev,* 55 (1969), 1243–1305.

1737 RICH, Bennett M. *The President and Civil Disorder.* Washington, D.C., 1941.

1738 ROBERTSON, David W. "The Debate among American International Lawyers about the Vietnam War." *Tex L Rev,* 46 (1968), 898–913.

1739 ROGERS, William P. "Congress, the President, and the War Powers." *Calif L Rev,* 59 (1971), 1194–1214.

1740 ROSSITER, Clinton. *Constitutional Dictatorship: Crisis Government in the Modern Democracies.* Princeton, N.J., 1948.

1741 ROSSITER, Clinton. *The Supreme Court and the Commander-in-Chief.* Ithaca, N.Y., 1951.

1742 ROSTOW, Eugene V. "The Japanese-American Cases—A Disaster." *Yale L J,* 54 (1945), 489–533.

1743 SCHICK, F. B. "Some Reflection on the Legal Controversies Concerning America's Involvement in Vietnam." *Int & Comp L Q,* 17 (1968), 953–995.

1744 SCHMIDHAUSER, John R. "The Butler Amendment: An Analysis." *Am Bar Assoc J,* 43 (1957), 714–717.

1745 SCHWARTZ, Bernard. "The War Power in Britain and America." *N Y U L Q Rev,* 20 (1945), 325–345, 465–498.

1746 *Selective Draft Law Cases.* 245 U.S. 366 (1918).

1747 SMITH, Louis. *American Democracy and Military Power. A Study of Civil Control of the Military Power in the United States.* Chicago, 1951.

1748 SPINDLER, John F. "Executive Agreements and the Proposed Constitutional Amendments to the Treaty Power." *Mich L Rev,* 51 (1953), 1202–1217.

1749 STEBBINS, Phillip E. "A History of the Role of the United States Supreme Court in Foreign Policy." Ph.D. dissertation, Ohio State University, 1966.

1750 STEIN, Harold, ed. *American Civil-Military Decisions: A Book of Case Studies.* University, Ala., 1963.

1751 SUTHERLAND, Arthur E. "Restricting the Treaty Power." *Harv L Rev,* 65 (1952), 1305–1338.

1752 SWISHER, Carl B. "The Control of War Preparations in the United States." *Am Pol Sci Rev,* 34 (1940), 1085–1103.

1753 U.S. House of Representatives. Committee on Foreign Affairs. Subcommittee on National Security Policy and Scientific Developments. *Congress, the President, and the War Powers.* 91st Cong., 2nd sess., 1970. Washington, D.C., 1970.

1754 *United States v. Belmont.* 301 U.S. 324 (1937).

1755 *United States v. Curtiss-Wright Export Corp.* 299 U.S. 304 (1936).

1756 VAN ALYSTYNE, William W. "Congress, the President and the Power to Declare War: A Requiem for Vietnam." *U Penn L Rev,* 121 (1972), 1–28.

1757 VANDERBILT, Arthur T. "War Powers and Their Administration." *Annual Survey of American Law, 1942.* New York, 1945.

1758 WESTIN, Alan F. *The Anatomy of a Constitutional Law Case.* New York, 1958.

1759 WHITING, William. *War Powers under the Constitution of the United States.* 10th ed. Boston, 1864.

1760 WILCOX, Francis O. *Congress, the Executive, and Foreign Policy.* New York, 1971.

1761 WILDHABER, Luzius. *Treaty-Making Power and Constitution: An International and Comparative Study.* Basel, Switzerland, and Stuttgart, West Germany, 1971.

1762 *Youngstown Sheet & Tube Co. v. Sawyer.* 343 U.S. 579 (1952).

The Judiciary and Other Agencies of Government

1763 BERGER, Raoul. *Congress v. the Supreme Court.* Cambridge, Mass., 1969.

1764 BERGER, Raoul. "The President, Congress, and the Courts." *Yale L J,* 83 (1974), 1111–1155.

1765 BOWMAN, Harold M. "Congress and the Supreme Court." *Pol Sci Q,* 25 (1910), 20–34.

1766 CARRINGTON, Paul D. "Political Questions: The Judicial Check on the Executive." *Va L Rev,* 42 (1956), 175–201.

1767 CHASE, Harold W. "The Warren Court and Congress." *Minn L Rev,* 44 (1960), 595–637.

1768 CHOPER, Jesse H. "The Supreme Court and the Political Branches: Democratic Theory and Practice." *U Penn L Rev,* 122 (1974), 810–858.

1769 COPE, Alfred H., and Fred KRINSKY, eds. *Franklin D. Roosevelt and the Supreme Court.* Boston, 1952.

1770 ELLIOTT, Sheldon D. "Court Curbing Proposals in Congress." *Not Dame Law,* 33 (1958), 597–616.

DOCTRINES AND POLITICS

1771 ETTRUDE, Dormin J. *Power of Congress to Nullify Supreme Court Decisions.* New York, 1924.

1772 FREEDMAN, Max, ed. *Roosevelt and Frankfurter. Their Correspondence, 1928–1945.* Boston, 1967.

1773 "The Function of the Supreme Court in the Development and Acquisition of Powers by Administrative Agencies." *Minn L Rev,* 42 (1957), 271–291.

1774 HORN, Robert A. "The Warren Court and the Discretionary Power of the Executive." *Minn L Rev,* 44 (1960), 639–672.

1775 JAFFE, Louis L. "Professors and Judges as Advisers to Government: Reflections on the Roosevelt-Frankfurter Relationship." *Harv L Rev,* 83 (1969), 366–375.

1776 LEE, Frederic P. "The Origins of Judicial Control of Federal Executive Action." *Geo L J,* 36 (1948), 287–309.

1777 LYTLE, Clifford M. "Congressional Response to Supreme Court Decisions in the Aftermath of the School Segregation Cases." *J Pub L,* 12 (1963), 290–312.

1778 McFARLAND, Carl. *Judicial Control of the Federal Trade Commission and the Interstate Commerce Commission Trust and Corporation Problems.* Cambridge, Mass., 1929.

1779 MELTZER, Bernard D. "The Supreme Court, Congress, and State Jurisdiction over Labor Relations." *Colum L Rev,* 59 (1959), 6–60, 269–302.

1780 MITCHELL, Claudia. "The Warren Court and Congress: A Civil Rights Partnership." *Neb L Rev,* 48 (1968), 91–128.

1781 MURPHY, Walter F. *Congress and the Court: A Case Study in the American Political Process.* Chicago, 1962.

1782 MURPHY, Walter F., and C. Herman PRITCHETT. *Courts, Judges, and Politics.* 2nd ed. New York, 1973.

1783 "The Nixon Busing Bills and Congressional Power." *Yale L J,* 81 (1972), 1542–1573.

1784 POST, Charles Gordon, Jr. *The Supreme Court and Political Questions.* Baltimore, 1936.

1785 PRITCHETT, C. Herman. *Congress Versus the Supreme Court: 1957–1960.* Minneapolis, 1961.

1786 SCHMIDHAUSER, John R., and Larry L. BERG. *The Supreme Court and Congress. Conflict and Interaction, 1945–1968.* New York, 1972.

1787 SCHUBERT, Glendon A. *The Presidency in the Courts.* Minneapolis, 1957.

1788 SCIGLIANO, Robert. *The Supreme Court and the Presidency.* New York, 1971.

1789 SHERWOOD, Foster H. "Judicial Control of Administrative Discretion, 1932–1952." *West Pol Q,* 6 (1953), 750–761.

1790 SIROTKIN, Phillip L. *The Supreme Court and the Legislative Process.* Chicago, 1951.

1791 WARREN, Charles. *Congress, the Constitution and the Supreme Court.* New York, 1968 (reprint of 1925 ed.).

1792 WARREN, Charles. "Legislative and Judicial Attacks on the Supreme Court of the United States." *Am L Rev,* 47 (1913), 1–34, 161–189.

B. The Judicial Process: The Supreme Court, the Lower Federal Courts, and the State Courts

General

1793 American Bar Association. *Code of Judicial Conduct.* Chicago, 1972.

1794 BICKEL, Alexander M. *The Least Dangerous Branch.* Indianapolis, 1962.

1795 BORKIN, Joseph. *The Corrupt Judge.* New York, 1962.

1796 BRAITHWAITE, William. *Who Judges the Judges? A Study of Procedures for Removal and Retirement.* Chicago 1971.

1797 BURTON, Harold H. "Unsung Services of the Supreme Court of the United States." *Ford L Rev,* 24 (1955), 169–177.

1798 CAHILL, Fred. *Judicial Legislation; A Study in American Legal Theory.* New York, 1952.

1799 CAHN, Edmond, ed. *Supreme Court and Supreme Law.* Bloomington, Ind., 1954.

1800 CARPENTER, William S. *Judicial Tenure in the United States with Especial Reference to the Tenure of Federal Judges.* New Haven, 1918.

1801 "Civil and Criminal Contempt in the Federal Courts." *Yale L J,* 57 (1947), 83–107.

1802 CLAYTON, James E. *The Making of Justice: The Supreme Court in Action.* New York, 1964.

1803 CURTIS, Charles P. *Law as Large as Life: A Natural Law for Today and the Supreme Court as Its Prophet.* New York, 1959.

1804 CURTIS, Charles P. *Lions under the Throne.* Boston, 1947.

1805 DAHL, Robert A. "Decision Making in a Democracy: The Role of the Supreme Court as a National Policy-Maker." *J Pub L,* 6 (1957), 279–295.

1806 DAVIS, Abraham L. *The United States Supreme Court and the Uses of Social Science Data.* New York, 1973.

1807 DAWSON, John P. *The Oracles of the Law.* Ann Arbor, Mich., 1968.

1808 DEUTSCH, Jan G. "Neutrality, Legitimacy, and the Supreme Court: Some Interactions Between Law and Political Science." *Stan L Rev,* 20 (1968), 169–261.

1809 DOBBS, Dan B. "Contempt of Court: A Survey." *Corn L Rev,* 56 (1971), 183–284.

1810 DOLBEARE, Kenneth M. *Trial Courts in Urban Politics.* New York, 1967.

1811 ERNST, Morris L. *The Great Reversals. Tales of the Supreme Court.* New York, 1973.

1812 FAIRMAN, Charles. "The Retirement of Federal Judges." *Harv L Rev,* 51 (1938), 397–443.

1813 FISS, Owen M. *Injunctions.* Chicago, 1971.

1814 Foundation of the Federal Bar Association. *Equal Justice under Law. The Supreme Court in American Life.* Washington, D.C., 1965.

1815 FRANK, John P. "Disqualification of Judges." *Yale L J,* 56 (1947), 605–639.

1816 FRANK, John P. *The Marble Palace.* New York, 1958.

1817 FRANKEL, J. E. "Judicial Discipline and Removal." *Tex L Rev,* 44 (1966), 1117–1135.

1818 FRANKEL, Marvin E. *Criminal Sentences; Law Without Order.* New York, 1973.

1819 FRANKFURTER, Felix. "Chief Justices I Have Known." *Va L Rev,* 39 (1953), 883–905.

1820 FRANKFURTER, Felix. "The Supreme Court in the Mirror of Justices." *U Penn L Rev,* 105 (1957), 781–796.

1821 FRANKFURTER, Felix, and N. V. GREENE. *The Labor Injunction.* New York, 1930.

1822 FREEDMAN, Max, *et al. Perspectives on the Court.* Evanston, Ill., 1967.

1823 FREUND, Paul A. *On Understanding the Supreme Court.* Boston, 1949.

1824 FREUND, Paul A. *The Supreme Court of the United States: Its Business, Purposes, and Performance.* Cleveland, Ohio, 1961.

1825 GLICK, Henry R. *Supreme Courts in State Politics; An Investigation of the Judicial Role.* New York, 1971.

1826 GOLDFARB, Ronald L. *The Contempt Power.* New York, 1963.

1827 GOLDMAN, Sheldon, and Thomas P. JAHNIGE. *The Federal Courts as a Political System.* New York, 1971.

1828 GROSMAN, Brian A. *Prosecutor, an Inquiry into the Exercise of Discretion.* Toronto, Canada, 1969.

1829 HUGHES, Charles E. *The Supreme Court of the United States.* New York, 1928.

1830 HYNEMAN, Charles S. *The Supreme Court on Trial.* New York, 1963.

1831 "Invoking Summary Criminal Contempt Procedures—The 'Chicago Seven' Contempts." *Mich L Rev,* 69 (1971), 1549–1575.

1832 JACKSON, Robert H. "Advocacy Before the Supreme Court." *Corn L Q,* 37 (1951), 1–16.

1833 JACKSON, Robert H. *The Supreme Court in the American System of Government.* Cambridge, Mass., 1955.

1834 JACOB, Herbert. *Justice in America: Courts, Lawyers, and the Judicial Process.* 2nd ed. Boston, 1972.

1835 JACOB, Herbert, ed. *Law, Politics and the Federal Courts.* Boston, 1970.

1836 JACOB, Herbert. *Urban Justice. Law and Order in American Cities.* Englewood Cliffs, N.J., 1973.

1837 JACOB, Herbert, and Kenneth N. VINES. *Studies in Judicial Politics.* New Orleans, La., 1963.

1838 JAFFE, Louis L. *English and American Judges as Lawmakers.* Oxford, 1969.

1839 JAHNIGE, Thomas P., and Sheldon GOLDMAN, eds. *The Federal Judicial System.* New York, 1968.

1840 JOINER, Charles W. *Civil Justice and the Jury.* Englewood Cliffs, N.J., 1962.

1841 KALVEN, Harry, Jr., and Hans ZEISEL. *The American Jury.* Boston, 1966.

1842 KEPHART, William M. *Racial Factors and Urban Law Enforcement.* Philadelphia, 1957.

1843 KIRCHHEIMER, Otto. *Political Justice. The Use of Legal Procedure for Political Ends.* Princeton, N.J., 1961.

1844 KRIER, James. *Environmental Law and Policy.* Indianapolis, 1971.

1845 KURLAND, Philip B. "The Constitution and the Tenure of Federal Judges: Some Notes from History." *U Chi L Rev,* 36 (1969), 665–698.

1846 LATHAM, Earl. "The Supreme Court as a Political Institution." *Minn L Rev,* 31 (1947), 205–231.

1847 LERNER, Max. "Constitution and Court as Symbols." *Yale L J,* 46 (1937), 1290–1319.

1848 LERNER, Max. "The Supreme Court and American Capitalism." *Yale L J,* 42 (1933), 668–701.

1849 LEWIS, Anthony. "The Supreme Court and Its Critics." *Minn L Rev,* 45 (1961), 305–332.

1850 McCUNE, Wesley. *The Nine Young Men.* New York, 1947.

1851 MacDONALD, James B., and John E. CONWAY. *Environmental Litigation.* Madison, Wis., 1972.

1852 MARSHALL, Thurgood. "Group Action in the Pursuit of Justice." *N Y U L Rev,* 44 (1969), 661–672.

1853 MASON, Alpheus T. "The Chief Justice of the United States: Primus Inter Pares." *J Pub L,* 17 (1968), 20–60.

1854 MASON, Alpheus T. "Myth and Reality in Supreme Court Decisions." *Va L Rev,* 48 (1962), 1385–1406.

1855 MASON, Alpheus T. "The Supreme Court: Temple and Forum." *Yale Rev,* 48 (1959), 524–540.

1856 MAVRINAC, A. A. "From *Lochner* to *Brown v. Topeka*: The Court and Conflicting Concepts of the Political Process." *Am Pol Sci Rev,* 52 (1958), 665–677.

1857 MAYERS, Lewis. *The American Legal System.* Rev. ed. New York, 1964.

1858 MILLER, Arthur S. *The Supreme Court and American Capitalism.* New York, 1968.

1859 MILLER, Charles A. *The Supreme Court and the Uses of History.* Cambridge, Mass., 1969.

1860 MILLER, Frank W. *Prosecution: The Decision to Charge a Suspect with a Crime.* Boston, 1969.

1861 MURPHY, Walter F. "The Contempt Power of the Federal Courts." *Fed Bar J,* 18 (1958), 34–55.

1862 MURPHY, Walter F., and Joseph TANENHAUS. "Public Opinion and the United States Supreme Court." *L & Soc Rev,* 2 (1968), 357–384.

1863 PATTERSON, C. Perry. "The Supreme Court as a Constituent Convention." *Tul L Rev,* 23 (1949), 431–451.

1864 PELTASON, Jack W. *Federal Courts in the Political Process.* New York, 1955.

1865 PRITCHETT, C. Herman, and Alan F. WESTIN, eds. *The Third Branch of Government: Eight Cases in Constitutional Politics.* New York, 1963.

1866 RAMASWAWY, M. *The Creative Role of the Supreme Court of the United States.* Stanford, Calif., 1956.

1867 RICHARDSON, Richard J., and Kenneth N. VINES. *The Politics of Federal Courts.* Boston, 1970.

1868 ROBERTS, Owen J. *The Court and the Constitution.* Cambridge, Mass., 1951.

1869 ROSEN, Paul L. *The Supreme Court and Social Science.* Urbana, Ill., 1973.

1870 ROSTOW, Eugene V. *The Sovereign Prerogative. The Supreme Court and the Quest for Law.* New Haven, 1962.

1871 ROSTOW, Eugene V. "The Supreme Court and the People's Will." *Not Dame Law,* 33 (1958), 573–596.

1872 SCHMIDHAUSER, John R. *The Supreme Court: Its Politics, Personalities and Procedures.* New York, 1960.

1873 SCHUBERT, Glendon A. *Judicial Policy-Making.* Rev. ed. Glenview, Ill., 1974.

1874 SHAPIRO, Martin. *Law and Politics in the Supreme Court: New Approaches to Political Jurisprudence.* New York, 1964.

1875 SHAPIRO, Martin. *The Supreme Court and Public Policy.* Glenview, Ill., 1969.

1876 SIGLER, Jay A. *An Introduction to the Legal System.* Homewood, Ill., 1968.

1877 STEPHENSON, D. Grier, Jr. "The Appellate Judiciary of Georgia and Contempt Out of Court." *Ga L Rev,* 2 (1968), 341–371.

1878 STERN, Robert L., and Eugene GROSSMAN. *Supreme Court Practice.* 4th ed. Washington, D.C., 1969.

1879 SUTHERLAND, Arthur E. "The Supreme Court and the General Will." *Proc Am Acad Arts & Sci,* 82 (1953), 169–197.

1880 SWISHER, Carl B. *The Supreme Court in the Modern Role.* Rev. ed. New York, 1965.

1881 Symposium. "Judicial Ethics." *L & Cont Prob,* 35 (1970), 3–228.

1882 "Symposium: Pivotal Decisions of the Supreme Court." *Ariz L Rev,* 15 (1973), 223–575.

1883 VAN DEVANTER, Willis. "The Supreme Court of the United States." *Ind L J,* 5 (1930), 553–562.

1884 WATSON, Richard A., and Rondal G. DOWNING. *The Politics of the Bench and the Bar: Judicial Selection under the Missouri Nonpartisan Plan.* New York, 1969.

1885 WESTIN, Alan F., ed. *The Supreme Court: Views from Inside.* New York, 1961.

Organization and Jurisdiction

1886 BATOR, Paul M., *et al. Hart and Wechsler's the Federal Courts and the Federal System.* Mineola, N.Y., 1973.

1887 BAZELON, David L. "New Gods for Old: 'Efficient' Courts in a Democratic Society." *N Y U L Rev,* 46 (1971), 653–674.

1888 BERGER, Raoul. "Standing to Sue in Public Actions." *Yale L J,* 83 (1969), 816–840.

1889 BLACK, Charles L., Jr. "The National Court of Appeals: An Unwise Proposal." *Yale L J,* 88 (1974), 883–899.

1890 BRENNAN, William J., Jr. "The National Court of Appeals: Another Dissent." *U Chi L Rev,* 40 (1973), 473–485.

1891 BURGER, Warren E. "Report on the Federal Judicial Branch—1973." *Am Bar Assoc J,* 59 (1973), 1125–1130.

1892 BURTON, Harold H. "Judging Is Also Administration: An Appreciation of Constructive Leadership." *Tem L Q,* 21 (1947), 77–90.

1893 "Developments in the Law—Federal Habeas Corpus." *Harv L Rev,* 83 (1970), 1038–1280.

1894 DOUGLAS, William O. "The Supreme Court and Its Caseload." *Corn L Q,* 45 (1960), 401–414.

1895 DOWNIE, Leonard, Jr. *Justice Denied; the Case for Reform of the Courts.* New York, 1971.

1896 DuPONCEAU, Peter S. *A Dissertation on the Nature and Extent of the Jurisdiction of the Courts of the United States.* Philadelphia, 1824.

1897 EISENBERG, Theodore. "Congressional Authority to Restrict Lower Federal Court Jurisdiction." *Yale L J,* 83 (1974), 498–533.

1898 "Federal Appellate Justice in an Era of Growing Demand." A Symposium. *Corn L Rev,* 59 (1974), 571–657.

1899 FISH, Peter Graham. *The Politics of Federal Judicial Administration.* Princeton, N.J., 1973.

1900 FRANKFURTER, Felix, and James M. LANDIS. *The Business of the Supreme Court. A Study in the Federal Judicial System.* New York, 1927.

1901 FREUND, Paul A. "Why We Need the National Court of Appeals." *Am Bar Assoc J,* 59 (1973), 247–252.

1902 FRIENDLY, Henry J. *Federal Jurisdiction: A General View.* New York, 1973.

1903 FRIESEN, Ernest C., *et al. Managing the Courts.* Indianapolis, 1971.

1904 GAZELL, James A., and Howard M. RIEGER. *Politics of Judicial Reform.* Berkeley, Calif., 1969.

1905 GOLDMAN, Sheldon. "Views of a Political Scientist: Political Selection of Federal Judges and the Proposal for a Judicial Service Commission." *J Am Jud Soc,* 53 (1968), 94–98.

1906 GRESSMAN, Eugene. "The National Court of Appeals: A Dissent." *Am Bar Assoc J,* 59 (1973), 253–258.

1907 HALL, Kermit L. "Federal Judicial Reform and Proslavery Constitutional Theory: A Retrospect on the Butler Bill." *Am J Leg Hist,* 17 (1973), 166–184.

1908 HARDIN, Mark. "Conservationists' Standing to Challenge the Actions of Federal Agencies." *Eco L Q,* 1 (1971), 305–329.

1909 HART, Henry M., Jr. "The Power of Congress to Limit the Jurisdiction of Federal Courts: An Exercise in Dialectic." *Harv L Rev,* 66 (1953), 1362–1402.

1910 HOLTZOFF, Alexander. "Judicial Procedure Reform: Leadership of the Supreme Court." *Am Bar Assoc J,* 43 (1957), 215–218.

1911 JAFFE, Louis L. "Standing to Secure Judicial Review: Public Actions." *Harv L Rev,* 74 (1961), 1265–1314.

1912 "Judicial Review of Agency Action: The Unsettled Law of Standing." *Mich L Rev* 69 (1971), 540–568.

1913 KARLEN, Delmar. *Judicial Administration: The American Experience.* Dobbs Ferry, N.Y., 1970.

1914 LEFLAR, Robert A. "The Task of the Appellate Court." *Not Dame Law,* 33 (1958), 548–572.

1915 *Ex parte McCardle.* 7 Wallace (74 U.S.) 506 (1869).

1916 McGOWAN, Carl. *The Organization of Judicial Power in the United States.* Evanston, Ill., 1967.

1917 *Massachusetts v. Mellon.* 262 U.S. 447 (1923).

1918 "The National Court of Appeals: A Constitutional 'Inferior Court'?" *Mich L Rev,* 72 (1973), 290–312.

1919 *The Propeller Genessee Chief v. Fitzhugh.* 12 Howard (53 U.S.) 443 (1851).

1920 SCOTT, Kenneth C. "Standing in the Supreme Court—A Functional Analysis." *Harv L Rev,* 86 (1973), 645–692.

1921 SEDLER, Robert Allen. "Dombrowski in the Wake of Younger: The View from Without and Within." *Wis L Rev,* 1972 (1972), 1–61.

1922 SEDLER, Robert Allen. "Standing, Justiciability, and All That: A Behavioral Analysis." *Vand L Rev,* 25 (1972), 479–512.

1923 STOKES, Isaac N. P. "National Court of Appeals: An Alternative Proposal." *Am Bar Assoc J,* 60 (1974), 179–181.

1924 Study Group on the Caseload of the Supreme Court. *Report.* Washington, D.C., 1972.

1925 "Symposium on Federal Jurisdiction and Procedure." *Vand L Rev,* 7 (1954), 441–675.

1926 TAFT, William Howard. "The Jurisdiction of the Supreme Court under the Act of February 13, 1925." *Yale L J,* 35 (1925), 1–12.

1927 TAFT, William Howard. "Possible and Needed Reforms in the Administration of Civil Justice in the Federal Courts." *Am L Rev,* 57 (1923), 1–23.

1928 ULMER, S. Sidney. "Revising the Jurisdiction of the Supreme Court: More Administrative Reform or Substantive Policy Change?" *Minn L Rev,* 58 (1973), 121–155.

1929 U.S. Senate. Committee on the Judiciary. Majority and Minority Report. *Limitation of Supreme Court Jurisdiction and Strengthening of Anti-Subversive Laws.* 85th Cong., 2nd sess., 1958. Washington, D.C., 1958.

1930 WARREN, Earl. "Let's Not Weaken the Supreme Court." *Am Bar Assoc J,* 60 (1974), 677–680.

Judicial Review, Constitutional Interpretation, and the Judicial Role

1931 ANDERSON, William. "The Intention of the Framers: A Note on Constitutional Interpretation." *Am Pol Sci Rev,* 49 (1955), 340–352.

DOCTRINES AND POLITICS

1932 BARNETT, Vincent M., Jr. "Constitutional Interpretation and Judicial Self-Restraint." *Mich L Rev,* 39 (1940), 213–237.

1933 BEARD, Charles A. "The Supreme Court: Usurper or Grantee?" *Pol Sci Q,* 27 (1912), 1–35.

1934 BECK, James M. "Nullification by Indirection." *Harv L Rev,* 23 (1910), 441–455.

1935 BERGER, Raoul. "Doctor Bonham's Case: Statutory Construction or Constitutional Theory?" *U Penn L Rev,* 117 (1969), 521–545.

1936 BLACK, Charles L., Jr. *The People and the Court.* New York, 1960.

1937 BORCHARD, Edwin. "The Constitutionality of Declaratory Judgments." *Colum L Rev,* 31 (1931), 561–616.

1938 BRADEN, George D. "The Search for Objectivity in Constitutional Law." *Yale L J,* 57 (1948), 571–594.

1939 BUCHANAN, G. Sidney. "Judicial Supremacy Re-examined: A Proposed Alternative." *Mich L Rev,* 70 (1972), 1279–1322.

1940 BURTON, Harold H. "The Cornerstone of Constitutional Law: The Extraordinary Case of *Marbury v. Madison.*" *Am Bar Assoc J,* 36 (1950), 850.

1941 CAPPELLETTI, Mauro. *Judicial Review in the Contemporary World.* Indianapolis, 1971.

1942 CARR, Robert K. *The Supreme Court and Judicial Review.* New York, 1942.

1943 CLARK, A. Inglis. "The Supremacy of the Judiciary." *Harv L Rev,* 17 (1903), 1–19.

1944 CLARK, Walter. "Where Does the Governing Power Reside?" *Am L Rev,* 52 (1918), 687–694.

1945 CLARKE, John H. "Judicial Power to Declare Legislation Unconstitutional." *Am Bar Assoc J,* 9 (1923), 689–692.

1946 *Cohens v. Virginia.* 6 Wheaton (19 U.S.) 264 (1821).

1947 COMMAGER, Henry Steele. "Judicial Review and Democracy." *Va Q Rev,* 19 (1943), 417–428.

1948 *Cooper v. Aaron.* 358 U.S. 1 (1958).

1949 CORWIN, Edward S. *Court over Constitution.* Princeton, N.J., 1938.

1950 CORWIN, Edward S. *The Doctrine of Judicial Review.* Princeton, N.J., 1914.

1951 CORWIN, Edward S. "The Establishment of Judicial Review." *Mich L Rev,* 9 (1910–1911), 102–125, 283–316.

1952 CORWIN, Edward S. "*Marbury v. Madison* and the Doctrine of Judicial Review." *Mich L Rev,* 12 (1914), 538–572.

1953 CORWIN, Edward S. "The Supreme Court and Unconstitutional Acts of Congress." *Mich L Rev,* 4 (1906), 616–630.

1954 CULP, Maurice S. "A Survey of the Proposals to Limit or Deny the Power of Judicial Review by the Supreme Court of the United States." *Ind L Rev,* 4 (1929), 386–398, 474–490.

1955 DAVIS, Horace A. "Annulment of Legislation by the Supreme Court." *Am Pol Sci Rev,* 7 (1913), 541–587.

1956 DAVIS, Horace A. *The Judicial Veto.* Boston, 1914.

82

1957 DAVIS, Kenneth Culp. "Ripeness of Governmental Action for Judicial Review." *Harv L Rev,* 68 (1955), 1122–1153, 1326–1373.

1958 DEAN, Howard E. *Judicial Review and Democracy.* New York, 1966.

1959 DODD, W. F. "The United States Supreme Court as the Final Interpreter of the Federal Constitution." *Ill L Rev,* 6 (1911), 289–312.

1960 DOUGHERTY, J. Hampden. *Power of Federal Judiciary over Legislation: Its Origin. . . .* New York, 1912.

1961 DOUGLAS, William O. "On Misconception of the Judicial Function and the Responsibility of the Bar." *Colum L Rev,* 59 (1959), 227–233.

1962 DOUGLAS, William O. "Stare Decisis." *Colum L Rev,* 49 (1949), 735–758.

1963 ELY, John Hart. "Legislative and Administrative Motivation in Constitutional Law." *Yale L J,* 79 (1970), 1205–1341.

1964 EPSTEIN, Leon D. "Justice Douglas: A Case Study in Judicial Review." Ph.D. dissertation, University of Chicago, 1949.

1965 *Fairfax's Devisee v. Hunter's Lessee.* 7 Cranch (11 U.S.) 603 (1813).

1966 FIELD, O. P. *Effect of an Unconstitutional Statute.* Minneapolis, 1935.

1967 FINKELSTEIN, Maurice. "From *Munn v. Illinois* to *Tyson v. Banton:* A Study in the Judicial Process." *Colum L Rev,* 27 (1927), 769–783.

1968 FINKELSTEIN, Maurice. "Judicial Self-Limitation." *Harv L Rev,* 37 (1924), 338–364.

1969 FRANK, Jerome. "Words and Music: Some Remarks on Statutory Interpretation." *Colum L Rev,* 47 (1947), 1259–1278.

1970 FRANKFURTER, Felix. "Some Reflections on the Reading of Statutes." *Colum L Rev,* 47 (1947), 527–546.

1971 GRANT, J. A. C. "*Marbury v. Madison* Today." *Am Pol Sci Rev,* 23 (1929), 673–681.

1972 GRIFFITH, Kathryn. *Judge Learned Hand and the Role of the Federal Judiciary.* Norman, Okla., 1973.

1973 GUNTHER, Gerald. "The Subtle Vices of the Passive Virtues—A Comment on Principle and Expediency in Judicial Review." *Colum L Rev,* 64 (1964), 1–25.

1974 HAINES, Charles G. *The American Doctrine of Judicial Supremacy.* 2nd ed. New York, 1959 (reprint of 1932 ed.).

1975 HAINES, Charles G. "Judicial Review of Acts of Congress and the Need for Constitutional Reform." *Yale L J,* 45 (1936), 816–856.

1976 HAINES, Charles G. "Judicial Review of Legislation in the United States and the Doctrine of Vested Rights." *Tex L Rev,* 2 (1924), 257–290, 387–421; 3 (1924), 1–43.

1977 HAND, Learned. *The Bill of Rights.* Cambridge, Mass., 1958.

1978 HARRIS, Robert J. "The Decline of Judicial Review." *J Pol,* 10 (1948), 1–19.

1979 HARRIS, Robert J. *The Judicial Power of the United States.* Baton Rouge, La., 1940.

1980 HOHFELD, Wesley Newcomb. *Fundamental Legal Conceptions as Applied in Judicial Reasoning.* New Haven, 1946.

1981 HUGHES, Graham. "Civil Disobedience and the Political Question Doctrine." *N Y U L Rev,* 43 (1968), 1–19.

1982 IRISH, Marian D. "Mr. Justice Douglas and Judicial Restraint." *U Fla L Rev,* 6 (1953), 537–553.

1983 JACKSON, Robert H. "The Meaning of Statutes: What Congress Says or What the Court Says." *Am Bar Assoc J,* 34 (1948), 535–538.

1984 JACKSON, Robert H. "The Task of Maintaining Our Liberties: The Role of the Judiciary." *Am Bar Assoc J,* 39 (1953), 961–965.

1985 JAFFE, Louis L. "Judicial Review: Constitutional and Jurisdictional Fact." *Harv L Rev,* 71 (1957), 953–985.

1986 JAFFE, Louis L. "The Right to Judicial Review." *Harv L Rev,* 71 (1958), 401–437, 769–814.

1987 "Judicial Review of the University-Student Relationship: Expulsion and Governance." *Stan L Rev,* 26 (1973), 95–130.

1988 KETCHAM, Ralph L. "James Madison and Judicial Review." *Syr L Rev,* 8 (1957), 158–165.

1989 "Legislative Purpose and Federal Constitutional Adjudication." *Harv L Rev,* 83 (1970), 1887–1903.

1990 LEVI, Edward H. *An Introduction to Legal Reasoning.* Chicago, 1948.

1991 *Luther v. Borden.* 7 Howard (48 U.S.) 1 (1849).

1992 McDONOUGH, James B. "The Alleged Usurpation of Power by the Federal Courts." *Am L Rev,* 46 (1912), 45–59.

1993 McMURTRIE, Richard C. "The Jurisdiction to Declare Void Acts of Legislation —When Is It Legitimate and When Mere Usurpation of Sovereignty?" *Am L Reg,* 32 (1893), 1093–1108.

1994 McWHINNEY, Edward. *Judicial Review.* 4th ed. Toronto, Canada, 1969.

1995 MACE, George. "The Anti-Democratic Character of Judicial Review." *Calif L Rev,* 60 (1972), 1140–1149.

1996 *Marbury v. Madison.* 1 Cranch (5 U.S.) 137 (1803).

1997 *Martin v. Hunter's Lessee.* 1 Wheaton (14 U.S.) 304 (1816).

1998 MASON, Alpheus T. "Judicial Activism: Old and New." *Va L Rev,* 55 (1969), 385–426.

1999 MASON, Alpheus T. "Judicial Restraint and Judicial Duty: An Historic Dichotomy." *NY State Bar J,* 38 (1966), 216–231.

2000 MILLER, Arthur S., and Ronald HOWELL. "The Myth of Neutrality in Constitutional Adjudication." *U Chi L Rev,* 27 (1960), 661–695.

2001 *Mississippi v. Johnson.* 4 Wallace (71 U.S.) 475 (1867).

2002 MOORE, Blaine F. "The Judicial Veto and Political Democracy." *Am Pol Sci Rev,* 10 (1916), 700–709.

2003 MOORE, Blaine F. *The Supreme Court and Unconstitutional Legislation.* New York, 1913.

2004 MURRAY, Craig C. "Chief Justice Gibson of the Pennsylvania Supreme Court and Judicial Review." *U Pitt L Rev,* 32 (1970), 127–166.

2005 PLUCKNETT, Theodore F. T. "Bonham's Case and Judicial Review." *Harv L Rev,* 40 (1926), 30–70.

2006 POTTER, William W. "Judicial Power in the United States." *Mich L Rev,* 27 (1928–1929), 1–22, 167–190, 285–313.

2007 RADIN, Max. "Statutory Interpretation." *Harv L Rev,* 43 (1930), 863–885.

2008 ROE, Gilbert E. *Our Judicial Oligarchy.* New York, 1912.

2009 ROSTOW, Eugene V. "The Democratic Character of Judicial Review." *Harv L Rev,* 66 (1952), 193–224.

2010 SCHARPF, Fritz W. "Judicial Review and the Political Question—A Functional Analysis." *Yale L J,* 75 (1966), 517–597.

2011 SHAPIRO, Martin. "Toward a Theory of Stare Decisis." *J Leg Stud,* 1 (1972), 125–134.

2012 THAYER, James Bradley. "Origin and Scope of the American Doctrine of Constitutional Law." *Harv L Rev,* 7 (1893), 129–156.

2013 *United States v. Carolene Products Co.* 304 U.S. 144 (1938).

2014 *United States v. Peters.* 5 Cranch (9 U.S.) 115 (1809).

2015 VON MOSCHZISKER, Robert. *Judicial Review of Legislation.* Washington, D.C., 1923.

2016 WECHSLER, Herbert. *Principles, Politics, and Fundamental Law.* Cambridge, Mass., 1961.

2017 WESTON, Melville F. "Political Questions." *Harv L Rev,* 38 (1925), 296–333.

2018 WRIGHT, J. Skelly. "The Courts and the Rulemaking Process: The Limits of Judicial Review." *Corn L Rev,* 59 (1974), 375–397.

2019 WRIGHT, J. Skelly. "The Role of the Supreme Court in a Democratic Society —Judicial Activism or Restraint?" *Corn L Rev,* 54 (1968), 1–28.

Judicial Decision Making

2020 AIKIN, Charles. "Stare Decisis, Precedent, and the Constitution." *West Pol Q,* 9 (1956), 87–92.

2021 ALBERTSWORTH, E. F. "The Federal Supreme Court and the Superstructure of the Constitution." *Am Bar Assoc J,* 16 (1930), 565–571.

2022 ALITO, Samuel A. "The 'Released Time' Cases Revisited: A Study of Group Decision Making by the Supreme Court." *Yale L J,* 83 (1974), 1202–1236.

2023 BIRKBY, Robert H., and Walter F. MURPHY. "Interest Group Conflict in the Judicial Arena: The First Amendment and Group Access to the Courts." *Tex L Rev,* 42 (1964), 1018–1048.

2024 CARDOZO, Benjamin N. *The Growth of the Law.* New Haven, 1924.

2025 CARDOZO, Benjamin N. *Law and Literature and Other Essays.* New York, 1931.

2026 CARDOZO, Benjamin N. *The Nature of the Judicial Process.* New Haven, 1921.

2027 CARDOZO, Benjamin N. *The Paradoxes of Legal Science.* New York, 1928.

2028 DANELSKI, David J. "The Influence of the Chief Justice in the Decisional Process." *Courts, Judges, and Politics.* Eds. W. F. Murphy and C. H. Pritchett. 2nd ed. New York, 1974.

2029 DANELSKI, David J. "Legislative and Judicial Decision-Making: The Case of Harold H. Burton." *Political Decision-Making.* Ed. S. Sidney Ulmer. New York, 1970.

2030 DANELSKI, David J. "Values as Variables in Judicial Decision-Making: Notes Toward a Theory." *Vand L Rev,* 19 (1966), 721–740.

2031 DOUGLAS, William O. *We the Judges.* New York, 1956.

2032 FRANK, Jerome. *Courts on Trial: Myth and Reality in American Justice.* Princeton, N.J., 1949.

2033 FRANK, Jerome. *Law and the Modern Mind.* New York, 1930.

2034 GROSSMAN, Joel B., and Joseph TANENHAUS, eds. *Frontiers of Judicial Research.* New York, 1969.

2035 GROSSMAN, Joel B., *et al. Social Science Approaches to the Judicial Process: A Symposium.* New York, 1971.

2036 HAKMAN, Nathan. "Lobbying the Supreme Court—An Appraisal of 'Political Science Folklore.' " *Ford L Rev,* 35 (1966), 15–50.

2037 HARPER, Fowler V., and Edwin D. ETHERINGTON. "Lobbyists Before the Court." *U Penn L Rev,* 101 (1953), 1172–1177.

2038 HOWARD, J. Woodford. "On the Fluidity of Judicial Choice." *Am Pol Sci Rev,* 62 (1968), 43–56.

2039 HUTCHESON, Joseph C., Jr. "The Judgment Intuitive: The Function of the 'Hunch' in Judicial Decision." *Corn L Q,* 14 (1929), 274–288.

2040 KRISLOV, Samuel. "The Amicus Curiae Brief: From Friendship to Advocacy." *Yale L J,* 72 (1963), 694–721.

2041 LEIMAN, Joan M. "The Rule of Four." *Colum L Rev,* 57 (1957), 975–992.

2042 LLEWELLYN, Karl N. *The Bramble Bush.* New York, 1951.

2043 LLEWELLYN, Karl N. *The Common Law Tradition: Deciding Appeals.* Boston, 1960.

2044 POUND, Roscoe. "The Theory of Judicial Decision." *Harv L Rev,* 36 (1923), 641–662, 802–825, 940–959.

2045 SCHUBERT, Glendon A. *The Judicial Mind. The Attitudes and Ideologies of Supreme Court Justices, 1946–1963.* Evanston, Ill., 1965.

2046 "Symposium: Empirical Approaches to Judicial Behavior." *U Cin L Rev,* 42 (1973), 589–677.

2047 "Symposium: Social Science Approaches to the Judicial Process." *Harv L Rev,* 79 (1966), 1551–1628.

2048 WASSERSTROM, Richard. *The Judicial Decision.* Stanford, Calif., 1961.

The Impact of Judicial Decisions

2049 BEANEY, William M., and Edward N. BEISER. "Prayer and Politics: The Impact of Engel and Schempp on the Political Process." *J Pub L,* 13 (1964), 475–503.

2050 BECKER, Theodore L., and Malcolm M. FEELEY, eds. *The Impact of Supreme Court Decisions.* 2nd ed. New York, 1973.

2051 BIRKBY, Robert H. "The Supreme Court and the Bible Belt: Tennessee Reaction to the 'Schempp' Decision." *Midw J Pol Sci,* 10 (1966), 304–319.

2052 DOLBEARE, Kenneth M., and Phillip E. HAMMOND. *The School Prayer Decisions: From Court Policy to Local Practice.* Chicago, 1971.

2053 "Enforcement of Court Orders." *R Rel L Rep,* 2 (1957), 1051–1079.

2054 EVERSON, David H., ed. *The Supreme Court as Policy-Maker: Three Studies on the Impact of Judicial Decisions.* Carbondale, Ill., 1968.

2055 JOHNSON, Richard M. *The Dynamics of Compliance: Supreme Court Decision-Making from a New Perspective.* Evanston, Ill., 1967.

2056 KRISLOV, Samuel, *et al.,* eds. *Compliance and the Law.* Beverly Hills, Calif., 1971.

2057 MANWARING, David R., *et al. The Supreme Court as Policy-Maker: Three Studies on the Impact of Judicial Decisions.* Carbondale, Ill., 1968.

2058 MUIR, William K., Jr. *Prayer in the Public Schools. Law and Attitude Change.* Chicago, 1967.

2059 MURPHY, Walter F. "Lower Court Checks on Supreme Court Power." *Am Pol Sci Rev,* 53 (1959), 1017–1031.

2060 NAGEL, Stuart S. "Causes and Effects of Constitutional Compliance." *Political and Legal Obligation, NOMOS XII.* Ed. J. Roland Pennock. New York, 1969.

2061 PATRIC, Gordon. "The Impact of a Court Decision: Aftermath of the McCollum Case." *J Pub L,* 6 (1957), 455–464.

2062 PELTASON, Jack W. *Fifty-Eight Lonely Men.* New York, 1961.

2063 ROBERTSON, John A., and Phyllis TEITELBAUM. "Optimizing Legal Impact: A Case Study in Search of a Theory." *Wis L Rev,* 1973 (1973), 665–726.

2064 SORAUF, Frank, Jr. "*Zorach v. Clauson*: The Impact of a Supreme Court Decision." *Am Pol Sci Rev,* 53 (1959), 777–791.

2065 WASBY, Stephen L. *The Impact of the United States Supreme Court: Some Perspectives.* Homewood, Ill., 1970.

The Bar

2066 BOROSAGE, Robert, *et al.* "The New Public Interest Lawyer." *Yale L J,* 79 (1970), 1069–1153.

2067 BRICKMAN, Lester. "Of Arterial Passageways Through the Legal Process: The Right of Universal Access to Courts and Lawyering Services." *N Y U L Rev,* 48 (1973), 595–668.

2068 CASPER, Jonathan D. *Lawyers Before the Warren Court.* Urbana, Ill., 1972.

2069 CHRISTENSEN, Barlow F. *Lawyers for People of Moderate Means; Some Problems of Availability of Legal Services.* Chicago, 1970.

2070 CHROUST, Anton-Hermann. *The Rise of the Legal Profession in America.* 2 vols. Norman, Okla., 1965.

2071 COUNTRYMAN, Vern, and Ted FINMAN, eds. *The Lawyer in Modern Society.* Boston, 1965.

2072 DRINKER, Henry S. *Legal Ethics.* New York, 1953.

2073 EULAU, Heinz, and John D. SPRAGUE. *Lawyers in Politics; A Study in Professional Convergence.* Indianapolis, 1964.

2074 GOEBEL, Julius, Jr., *et al. The Law Practice of Alexander Hamilton: Documents and Commentary.* 2 vols. New York, 1964–1969.

2075 GOULDEN, Joseph C. *The Superlawyers: The Small and Powerful World of the Great Washington Law Firms.* New York, 1971.

2076 GROSSMAN, Joel B. *Lawyers and Judges: The ABA and the Politics of Judicial Selection.* New York, 1965.

2077 HARBAUGH, William H. *Lawyer's Lawyer: The Life of John W. Davis.* New York, 1973.

2078 HOFFMAN, Paul. *Lions in the Street: The Inside Story of the Great Wall Street Law Firms.* New York, 1973.

2079 "Inciting Litigation." *R Rel L Rep,* 3 (1958), 1257–1277.

2080 McKEAN, Dayton D. *The Integrated Bar.* Boston, 1963.

2081 MARKS, F. Raymond, *et al. The Lawyer, the Public and Professional Responsibility.* Chicago, 1972.

2082 MAYER, Andrew C. "The Lawyer in the Executive Branch of Government." *L & Soc Rev,* 4 (1970), 425–444.

2083 MAYER, Martin. *The Lawyers.* New York, 1966.

2084 POUND, Roscoe. *The Lawyer from Antiquity to Modern Times.* Minneapolis, 1953.

2085 "Private Attorneys General." *Yale L J,* 58 (1949), 574–598.

2086 REHNQUIST, William H. "The Bar Admission Cases: A Strange Judicial Aberration." *Am Bar Assoc J,* 44 (1958), 229–232.

2087 RHYNE, Charles S. "Defending Our Courts: The Duty of the Legal Profession." *Am Bar Assoc J,* 44 (1958), 121–124.

2088 RODELL, Fred. *Woe unto You, Lawyers.* New York, 1939.

2089 "The South's Amended Barratry Laws: An Attempt to End Group Pressure Through the Courts." *Yale L J,* 72 (1963), 1613–1645.

2090 THURMAN, Samuel David, *et al. Cases and Materials on the Legal Profession.* Mineola, N.Y., 1970.

2091 WARKOV, Seymour, and Joseph ZELAN. *Lawyers in the Making.* Chicago, 1965.

2092 WARREN, Charles. *A History of the American Bar.* Boston, 1911.

Judicial Federalism

2093 American Law Institute. *Study of the Division of Jurisdiction Between State and Federal Courts.* Philadelphia, 1969.

2094 BERMAN, Bayard F. "Supreme Court Review of State Court 'Findings of Fact' in Certain Criminal Cases: The Fact-Law Dichotomy in a Narrow Area." *So Calif L Rev,* 23 (1950), 334–343.

2095 BRENNAN, William J., Jr. "The Bill of Rights and the States." *N Y U L Rev,* 36 (1961), 761–778.

2096 BRENNAN, William J., Jr. "State Court Decisions and the Supreme Court." *Penn Bar Assoc Q,* 31 (1960), 393–407.

2097 DODD, E. Merrick, Jr. "The Power of the Supreme Court to Review State Decisions in the Field of Conflict of Laws." *Harv L Rev,* 39 (1926), 533–562.

2098 DUMBAULD, Edward. "Judicial Interference with Litigation in Other Courts." *Dick L Rev,* 74 (1970), 369–388.

2099 ELY, John Hart. "The Irrepressible Myth of Erie." *Harv L Rev,* 87 (1974), 693–740.

2100 *Erie Railroad v. Tompkins.* 304 U.S. 64 (1938).

2101 "The Federal Common Law." *Harv L Rev,* 82 (1970), 1512–1535.

2102 FRANKFURTER, Felix. "Distribution of Judicial Power Between United States and State Courts." *Corn L Q,* 13 (1928), 499–530.

2103 HUFSTEDLER, Shirley M. "Comity and the Constitution: The Changing Role of the Federal Judiciary." *N Y U L Rev,* 47 (1972), 841–870.

2104 KURLAND, Philip B. "The Supreme Court, the Due Process Clause, and the In Personam Jurisdiction of State Courts." *U Chi L Rev,* 25 (1958), 569–624.

2105 MARAIST, Frank L. "Federal Injunctive Relief Against State Court Proceedings." *Tex L Rev,* 48 (1970), 535–607.

2106 "Protecting Civil Liberties Through Federal Court Intervention in State Criminal Matters." *Calif L Rev,* 59 (1971), 1549–1575.

2107 "Supreme Court Disposition of State Decisions Involving Non-Federal Questions." *Yale L J,* 49 (1940), 1463–1469.

2108 *Swift v. Tyson.* 16 Peters (41 U.S.) 1 (1842).

2109 *"Swift v. Tyson* Exhumed." *Yale L J,* 79 (1969), 284–310.

2110 WENDELL, Mitchell. *Relations Between the Federal and State Courts.* New York, 1949.

2111 WHITE, Welsh S. "Federal Habeas Corpus: The Impact of the Failure to Assert a Constitutional Right at Trial." *Va L Rev,* 58 (1972), 67–95.

C. Federalism

2112 *Ableman v. Booth.* 21 Howard (62 U.S.) 506 (1859).

2113 ADAMS, Henry, ed. *Documents Relating to New England Federalism, 1800–1815.* Boston, 1877.

2114 Advisory Commission on Intergovernmental Relations. *Federalism in 1973: The System under Stress.* Washington, D.C., 1974.

2115 AMES, Herman V., ed. *State Documents on Federal Relations.* Philadelphia, 1900.

2116 BENNETT, Walter Hartwell. *American Theories of Federalism.* University, Ala., 1964.

2117 BERNS, Walter. "The Meaning of the 10th Amendment." *A Nation of States.* Ed. R. A. Goldwin. Chicago, 1953.

2118 BITTERMAN, H. J. *State and Federal Grants in Aid.* Chicago, 1938.

2119 BORDEN, Morton. *The Anti-Federalist Papers.* East Lansing, Mich., 1965.

2120 BOWIE, Robert R., and Carl J. FRIEDRICH, eds. *Studies in Federalism.* Boston, 1954.

2121 BURDICK, Charles K. "Federal Aid Legislation." *Corn L Q,* 8 (1923), 324–337.

2122 CARY, William L. "Federalism and Corporate Law: Reflections upon Delaware." *Yale L J,* 83 (1974), 663–705.

2123 *Chisholm v. Georgia.* 2 Dallas (2 U.S.) 419 (1793).

2124 CLARK, Jane Perry. *The Rise of a New Federalism.* New York, 1938.

2125 Council of State Governments. Committee on Federal Grants-in-Aid. *Federal Grants in Aid.* Chicago, 1949.

2126 Conference of Chief Justices. "Report of the Committee on Federal-State Relationships as Affected by Judicial Decisions." *State Govt,* 32 (1959), 60–74.

2127 CORWIN, Edward S. "National Power and State Interposition, 1787–1861." *Mich L Rev,* 10 (1912), 535–551.

2128 CORWIN, Edward S. *National Supremacy. Treaty Power vs. State Power.* New York, 1913.

2129 CORWIN, Edward S. "The Passing of Dual Federalism." *Va L Rev,* 36 (1950), 1–24.

2130 CRAMTON, Roger C. *"Pennsylvania v. Nelson;* A Case Study in Federal Preemption." *U Chi L Rev,* 26 (1958), 85–108.

2131 DOUGLAS, William O. "Interposition and the Peters Case, 1778–1809." *Stan L Rev,* 9 (1956), 3–12.

2132 ELAZAR, Daniel J. *American Federalism: A View from the States.* New York, 1966.

2133 ELAZAR, Daniel J. *The American Partnership.* Chicago, 1962.

2134 FLAHERTY, Donald W. *The Role of the United States Supreme Court in the Settlement of Inter-sovereign Disputes.* Ann Arbor, Mich., 1954.

2135 FOX, Douglas M. *New Urban Politics: Cities and the Federal Government.* Pacific Palisades, Calif., 1972.

2136 FRANKFURTER, Felix, and James M. LANDIS. "The Compact Clause of the Constitution—A Study in Interstate Adjustments." *Yale L J,* 34 (1925), 685–758.

2137 FREUND, Paul A. "Umpiring the Federal System." *Colum L Rev,* 54 (1954), 561–578.

2138 *Hammer v. Dagenhart.* 247 U.S. 251 (1918).

2139 HANSEN, Niles M. *Rural Poverty and the Urban Crisis: A Strategy for Regional Development.* Bloomington, Ind., 1970.

2140 HARRIS, Fred R., and John V. LINDSAY. *State of the Cities: Report of the Commission on the Cities in the 70's.* New York, 1972.

2141 "Interposition Versus Judicial Power." *R Rel L Rep,* 1 (1956), 465–499.

2142 JACKSON, Robert H. *Full Faith and Credit: The Lawyer's Clause of the Constitution.* New York, 1945.

2143 JACOBS, Clyde E. *The Eleventh Amendment and Sovereign Immunity.* Greenwood, Conn., 1972.

2144 *Kentucky v. Dennison.* 24 Howard (65 U.S.) 66 (1861).

2145 KEY, V. O., Jr. *Administration of Federal Grants to States.* Chicago, 1937.

2146 LEACH, Richard H. *American Federalism.* New York, 1970.

2147 LIVINGSTON, William S. *Federalism and Constitutional Change.* Oxford, 1956.

2148 *McCulloch v. Maryland.* (See 1516.)

2149 MacDONALD, A. F. *Federal Aid: A Study of the American Subsidy System.* New York, 1928.

2150 McLAUGHLIN, Andrew C. "The Background of American Federalism." *Am Pol Sci Rev,* 12 (1918), 215–240.

2151 MARSHALL, Burke. *Federalism and Civil Rights.* New York, 1964.

2152 MASON, Alpheus T. "The Nature of Our Federal Union Reconsidered." *Pol Sci Q,* 65 (1950), 502–521.

2153 MASON, Alpheus T. *The States Rights Debate* (see 456).

2154 METCALFE, William K. "The Tidelands Controversy: A Study in the Development of a Political-Legal Problem." *Syr L Rev,* 4 (1952), 39–89.

2155 NAGEL, Paul C. *One Nation Indivisible. The Union in American Thought, 1776–1861.* New York, 1964.

2156 OWSLEY, Frank L. *State Rights in the Confederacy.* Glouster, Mass., 1961 (reprint of 1925 ed.).

2157 PARKER, John J. "Dual Sovereignty and the Federal Courts." *Northw U L Rev,* 51 (1956), 407–423.

2158 *Pennsylvania v. Nelson.* 350 U.S. 497 (1956).

2159 POUND, Roscoe, *et al. Federalism as a Democratic Process.* New Brunswick, N.J., 1942.

2160 RANNEY, John C. "The Basis of American Federalism." *Wm & M Q,* 3 (1946), 1–35.

2161 REAGAN, Michael D. *The New Federalism.* New York, 1972.

2162 REUSS, Henry S. *Revenue-Sharing: Crutch or Catalyst for State and Local Governments?* New York, 1970.

2163 RIDGEWAY, Marian E. *Interstate Compacts. A Question of Federalism.* Carbondale, Ill., 1971.

2164 ROBERTSON, David W. *Admiralty and Federalism: History and Analysis of Problems of Federal-State Relations in the Maritime Law of the United States.* Mineola, N.Y., 1970.

2165 SCHMIDHAUSER, John R. *The Supreme Court as Final Arbiter in Federal-State Relations, 1789-1957.* Chapel Hill, N.C., 1958.

2166 SCHOENFELD, Benjamin. "American Federalism and the Abstention Doctrine in the Supreme Court." *Dick L Rev,* 73 (1969), 605–638.

2167 SCOTT, James B. "The Role of the Supreme Court of the United States in the Settlement of Interstate Disputes." *Geo L J,* 15 (1927), 146–167.

2168 SPRAGUE, John D. *Voting Patterns of the United States Supreme Court. Cases in Federalism, 1889-1959.* Indianapolis, 1968.

2169 STOLZ, Otto G. "Revenue Sharing—New American Revolution or Trojan Horse?" *Minn L Rev,* 58 (1973), 1–120.

2170 SWINDLER, William F. "The Current Challenge to Federalism: The Confederating Proposals." *Geo L J,* 52 (1963), 1–41.

2171 *Texas v. White.* 7 Wallace (74 U.S.) 700 (1869).

2172 THILLY, John Leroy. "Suing the State under Title VII in the Face of the Eleventh Amendment." *Wis L Rev,* 1973 (1973), 1099–1123.

2173 U.S. Commission on Intergovernmental Relations. *A Report to the President for Transmittal to the Congress.* Washington, D.C., 1955.

2174 *United States v. Darby Lumber Co.* 312 U.S. 100 (1941).

2175 VILE, M. J. C. *The Structure of American Federalism.* London, 1961.

2176 *Ware v. Hylton.* 3 Dallas (3 U.S.) 199 (1796).

2177 WARREN, Charles. *The Supreme Court and Sovereign States.* Princeton, N.J., 1924.

2178 WIECEK, William M. *The Guarantee Clause of the U.S. Constitution.* Ithaca, N.Y., 1972.

2179 WILKINSON, J. Harvie, III. "Justice John M. Harlan and the Values of Federalism." *Va L Rev,* 57 (1971), 1185–1221.

2180 *Williams v. North Carolina.* 325 U.S. 226 (1945).

D. *Constitutional Amendment*

2181 American Bar Association. Constitutional Convention Study Committee. *Amendment of the Constitution by the Convention Method under Article V.* Chicago, 1973.

2182 AMES, Herman V. *The Proposed Amendments to the Constitution of the United States During the First Century of Its History.* New York, 1970 (reprint of 1896 ed.).

2183 BIRCHFIELD, Cyril F. *Problems Relating to a Federal Constitutional Convention.* Washington, D.C., 1957.

2184 BROWN, Everett S. *Proposed Amendments to the Constitution of the United States, January 3, 1947–January 3, 1953.* Ann Arbor, Mich., 1953.

2185 BROWN, Everett S. *Ratification of the Twenty-First Amendment to the Constitution of the United States.* Ann Arbor, Mich., 1938.

2186 CLARK, Homer. "The Supreme Court and the Amending Process." *Va L Rev,* 39 (1953), 621–652.

2187 GILLETTE, William. *The Right to Vote: Politics and the Passage of the Fifteenth Amendment.* Baltimore, 1965.

2188 GRAHAM, Fred P. "The Role of the States in Proposing Constitutional Amendments." *Am Bar Assoc J,* 49 (1963), 1175–1183.

2189 GRINNEL, Frank W. "Constitutional Amendments Proposed Relative to the Supreme Court of the United States." *Mass L Q,* 34 (1949), 33–38.

2190 MARBURY, William L. "The Limitations upon the Amending Power." *Harv L Rev,* 33 (1919), 223–235.

2191 MARBURY, William L. "The Nineteenth and After." *Va L Rev,* 7 (1920), 1–29.

2192 MARTIN, Philip L. "The Application Clause of Article Five." *Pol Sci Q,* 85 (1970), 616–628.

2193 MARTIN, Philip L. "Convention Ratification of Federal Constitutional Amendments." *Pol Sci Q,* 82 (1967), 61–71.

2194 OBERST, Paul. "The Genesis of the Three States-rights Amendments of 1963." *Not Dame Law,* 39 (1964), 644–658.

2195 ORFIELD, Lester B. *The Amending of the Federal Constitution.* Chicago, 1942.

2196 SILVA, Edward T. "States and the Nation: State Cohorts and Amendment Clusters in the Process of Federal Constitutional Amendment in the United States, 1869–1931." *L & Soc Rev,* 4 (1970), 445–466.

2197 TUCKER, Henry St. George. *Woman Suffrage by Constitutional Amendment.* New Haven, 1916.

2198 TUGWELL, Rexford Guy. *The Emerging Constitution.* New York, 1974.

2199 United States Senate. Library. *Proposed Amendments to the Constitution of the United States Introduced in Congress from the 69th Congress, 2nd session, Through the 84th Congress, 2nd session, December 6, 1926, to January 3, 1957.* Washington, D.C., 1957.

2200 VOSE, Clement E. *Constitutional Change.* Lexington, Mass., 1972.

2201 WILLIS, Paul G., and George L. WILLIS. "The Politics of the Twenty-Second Amendment." *West Pol Q,* 5 (1952), 469–482.

E. Civil Liberties and Civil Rights

General

2202 ABRAHAM, Henry J. *Freedom and the Court. Civil Rights and Liberties in the United States.* 2nd ed. New York, 1972.

2203 ADLER, Mortimer J. *The Idea of Freedom.* 2 vols. New York, 1958–1961.

2204 BAKAL, Carl. *The Right to Bear Arms.* New York, 1966.

2205 BARKER, Lucius J., and Twiley W. BARKER, Jr. *Freedoms, Courts, Politics. Studies in Civil Liberties.* Rev. ed. Englewood Cliffs, N.J., 1972.

2206 BARNETT, Vincent M., Jr. "Mr. Justice Murphy, Civil Liberties and the Holmes Tradition." *Corn L Q,* 32 (1946), 177–221.

2207 BARRETT, Edward L., Jr. "Personal Rights, Property Rights and the Fourth Amendment." *S Ct Rev* (1960), 46–74.

2208 BASKIN, Alex. *The American Civil Liberties Union Papers; A Guide to the Records, A.C.L.U. Cases 1912–1946.* Stony Brook, N.Y., 1971.

2209 BASON, George F. "To Enforce These Rights." *Wis L Rev,* 1973 (1973), 1085–1098.

2210 BEANEY, William M. "Civil Liberties and Statutory Construction." *J Pub L,* 8 (1959), 66–80.

2211 BECKER, Carl, *et al. Safeguarding Civil Liberties Today.* Ithaca, N.Y., 1945.

2212 BIDDLE, Francis. *The Fear of Freedom.* Garden City, N.Y., 1951.

2213 BIRKBY, Robert H. "Justice Wiley B. Rutledge and Individual Liberties." Ph.D. dissertation, Princeton University, 1963.

2214 BISCHOFF, Ralph F. "Constitutional Law and Civil Rights." *N Y U L Rev,* 31 (1956), 60–92.

2215 BORCHARD, Edwin. "The Supreme Court and Private Rights." *Yale L J,* 47 (1938), 1051–1078.

2216 BRANT, Irving. *The Bill of Rights. Its Origin and Meaning.* Indianapolis, 1965.

2217 BRANT, Irving. *The Constitution and the Right to Know.* Columbia, Mo., 1967.

2218 CAHN, Edmond, ed. *The Great Rights.* New York, 1963.

2219 *Calder v. Bull.* 3 Dallas (3 U.S.) 386 (1798).

2220 CASPER, Jonathan D. *The Politics of Civil Liberties.* New York, 1972.

2221 CASSINELLI, C. W. *The Politics of Freedom.* Seattle, Wash., 1961.

2222 CAUGHEY, John W. *In Clear and Present Danger: The Crucial State of Our Freedoms.* Chicago, 1958.

2223 CHAFEE, Zechariah, Jr. *The Blessings of Liberty.* Philadelphia, 1956.

2224 CHAFEE, Zechariah, Jr., ed. *Documents in Fundamental Human Rights.* 3 vols. Cambridge, Mass., 1951–1952.

2225 CHAFEE, Zechariah, Jr. "Federal and State Powers under the U.N. Covenant on Human Rights." *Wis L Rev,* 1951 (1951), 389–473, 623–656.

2226 CHAFEE, Zechariah, Jr. *How Human Rights Got into the Constitution.* Boston, 1952.

2227 "Civil Liberties—A Symposium." *U Chi L Rev,* 20 (1953), 363–545.

2228 "Civil Liberties Problems in Welfare Administration." *N Y U L Rev,* 43 (1968), 836–915.

2229 COMMAGER, Henry Steele. *Majority Rule and Minority Rights.* New York, 1943.

2230 COX, Archibald. "Foreward: Constitutional Adjudication and the Promotion of Human Rights." *Harv L Rev,* 80 (1966), 91–122.

2231 DELLINGER, Walter E. "Of Rights and Remedies: The Constitution as a Sword." *Harv L Rev,* 85 (1972), 1532–1564.

2232 DORSEN, Norman. *Frontiers of Civil Liberties.* New York, 1968.

2233 DOUGLAS, William O. *A Living Bill of Rights.* Garden City, N.Y., 1961.

2234 DOUGLAS, William O. *The Right of the People.* New York, 1958.

2235 EMERSON, Thomas I., et al. *Political and Civil Rights in the United States.* 3rd ed. 2 vols. Boston, 1967.

2236 EPSTEIN, Leon D. "Justice Douglas and Civil Liberties." *Wis L Rev,* 1951 (1951), 125–157.

2237 FRAENKEL, O. K. *The Supreme Court and Civil Liberties.* 2nd ed. New York, 1963.

2238 FREUND, Paul A. "The Supreme Court and Civil Liberties." *Vand L Rev,* 4 (1951), 533–554.

2239 FRIEDMANN, Wolfgang. "Interference with Human Life: Some Jurisprudential Reflections." *Colum L Rev,* 70 (1970), 1058–1078.

2240 FRIEDMANN, Wolfgang. "Property, Freedom, Security and the Supreme Court of the United States." *Mod L Rev,* 19 (1956), 461–477.

2241 GARVEY, George E. "Unenumerated Rights—Substantive Due Process, the Ninth Amendment, and John Stuart Mill." *Wis L Rev,* 1971 (1971), 922–938.

2242 GELLHORN, Walter. *American Rights: The Constitution in Action.* New York, 1960.

2243 GELLHORN, Walter. *Individual Freedom and Governmental Restraints.* New York, 1956.

2244 GINGER, Ann Fagan. *The Law, the Supreme Court, and the People's Rights.* Woodbury, N.Y., 1973.

2245 HILL, Alfred. "The Bill of Rights and the Supervisory Power." *Colum L Rev,* 69 (1969), 181–215.

2246 HILL, Alfred. "Constitutional Remedies." *Colum L Rev,* 69 (1969), 1109–1161.

2247 JACOBS, Clyde E. *Justice Frankfurter and Civil Liberties.* Berkeley, Calif., 1961.

2248 JENSEN, Joan M. *The Price of Vigilance.* Chicago, 1968.

2249 KAUPER, Paul G. *Civil Liberties and the Constitution.* Ann Arbor, Mich., 1962.

2250 KAUPER, Paul G. *Frontiers of Constitutional Liberty.* Ann Arbor, Mich., 1956.

2251 KONVITZ, Milton R., ed. *Bill of Rights Reader.* Ithaca, N.Y., 1965.

2252 KONVITZ, Milton R. *Expanding Liberties.* New York, 1966.

2253 KONVITZ, Milton R. *Fundamental Liberties of a Free People: Religion, Speech, Press, Assembly.* Ithaca, N.Y., 1957.

2254 KONVITZ, Milton R., and Clinton ROSSITER, eds. *Aspects of Liberty: Essays Presented to Robert E. Cushman.* Ithaca, N.Y., 1958.

2255 KRISLOV, Samuel. *The Supreme Court and Political Freedom.* New York, 1968.

2256 LASKI, Harold J. *Liberty in the Modern State.* London, 1930.

2257 LEVY, Leonard W. *Jefferson and Civil Liberties: The Darker Side.* Cambridge, Mass., 1963.

2258 MEIKLEJOHN, Alexander. *Political Freedom: The Constitutional Powers of the People.* New York, 1960.

2259 "The 'New' Thirteenth Amendment: A Preliminary Analysis. *Harv L Rev,* 82 (1969), 1294–1321.

2260 O'NEIL, Robert M. *Price of Dependency: Civil Liberties in the Welfare State.* New York, 1970.

2261 PRITCHETT, C. Herman. *Civil Liberties and the Vinson Court.* Chicago, 1954.

2262 RATLIFF, Richard C. *Constitutional Rights of College Students.* Metuchen, N.J., 1972.

2263 ROGGE, O. John. *The First and the Fifth, with Some Incursions into Others.* New York, 1960.

2264 SCHEIBER, Harry N. *The Wilson Administration and Civil Liberties, 1917–1921.* Ithaca, N.Y., 1960.

2265 SMITH, James Morton. *Freedom's Fetters: The Alien and Sedition Acts and American Civil Liberties.* Ithaca, N.Y., 1956.

2266 SPICER, George W. *The Supreme Court and Fundamental Freedoms.* 2nd ed. New York, 1967.

2267 SPINRAD, William. *Civil Liberties.* New York, 1970.

2268 SPRAGUE, Dean. *Freedom under Lincoln.* Boston, 1965.

2269 SWISHER, Carl B. "Civil Liberties in War Time." *Pol Sci Q,* 55 (1940), 321–347.

2270 THURMAN, Samuel David. *The Right of Access to Information from the Government.* New York, 1973.

2271 WHIPPLE, Leon. *The Story of Civil Liberty in the United States.* New York, 1927.

Property Rights and the Police Power

2272 *Adkins v. Children's Hospital.* 261 U.S. 525 (1923).

2273 *Allgeyer v. Louisiana.* 165 U.S. 578 (1897).

2274 BOSSELMAN, Fred, *et al. Taking Issue: An Analysis of the Constitutional Limits of Land Use Control.* Washington, D.C., 1973.

2275 BROWN, Ray A. "Police Power—Legislation for Health and Personal Safety." *Harv L Rev,* 42 (1929), 866–898.

2276 *Charles River Bridge v. Warren Bridge.* 11 Peters (36 U.S.) 420 (1837).

2277 *Chicago, Milwaukee, and St. Paul Railway Co. v. Minnesota.* 134 U.S. 418 (1890).

2278 CLARK, Jane Perry. "Emergencies and the Law." *Pol Sci Q,* 49 (1934), 268–283.

2279 COKER, F. W. "American Traditions Concerning Property and Liberty." *Am Pol Sci Rev,* 30 (1936), 1–23.

2280 COOLEY, Thomas M. "Limits to State Control of Private Business." *Princeton Rev* (1878), 233–271.

2281 CORWIN, Edward S. *Liberty Against Government.* Baton Rouge, La., 1948.

2282 COWLES, Willard Bunce. *Treaties and Constitutional Law: Property Interferences and Due Process of Law.* Washington, D.C., 1941.

2283 CROSSKEY, William W. "The Ex-Post-Facto and the Contracts Clauses in the Federal Convention: A Note on the Editorial Integrity of James Madison." *U Chi L Rev,* 35 (1968), 248–254.

2284 CUSHMAN, Robert E. "The Social and Economic Interpretation of the Fourteenth Amendment." *Mich L Rev,* 20 (1922), 737–764.

2285 *Dartmouth College v. Woodward.* 4 Wheaton (17 U.S.) 518 (1819).

2286 DODD, W. F. "Social Legislation and the Courts." *Pol Sci Q,* 28 (1913), 1–17.

2287 FAIRMAN, Charles. "The So-Called Granger Cases, Lord Hale, and Justice Bradley." *Stan L Rev,* 5 (1953), 587–679.

2288 *Ferguson v. Skrupa.* 372 U.S. 726 (1963).

2289 *Fletcher v. Peck.* 6 Cranch (10 U.S.) 87 (1810).

2290 FRANKFURTER, Felix. "Hours of Labor and Realism in Constitutional Law." *Harv L Rev,* 29 (1916), 353–373.

2291 FREUND, Ernst. *The Police Power.* Chicago, 1904.

2292 HADLEY, Arthur Twining. "The Constitutional Position of Property in America." *Ind,* 64 (1908), 834–838.

2293 HALE, Robert L. "The Supreme Court and the Contract Clause." *Harv L Rev,* 57 (1944), 512–557, 621–674, 852–892.

2294 HAMILTON, Walton H. "Affectation with a Public Interest." *Yale L J,* 39 (1930), 1089–1112.

2295 HETHERINGTON, John A. "State Economic Regulation and Substantive Due Process of Law." *Northw U L Rev,* 53 (1953), 13–32.

2296 HORWITZ, Morton J. "The Transformation in the Conception of Property in American Law, 1780–1860." *U Chi L Rev,* 40 (1973), 248–290.

2297 KUTLER, Stanley I. *Privilege and Creative Destruction: The Charles River Bridge Case.* Philadelphia, 1972.

2298 "Land Use Regulation and the Concept of Takings in Nineteenth Century America." *U Chi L Rev,* 40 (1973), 854–872.

2299 LARGE, Donald W. "This Land Is Whose Land? Changing Concepts of Land as Property." *Wis L Rev,* 1973 (1973), 1039–1084.

2300 LIEBERMAN, Elias. *Unions Before the Bar: Historic Trials Showing the Evolution of Labor Rights in the United States.* Rev. ed. New York, 1960.

2301 *Lochner v. New York.* 198 U.S. 45 (1905).

2302 LUCAS, Jo D. "Constitutional Law and Economic Liberty." *J L & Econ,* 11 (1968), 5–33.

2303 McALLISTER, B. P. "Lord Hale and Business Affected with a Public Interest." *Harv L Rev,* 43 (1930), 759–791.

2304 McCLOSKEY, Robert G. "Economic Due Process and the Supreme Court: An Exhumation and Reburial." *S Ct Rev* (1962), 34–62.

2305 McLAUGHLIN, Andrew C. "The Court, the Corporation, and Conkling." *Am Hist Rev,* 46 (1940), 45–63.

2306 MAGRATH, C. Peter. *Yazoo—Law and Politics in the New Republic: The Case of Fletcher v. Peck.* Providence, R.I., 1966.

2307 MARSHALL, Charles C. "A New Constitutional Amendment." *Am L Rev,* 24 (1890), 908–931.

2308 MICHELMAN, Frank I. "Property, Utility, and Fairness: Comments on the Ethical Foundations of 'Just Compensation' Law." *Harv L Rev,* 80 (1967), 1165–1258.

2309 MORIN, Richard W. "Will to Resist: The Dartmouth College Case." *Dart Alum Mag,* 61 (April 1969), 17–36.

2310 *Mugler v. Kansas.* 123 U.S. 623 (1887).

2311 *Muller v. Oregon.* 208 U.S. 412 (1908).

2312 *Munn v. Illinois.* 94 U.S. 113 (1877).

2313 National Consumers' League. *The Supreme Court and Minimum Wage Legislation.* New York, 1925.

2314 *Nebbia v. New York.* 291 U.S. 502 (1934).

2315 *New York v. Miln.* 11 Peters (36 U.S.) 102 (1837).

2316 PAULSON, Monrad. "The Persistence of Substantive Due Process in the States." *Minn L Rev,* 34 (1950), 91–118.

2317 POUND, Roscoe. "Liberty of Contract." *Yale L J,* 18 (1909), 454–487.

2318 POWELL, Thomas Reed. "The Judiciality of Minimum Wage Legislation." *Harv L Rev,* 37 (1924), 545–573.

2319 POWELL, Thomas Reed. "The Oregon Minimum-Wage Cases." *Pol Sci Q,* 32 (1917), 296–311.

2320 POWELL, Thomas Reed. "Protecting Property and Liberty, 1922–1924." *Pol Sci Q,* 40 (1925), 404–437.

2321 POWELL, Thomas Reed. "The Supreme Court and State Police Power, 1922–1930." *Va L Rev,* 17 (1931), 529–556, 653–675, 765–799.

2322 *Providence Bank v. Billings.* 4 Peters (29 U.S.) 514 (1830).

2323 REOTTINGER, Ruth Locke. *The Supreme Court and State Police Power. A Study in Federalism.* Washington, D.C., 1957.

2324 RODES, Robert E., Jr. "Due Process and Social Legislation in the Supreme Court 1873–1937—A Post Mortem." *Not Dame Law,* 33 (1957), 5–33.

2325 SAX, Joseph L. "Takings, Private Property and Public Rights." *Yale L J,* 81 (1971), 149–186.

2326 SCHMIDHAUSER, John R. "Jeremy Bentham, the Contract Clause and Justice John Archibald Campbell." *Vand L Rev,* 11 (1958), 801–820.

2327 SHIRLEY, John M. *The Dartmouth College Causes and the Supreme Court of the United States.* Chicago, 1895.

2328 STITES, Francis. *Private Interest and Public Gain: The Dartmouth College Case, 1819.* Amherst, Mass., 1972.

2329 TIEDEMAN, Christopher G. *A Treatise on the Limitations of Police Power in the United States.* St. Louis, Mo., 1886.

2330 "Towards a Constitutionally Protected Environment." *Va L Rev,* 56 (1970), 458–486.

2331 *West Coast Hotel Co. v. Parrish.* 300 U.S. 379 (1937).

2332 WRIGHT, Benjamin F. *The Contract Clause of the Constitution.* Cambridge, Mass., 1938.

The Fourteenth Amendment

2333 ABERNATHY, Glenn. "Expansion of the State Action Concept under the Fourteenth Amendment." *Corn L Q,* 43 (1958), 375–418.

2334 *Adamson v. California.* 332 U.S. 46 (1947).

2335 *Barron v. Baltimore.* 7 Peters (32 U.S.) 243 (1833).

2336 BETH, Loren P. "The Slaughterhouse Cases." *La L Rev,* 23 (1963), 487–505.

2337 BLACK, Hugo L. "The Bill of Rights." *N Y U L Rev,* 35 (1960), 865–881.

2338 BOUDIN, Louis B. "Truth and Fiction about the Fourteenth Amendment." *N Y U L Rev,* 16 (1938), 19–82.

DOCTRINES AND POLITICS

2339 CANCIAN, John. "Justice Jackson: Civil Liberties and State Action under the Due Process Clause of the Fourteenth Amendment." *Northe L Rev,* 1951 (1951), 3–48.

2340 CORWIN, Edward S. "The Supreme Court and the Fourteenth Amendment." *Mich L Rev,* 7 (1909), 643–672.

2341 CUSHMAN, Robert F. "Incorporation: Due Process and the Bill of Rights." *Corn L Q,* 51 (1966), 467–581.

2342 FAIRMAN, Charles. "Does the Fourteenth Amendment Incorporate the Bill of Rights: The Original Understanding." *Stan L Rev,* 2 (1949), 5–139.

2343 FAIRMAN, Charles, and Stanley E. MORRISON. *Fourteenth Amendment and the Bill of Rights. The Incorporation Theory.* New York, 1970 (reprint of 1949 ed.).

2344 FLACK, Horace. *The Adoption of the Fourteenth Amendment.* Baltimore, 1908.

2345 FRANKFURTER, Felix. "Memorandum on 'Incorporation' of the Bill of Rights into the Due Process Clause of the Fourteenth Amendment." *Harv L Rev,* 78 (1965), 746–783.

2346 GRAHAM, Howard Jay. "The Conspiracy Theory of the Fourteenth Amendment." *Yale L J,* 47 (1938), 371–403.

2347 GRAHAM, Howard Jay. "The Early Anti-Slavery Backgrounds of the Fourteenth Amendment." *Wis L Rev,* 23 (1950), 610–661.

2348 GRAHAM, Howard Jay. "Justice Field and the Fourteenth Amendment." *Yale L J,* 52 (1943), 851–889.

2349 GRAHAM, Howard Jay. "Our Declaratory Fourteenth Amendment." *Stan L Rev,* 7 (1954), 3–39.

2350 JAMES, Joseph B. *Framing of the Fourteenth Amendment.* Urbana, Ill., 1956.

2351 JAMES, Joseph B. "Southern Reaction to the Proposal of the Fourteenth Amendment." *J So Hist,* 22 (1956), 477–497.

2352 KURLAND, Philip B. "The Privileges and Immunities Clause: 'Its Hour Come Round at Last'?" *Wash U L Q,* 1972 (1972), 405–420.

2353 LIEN, A. J. *Concurring Opinion: The Privileges and Immunities Clause of the Fourteenth Amendment.* St. Louis, Mo., 1957.

2354 MORRISON, Stanley E. "Does the Fourteenth Amendment Incorporate the Bill of Rights: The Judicial Interpretation." *Stan L Rev,* 2 (1949), 140–173.

2355 *Palko v. Connecticut.* 302 U.S. 319 (1937).

2356 *Pointer v. Texas.* 380 U.S. 400 (1965).

2357 RUSSELL, James. "The Railroads and the Conspiracy Theory of the Fourteenth Amendment." *Miss Val Hist Rev,* 41 (1955), 601–622.

2358 SCHWARTZ, Bernard, ed. *Fourteenth Amendment: A Century in American Law and Life.* New York, 1972.

2359 *Slaughter-House Cases.* 16 Wallace (83 U.S.) 36 (1873).

2360 TEN BROEK, Jacobus. *Equal under Law (Anti-Slavery Origins of the 14th Amendment).* New York, 1965.

2361 *Twining v. New Jersey.* 211 U.S. 78 (1908).

99

Due Process of Law: General

2362 BERNS, Walter. "*Buck v. Bell*: Due Process of Law?" *West Pol Q*, 6 (1953), 762–773.

2363 CORWIN, Edward S. "The Doctrine of Due Process of Law Before the Civil War." *Harv L Rev*, 24 (1911), 366–385, 460–479.

2364 FERNANDEZ, Ferdinand F. "Due Process and Pollution: The Right to a Remedy." *Vill L Rev*, 16 (1971), 789–814.

2365 GRAHAM, Howard Jay. "Procedure to Substance—Extra-Judicial Rise of Due Process." *Calif L Rev*, 40 (1952–1953), 483–500.

2366 GRANT, J. A. C. "Natural Law Background of Due Process." *Colum L Rev*, 31 (1931), 56–81.

2367 HOUGH, Charles. "Due Process of Law Today." *Harv L Rev*, 32 (1919), 218–233.

2368 HOWE, Lowell J. "The Meaning of Due Process Prior to the Adoption of the Fourteenth Amendment." *Calif L Rev*, 18 (1930), 583–610.

2369 *Hurtado v. California.* 110 U.S. 516 (1884).

2370 KALES, A. M. "New Methods in Due Process Cases." *Am Pol Sci Rev*, 12 (1918), 241–250.

2371 KARST, Kenneth L. "Invidious Discrimination: Justice Douglas and the Return of the Natural Law—Due Process Formula." *U C L A L Rev*, 16 (1969), 716–750.

2372 MARAIST, Frank L., and T. Page SHARP. "Federal Procedure's Troubled Marriage: Due Process and the Class Action." *Tex L Rev*, 49 (1970), 1–24.

2373 MILLER, Arthur S. "An Affirmative Thrust of Due Process of Law?" *Geo Wash L Rev*, 30 (1962), 399–428.

2374 MISHKIN, Paul J. "Foreward: The High Court, the Great Writ, and the Due Process of Time and Law." *Harv L Rev*, 79 (1965), 56–102.

2375 MOTT, R. L. *Due Process of Law.* Indianapolis, 1926.

2376 *Murray's Lessee v. Hoboken Land & Improvement Co.* 18 Howard (59 U.S.) 272 (1856).

2377 SHATTUCK, C. E. "The True Meaning of the Term 'Liberty' in Those Clauses in the Federal and State Constitutions Which Protect Life, Liberty, and Property." *Harv L Rev*, 4 (1891), 365–392.

2378 WOOD, Virginia. *Due Process of Law, 1939–1949. The Supreme Court's Use of a Constitutional Tool.* Baton Rouge, La., 1951.

2379 *Wynehamer v. New York.* 13 N.Y. 378 (1856).

Due Process of Law: Procedural Rights

General

2380 AMSTERDAM, Anthony G. "The Supreme Court and the Rights of Suspects in Criminal Cases." *N Y U L Rev*, 45 (1970), 785–815.

2381 BAILEY, F. Lee. *The Defense Never Rests.* New York, 1971.

2382 BEISEL, Albert R., Jr. "Control over Illegal Enforcement of the Criminal Law: Role of the Supreme Court." *Bos U L Rev,* 35 (1955), 1–76.

2383 BENDER, Paul. "The Retroactive Effect of an Overruling Constitutional Decision." *U Penn L Rev,* 110 (1962), 650–679.

2384 BING, Stephen R., and S. Stephen ROSENFELD. *Quality of Justice in the Lower Criminal Courts of Metropolitan Boston.* Boston, 1970.

2385 BLUMBERG, Abraham. *Criminal Justice.* Chicago, 1967.

2386 BOSKEY, Bennett, and John H. PICKERING. "Federal Restrictions on State Criminal Procedure." *U Chi L Rev,* 13 (1946), 266–299.

2387 CASPER, Jonathan D. *American Criminal Justice: The Defendant's Perspective.* Englewood Cliffs, N.J., 1972.

2388 CHAMBLISS, William J. *Crime and the Legal Process.* New York, 1969.

2389 COLE, George F. *Criminal Justice: Law and Politics.* Belmont, Calif., 1972.

2390 Editors of the Criminal Law Reporter. *Criminal Law Revolution and Its Aftermath: 1960–1972.* Washington, D.C., 1973.

2391 ENNIS, Bruce J. *Prisoners of Psychiatry: Mental Patients, Psychiatrists, and the Law.* New York, 1972.

2392 FAHLUND, G. Gregory. "Retroactivity and the Warren Court: The Strategy of a Revolution." *J Pol,* 35 (1973), 570–593.

2393 FELLMAN, David. *The Defendant's Rights.* New York, 1958.

2394 FRIENDLY, Henry J. "The Bill of Rights as a Code of Criminal Procedure." *Calif L Rev,* 53 (1965), 929–956.

2395 HOCKMAN, Charles B. "The Supreme Court and the Constitutionality of Retroactive Legislation." *Harv L Rev,* 73 (1960), 692–727.

2396 HOGAN, John C. "Blackstone and Joseph Story—Their Influence on the Development of Criminal Law in America." *Minn L Rev,* 40 (1956), 107–124.

2397 KAMISAR, Yale. *Criminals, Cops and the Constitution.* New York, 1964.

2398 KAMISAR, Yale, *et al. Criminal Justice in Our Time.* Charlottesville, Va., 1965.

2399 KARLEN, Delmar. *Anglo-American Criminal Justice.* New York, 1967.

2400 KATZ, Jay. *Experimentation with Human Beings.* New York, 1972.

2401 "The Legitimate Scope of Police Discretion to Restrict Ordinary Public Activity." *Harv Civ R—Civ Lib L Rev,* 4 (1969), 233–344.

2402 NAGEL, Stuart S., ed. *The Rights of the Accused: In Law and Action.* Beverly Hills, Calif., 1972.

2403 NEWMAN, Frank C. "Federal Agency Investigations: Procedural Rights of the Subpoenaed Witness." *Mich L Rev,* 60 (1961), 169–186.

2404 NUTTING, Charles B. "The Supreme Court, the Fourteenth Amendment and State Criminal Cases." *U Chi L Rev,* 3 (1936), 244–260.

2405 OAKS, Dallin H., and Warren LEHMAN. *A Criminal Justice System and the Indigent: A Study of Chicago and Cook County.* Chicago, 1968.

2406 ORFIELD, Lester B. *Criminal Procedure from Arrest to Appeal.* New York, 1947.

2407 ROGGE, O. John. "Inquisitions by Officials: A Study of Due Process Requirements in Administrative Investigations." *Minn L Rev,* 47 (1963), 939–996; 48 (1964), 557–596, 1081–1107.

2408 SCHAEFER, Walter V. *The Suspect and Security: Criminal Procedure and Converging Constitutional Doctrines.* Evanston, Ill., 1967.

2409 SCOTT, Robert E. "The Reality of Procedural Due Process—A Study of the Implementation of Fair Hearing Requirements by the Welfare Caseworker." *Wm & M L Rev,* 13 (1972), 725–768.

2410 SKOLNICK, Jerome H. *Justice Without Trial: Law Enforcement in Democratic Society.* New York, 1966.

2411 TAYLOR, Telford. *Two Studies in Constitutional Interpretation. Search, Seizure, and Surveillance and Fair Trial and Free Press.* Columbus, Ohio, 1969.

2412 TRAYNOR, Roger J. *Riddle of Harmless Error.* Columbus, Ohio, 1970.

2413 TREBACH, Arnold S. *The Rationing of Justice: Constitutional Rights and the Criminal Process.* New Brunswick, N.J., 1964.

2414 "The Unconstitutionality of Plea Bargaining." *Harv L Rev,* 83 (1970), 1387–1411.

2415 "Vagueness Doctrine in the Federal Courts: A Focus on the Military, Prison, and Campus Contexts." *Stan L Rev,* 26 (1974), 855–892.

2416 WILSON, Paul. *Sexual Dilemma: Abortion, Homosexuality, Prostitution, and the Criminal Threshold.* New York, 1971.

Search and Seizure and the Exclusionary Rule

2417 ALLEN, Francis A. "Federalism and the Fourth Amendment: A Requiem for Wolf." *S Ct Rev* (1961), 1–48.

2418 AMSTERDAM, Anthony G. "Perspectives on the Fourth Amendment." *Minn L Rev,* 58 (1974), 349–477.

2419 ANTROBUS, Louis A. *The Federal Exclusionary Rule in Relation to the Fourth Amendment as Applied and Interpreted by the United States Supreme Court.* Ann Arbor, Mich., 1956.

2420 BROEDER, Dale W. "The Decline and Fall of *Wolf v. Colorado.*" *Neb L Rev,* 41 (1961), 185–219.

2421 *Chimel v. California.* 395 U.S. 752 (1969).

2422 "The Constitutionality of Airport Searches." *Mich L Rev,* 72 (1973), 128–156.

2423 COOK, Joseph G. "Probable Cause to Arrest." *Vand L Rev,* 24 (1971), 317–339.

2424 FISHER, Edward C. *Search and Seizure.* Evanston, Ill., 1970.

2425 KAPLAN, John. "The Limits of the Exclusionary Rule." *Stan L Rev,* 26 (1974), 1027–1056.

2426 LaFAVE, Wayne R. *Arrest: The Decision to Take a Suspect into Custody.* Boston, 1965.

2427 LaFAVE, Wayne R. " 'Street Encounters' and the Constitution: *Terry, Sibron, Peters,* and Beyond." *Mich L Rev,* 67 (1968), 39–126.

2428 LANDYNSKI, Jacob W. *Search and Seizure and the Supreme Court: A Study in Constitutional Interpretation.* Baltimore, 1966.

2429 LANDYNSKI, Jacob W. "The Supreme Court's Search for Fourth Amendment Standards: The Warrantless Search." *Conn Bar J,* 45 (1971), 2–39.

2430 LASSON, Nelson B. *History and Development of the Fourth Amendment to the United States Constitution.* Baltimore, 1937.

2431 *Mapp v. Ohio.* 367 U.S. 643 (1961).

2432 "No-Knock and the Constitution: The District of Columbia Court Reform and Criminal Procedure Act of 1970." *Minn L Rev,* 55 (1971), 871–894.

2433 PLAYER, Mack Allen. "Warrantless Searches and Seizures." *Ga L Rev,* 5 (1971), 269–293.

2434 REBELL, Michael A. "The Undisclosed Informant and the Fourth Amendment: A Search for Meaningful Standards." *Yale L J,* 81 (1972), 703–724.

2435 SPIOTTO, James E. "Search and Seizure: An Empirical Study of the Exclusionary Rule and Its Alternatives." *J Leg Stud,* 2 (1973), 243–278.

2436 *Terry v. Ohio.* 392 U.S. 1 (1968).

2437 *Weeks v. United States.* 232 U.S. 383 (1914).

2438 *Wolf v. Colorado.* 338 U.S. 25 (1949).

Interrogations, Confessions, and Right to Counsel

2439 BEANEY, William M. *The Right to Counsel in American Courts.* Ann Arbor, Mich., 1955.

2440 CARTER, Dan T. *Scottsboro: A Tragedy of the American South.* Baton Rouge, La., 1969.

2441 COOK, Joseph G. *Constitutional Rights of the Accused: Pre-Trial Rights.* Rochester, N.Y., 1972.

2442 ELSEN, Sheldon H., and Arthur ROSETT. "Protections for the Suspects under *Miranda v. Arizona.*" *Colum L Rev,* 67 (1967), 645–670.

2443 FRIENDLY, Henry J. "The Fifth Amendment Tomorrow: The Case for Constitutional Change." *Cincin L Rev,* 37 (1968), 671–726.

2444 *Gideon v. Wainwright.* 372 U.S. 335 (1963).

2445 GRISWOLD, Erwin N. *The Fifth Amendment Today.* Cambridge, Mass., 1955.

2446 HELLER, Francis H. *Sixth Amendment to the Constitution of the United States: A Study in Constitutional Development.* Lawrence, Kan., 1951.

2447 HERMAN, Lawrence. *The Right to Counsel in Misdemeanor Court.* Columbus, Ohio, 1973.

2448 HERMAN, Lawrence. "The Supreme Court and Restrictions on Police Interrogation." *O State L J,* 25 (1964), 1–59.

2449 HOFSTADTER, Samuel H. *The Fifth Amendment and the Immunity Act of 1954.* New York, 1955.

2450 HOGAN, James E., and Joseph M. SNEE. "The McNabb-Mallory Rule: Its Use, Rationale and Rescue." *Geo L J,* 47 (1958), 1–46.

2451 HOOK, Sidney. *Common Sense and the Fifth Amendment.* New York, 1957.

2452 INBAU, Fred E., and John E. REID. *Criminal Interrogation and Confessions.* Baltimore, 1962.

2453 KAMISAR, Yale. "A Dissent from the Miranda Dissents: Some Comments on the 'New' Fifth Amendment and the Old 'Voluntariness' Test." *Mich L Rev,* 65 (1966), 59–104.

2454 LEVY, Leonard W. *Origins of the Fifth Amendment. The Right Against Self-Incrimination.* New York, 1968.

2455 LEWIS, Anthony. *Gideon's Trumpet.* New York, 1964.

2456 MAYERS, Lewis. *Shall We Amend the Fifth Amendment?* New York, 1959.

2457 MEDALIE, Richard J. *From Escobedo to Miranda: The Anatomy of a Supreme Court Decision.* Washington, D.C., 1966.

2458 MEDALIE, Richard J., *et al.* "Custodial Police Interrogation in Our Nation's Capital: The Attempt to Implement Miranda." *Mich L Rev,* 66 (1968), 1347–1422.

2459 MILNER, Neal A. *The Court and Local Law Enforcement: The Impact of Miranda.* Beverly Hills, Calif., 1971.

2460 *Miranda v. Arizona.* 384 U.S. 436 (1966).

2461 ORSBON, R. Anthony. "Immunity from Prosecution and the Fifth Amendment: An Analysis of Constitutional Standards." *Vand L Rev,* 25 (1972), 1207–1235.

2462 *Powell v. Alabama.* 287 U.S. 45 (1932).

2463 "The Right to Counsel: A Symposium." *Minn L Rev,* 45 (1961), 693–896.

2464 SILVERSTEIN, Lee. *Defense of the Poor in Criminal Cases in American State Courts: A Field Study and Report. Vol. 1: National Report.* Chicago, 1965.

2465 STAPLETON, W. Vaughan, and Lee E. TEITELBAUM. *In Defense of Youth: A Study of the Role of Counsel in American Juvenile Courts.* New York, 1972.

2466 STEPHENS, Otis H., Jr. *The Supreme Court and Confessions of Guilt.* Knoxville, Tenn., 1973.

2467 "Waiver of Rights in Police Interrogation: *Miranda* in the Lower Courts." *U Chi L Rev,* 36 (1969), 413–447.

2468 WALD, Michael S., *et al.* "Interrogations in New Haven: The Impact of Miranda." *Yale L J,* 76 (1967), 1519–1648.

Fair Trial

2469 American Bar Association. *Fair Trial and Free Press.* Chicago, 1966.

2470 American Newspaper Publishers Association. *Free Press and Fair Trial.* New York, 1967.

2471 BUSH, Chilton R., ed. *Free Press and Fair Trial.* Athens, Ga., 1970.

2472 Conference on Prejudicial News Reporting in Criminal Cases: Northwestern School of Law and Medill School of Journalism. *Papers and Proceedings: Free Press, Fair Trial.* Evanston, Ill., 1964.

2473 ERLANGER, Howard S. "Jury Research in America: Its Past and Future." *L & Soc Rev,* 4 (1970), 345–370.

2474 FRIENDLY, Alfred, and Ronald L. GOLDFARB. *Crime and Publicity: The Impact of News on the Administration of Justice.* New York, 1967.

2475 GILLMOR, Donald M. *Free Press and Fair Trial.* Washington, D.C., 1966.

2476 HENDERSON, Edith Guild. "The Background of the Seventh Amendment." *Harv L Rev,* 80 (1966), 289–337.

2477 MEDINA, Harold R. *Freedom of the Press and Fair Trial.* New York, 1967.

2478 POLLITT, Daniel H. "The Right of Confrontation: Its History and Modern Dress." *J Pub L,* 8 (1959), 381–413.

2479 ROGGE, O. John. "*Williams v. Florida:* End of a Theory." *Vill L Rev,* 16 (1971), 441–466, 607–709.

2480 SCOTT, Austin W., Jr. "The Supreme Court's Control over State and Federal Criminal Juries." *Iowa L Rev,* 34 (1949), 577–604.

2481 *Sheppard v. Maxwell.* 384 U.S. 333 (1966).

2482 Special Committee on Radio and Television of the Association of the Bar of the City of New York. *Freedom of the Press and Fair Trial: Final Report with Recommendations.* New York, 1967.

2483 Special Committee on Radio and Television of the Association of the Bar of the City of New York. *Radio, Television, and the Administration of Justice: A Documented Survey of Materials.* New York, 1965.

2484 STANGA, John E., Jr. "Judicial Protection of the Criminal Defendant Against Adverse Press Coverage." *Wm & M L Rev,* 13 (1971), 1–74.

2485 "Symposium on a Free Press and a Fair Trial." *Vill L Rev,* 11 (1966), 677–741.

2486 WALSH, Michael H. "The American Jury: A Reassessment." *Yale L J,* 79 (1969), 142–158.

2487 WILLCOX, Bertram F., and Edward J. BLOUSTEIN. "The Griffin Case—Poverty and the Fourteenth Amendment." *Corn L Q,* 43 (1957), 1–26.

2488 WOLFRAM, Charles W. "The Constitutional History of the Seventh Amendment." *Minn L Rev,* 57 (1973), 639–747.

2489 ZEISEL, Hans. ". . . And Then There Were None: The Diminution of the Federal Jury." *U Chi L Rev,* 38 (1971), 710–725.

Double Jeopardy, Detention, and Punishment

2490 BASES, Nan C., and William F. McDONALD. *Preventive Detention in the District of Columbia: The First Ten Months.* New York, 1972.

2491 "Double Jeopardy and Dual Sovereignty: A Critical Analysis." *Wm & M L Rev,* 11 (1970), 946–959.

2492 *Furman v. Georgia.* 408 U.S. 238 (1972).

2493 GOLDBERG, Arthur J. and Alan M. DERSHOWITZ. "Declaring the Death Penalty Unconstitutional." *Harv L Rev,* 83 (1970), 1773–1819.

2494 GOLDFARB, Ronald L. *Ransom: A Critique of the American Bail System.* New York, 1965.

2495 GREENAWALT, Kent. " 'Uncontrollable' Actions and the Eighth Amendment: Implications of *Powell v. Texas."* *Colum L Rev,* 69 (1969), 927–979.

2496 MELTSNER, Michael. *Cruel and Unusual.* New York, 1973.

2497 MILLER, Leonard G. *Double Jeopardy and the Federal System.* Chicago, 1968.

2498 NEWMAN, Lawrence. "Double Jeopardy and the Problem of Successive Prosecutions: A Suggested Solution." *So Calif L Rev,* 34 (1961), 252–267.

2499 PALMER, John W. *Constitutional Rights of Prisoners.* Cincinnati, Ohio, 1973.

2500 PRETTYMAN, Barrett, Jr. *Death and the Supreme Court.* New York, 1961.

2501 "Preventive Detention: An Empirical Analysis." *Harv Civ R—Civ Lib L Rev,* 6 (1971), 289–396.

2502 "Prisoners' Rights and the Correctional Scheme: The Legal Controversy and Problems of Implementation—A Symposium." *Vill L Rev,* 16 (1971), 1029–1118.

2503 SIGLER, Jay A. *Double Jeopardy: The Development of a Legal and Social Policy.* Ithaca, N. Y., 1969.

2504 TURNER, William Bennett. "Establishing the Rule of Law in Prisons: A Manual for Prisoners' Rights Litigation." *Stan L Rev,* 23 (1971), 473–518.

2505 WHEELER, Malcolm E. "Toward a Theory of Limited Punishment: An Examination of the Eighth Amendment." *Stan L Rev,* 24 (1972), 838–873.

Freedom of Expression and Association

General

2506 ABERNATHY, Glenn. *The Right of Assembly and Association.* Columbia, S. C., 1961.

2507 ANASTAPLO, George. *Constitutionalists: Notes on the First Amendment.* Dallas, Tex., 1971.

2508 ASKIN, Frank. "Police Dossiers and Emerging Principles of First Amendment Adjudication." *Stan L Rev,* 22 (1970), 196–220.

2509 BERNS, Walter. *Freedom, Virtue and the First Amendment.* Baton Rouge, La., 1956.

2510 BETH, Loren P. "Group Libel and Free Speech." *Minn L Rev,* 39 (1955), 167–184.

2511 BRENNAN, William J., Jr. "The Supreme Court and the Meiklejohn Interpretation of the First Amendment." *Harv L Rev,* 79 (1965), 1–20.

2512 "Cable Television and the First Amendment." *Colum L Rev,* 71 (1971), 1008–1038.

2513 CAHN, Edmond. "Justice Black and First Amendment 'Absolutes.'" *N Y U L Rev,* 37 (1962), 981–1000.

2514 CHAFEE, Zechariah, Jr. *Free Speech in the United States.* Cambridge, Mass., 1941.

2515 CORWIN, Edward S. "Bowing Out 'Clear and Present Danger.'" *Not Dame Law,* 27 (1952), 325–359.

2516 "Developments in the Law—Academic Freedom." *Harv L Rev,* 81 (1968), 1045–1159.

2517 EMERSON, Thomas I. "The Doctrine of Prior Restraint." *L & Cont Prob,* 20 (1955), 648–671.

2518 EMERSON, Thomas I. *The System of Freedom of Expression.* New York, 1970.

2519 EMERSON, Thomas I. *Toward a General Theory of the First Amendment.* New York, 1966.

2520 FELLMAN, David. *The Constitutional Right of Association.* Chicago, 1963.

2521 FINE, David J. "Federal Grand Jury Investigation of Political Dissidents." *Harv Civ R—Civ Lib L Rev,* 7 (1972), 432–499.

2522 FINMAN, Ted, and Stewart MACAULAY. "Freedom to Dissent: The Vietnam Protests and the Words of Public Officials." *Wis L Rev,* 1966 (1966), 632–723.

2523 "The First Amendment and Regulation of Television News." *Colum L Rev,* 72 (1972), 746–771.

2524 "The First Amendment Overbreadth Doctrine." *Harv L Rev,* 83 (1970), 844–927.

2525 FORTAS, Abe. *Concerning Dissent and Civil Disobedience.* New York, 1968.

2526 "Freedom of Association." *R Rel L Rep,* 4 (1959), 207–236.

2527 GOLDSTEIN, Paul. "Copyright and the First Amendment." *Colum L Rev,* 70 (1970), 983–1057.

2528 HEBERLE, Klaus H. "From Gitlow to Near: Judicial 'Amendment' by Absent-Minded Incrementalism." *J Pol,* 34 (1972), 458–483.

2529 HIMES, Jay L. "Of Shadows and Substance: Freedom of Speech, Expression, and Action." *Wis L Rev,* 1971 (1971), 1209–1235.

2530 HUDSON, Edward G. *Freedom of Speech and Press in America.* Washington, D.C., 1963.

2531 "Justice Black and the First Amendment—'Absolutes': A Public Interview." *N Y U L Rev,* 37 (1962), 549–563.

2532 KAUFMAN, Irving R. "The Medium, the Message and the First Amendment." *N Y U L Rev,* 45 (1970), 761–784.

2533 KRISLOV, Samuel. "Mr. Justice Black Reopens the Free Speech Debate." *UCLA L Rev,* 2 (1964), 63–64, 189–211.

2534 LEVY, Leonard W. *Legacy of Suppression. Freedom of Speech and Press in Early American History.* Cambridge, Mass., 1960.

2535 LINDE, Hans A. " 'Clear and Present Danger' Reexamined: Dissonance in the *Brandenburg* Concerto." *Stan L Rev,* 22 (1970), 1163–1186.

2536 MEIKLEJOHN, Alexander. *Free Speech in Relation to Self-Government.* New York, 1948.

2537 MENDELSON, Wallace. "Clear and Present Danger: From Schenck to Dennis." *Colum L Rev,* 52 (1952), 313–333.

2538 MENDELSON, Wallace. "On the Meaning of the First Amendment: Absolutes in the Balance." *Calif L Rev,* 50 (1962), 821–828.

2539 MILLER, John C. *Crisis in Freedom: The Alien and Sedition Acts.* Boston, 1951.

2540 MONAGHAN, Henry P. "First Amendment 'Due Process.' " *Harv L Rev,* 83 (1970), 518–551.

2541 MURPHY, Paul L. *Meaning of Freedom of Speech: First Amendment Freedoms from Wilson to F.D.R.* Westport, Conn., 1972.

2542 MURPHY, Walter F. "Mr. Justice Jackson, Free Speech, and the Judicial Function." *Vand L Rev,* 22 (1959), 1019–1046.

2543 *National Association for the Advancement of Colored People v. Alabama.* 357 U.S. 449 (1958).

2544 NIMMER, Melville B. "National Security Secrets v. Free Speech: The Issues Left Undecided in the Ellsberg Case." *Stan L Rev,* 26 (1974), 311–333.

2545 O'BRIEN, F. William. *Justice Reed and the First Amendment.* Washington, D.C., 1958.

2546 POWE, L. A., Jr. "Evolution to Absolutism: Justice Douglas and the First Amendment." *Colum L Rev,* 74 (1974), 371–411.

2547 PRESTON, William, Jr. *Aliens and Dissenters: Federal Suppression of Radicals, 1900–1933.* Cambridge, Mass., 1963.

2548 RAGAN, Fred D. "Justice Oliver Wendell Holmes, Jr., Zechariah Chafee, Jr., and the Clear and Present Danger Test for Free Speech: The First Year, 1919." *J Am Hist,* 58 (1971), 24–45.

2549 REDISH, Martin H. "Campaign Spending Laws and the First Amendment." *N Y U L Rev,* 46 (1971), 900–934.

2550 RICE, Charles E. *Freedom of Association.* New York, 1962.

2551 RICHARDSON, Elliott L. "Freedom of Expression and the Function of Courts." *Harv L Rev,* 65 (1951), 1–54.

2552 ROBISON, Joseph B. "Protection of Association from Compulsory Disclosure." *Colum L Rev,* 58 (1958), 614–649.

2553 ROGGE, O. John. "Congress Shall Make No Law." *Mich L Rev,* 56 (1958), 331–374, 579–618.

2554 SAVAGE, William Sherman. *The Controversy over the Distribution of Abolition Literature, 1830–1860.* Washington, D.C., 1938.

2555 *Schenck v. United States.* 249 U.S. 47 (1919).

2556 SHAPIRO, Martin. *Freedom of Speech: The Supreme Court and Judicial Review.* Englewood Cliffs, N.J., 1966.

2557 STRONG, Frank E. "Fifty Years of Clear and Present Danger: From Schenck to Brandenburg—and Beyond." *S Ct Rev* (1969), 41–80.

2558 *Tinker v. Des Moines School District.* 393 U.S. 503 (1969).

2559 TORKE, J. W. "The Future of First Amendment Overbreadth." *Vand L Rev,* 27 (1974), 289–310.

2560 *Tribute of William Ellery Channing to the American Abolitionists for Their Vindication of Freedom of Speech.* New York, 1861.

2561 U.S. Commission on Political Activity of Government Personnel. *A Commission Report.* Washington, D.C., 1968.

2562 VAN ALSTYNE, William W. "Political Speech at State Universities: Some Constitutional Considerations." *U Penn L Rev,* 111 (1963), 328–342.

2563 VELVEL, Lawrence R. "Freedom of Speech and the Draft-Card Burning Cases." *Kan L Rev,* 16 (1968), 449–503(e).

2564 WARREN, Charles. "The New Liberty under the Fourteenth Amendment." *Harv L Rev,* 39 (1926), 431–465.

2565 WEINGARTEN, I. Jacob. "Academic Freedom in the Public Schools: The Right to Teach." *N Y U L Rev,* 48 (1973), 1176–1199.

2566 *Whitney v. California.* 274 U.S. 357 (1927).

The Public Forum

2567 ALFANGE, Dean, Jr. "Free Speech and Symbolic Conduct; The Draft-Card Burning Cases." *S Ct Rev* (1968), 1–52.

2568 BLASI, Vince. "Prior Restraints on Demonstrations." *Mich L Rev,* 68 (1970), 1481–1574.

2569 DODD, E. Merrick, Jr. "Picketing and Free Speech: A Dissent." *Harv L Rev,* 56 (1943), 513–531.

2570 *Feiner v. New York.* 340 U.S. 315 (1951).

2571 FINE, Sidney. "Frank Murphy, the Thornhill Decision, and Picketing as Free Speech." *Lab Hist,* 6 (1965), 99–120.

2572 GARDNER, George K. "Free Speech in Public Places." *Bos U L Rev,* 36 (1956), 239–252.

2573 JARRETT, James M., and Vernon A. MUND. "The Right of Assembly." *N Y U L Q Rev,* 9 (1931), 1–38.

2574 JONES, Edgar A., Jr. "The Right to Picket: Twilight Zone of the Constitution." *U Penn L Rev,* 102 (1954), 995–1029.

2575 KALVEN, Harry, Jr. "The Concept of the Public Forum: *Cox v. Louisiana.*" *S Ct Rev* (1965), 1–32.

2576 KALVEN, Harry, Jr. *The Negro and the First Amendment.* Columbus, Ohio, 1965.

2577 KAMIN, Alfred. "Residential Picketing and the First Amendment." *Northw U L Rev,* 61 (1966), 177–236.

2578 POLLITT, Daniel H. "Dime Store Demonstrations: Events and Legal Problems of the First Sixty Days." *Duke L J,* 1960 (1960), 315–365.

2579 STEPHENSON, D. Grier, Jr. "A Seat on the Sidelines: The Georgia Appellate Judiciary and the Public Forum." *Ga L Rev,* 3 (1969), 80–109.

2580 STEPHENSON, D. Grier, Jr. "State Appellate Courts and the Political Process: Florida and the Public Forum." *U Miami L Rev,* 23 (1968), 182–210.

2581 "Symposium: The Draft, the War and Public Protest." *Geo Wash L Rev,* 37 (1969), 433–588.

2582 TANENHAUS, Joseph. "Picketing as Free Speech: Early Stages in the Growth of the New Law of Picketing." *U Pitt L Rev,* 14 (1953), 397–418.

2583 TANENHAUS, Joseph. "Picketing as Free Speech: The Growth of the New Law of Picketing from 1940 to 1952." *Corn L Q,* 38 (1952), 1–50.

2584 TELLER, Ludwig. "Picketing and Free Speech." *Harv L Rev,* 56 (1942), 180–218.

Loyalty and National Security

2585 *American Communications Association v. Douds.* 339 U.S. 382 (1950).

2586 BARBER, Kathleen L. "The Legal Status of the American Communist Party, 1965." *J Pub L,* 15 (1966), 94–121.

2587 BARTH, Alan. *Government by Investigation.* New York, 1955.

2588 BARTH, Alan. *The Loyalty of Free Men.* New York, 1951.

2589 BECKER, Theodore L., ed. *Political Trials.* Indianapolis, 1971.

2590 BONSAL, Dudley B. *The Federal Loyalty—Security Program: Report of the Special Committee of the Association of the Bar of the City of New York.* New York, 1956.

2591 BONTECOU, Eleanor. *The Federal Loyalty—Security Program.* Ithaca, N.Y., 1953.

2592 BOUDIN, Louis B. " 'Seditious Doctrines' and 'Clear and Present Danger' Rule." *Va L Rev,* 38 (1952), 143–186, 315–356.

DOCTRINES AND POLITICS

2593 BROWN, Ralph S. *Loyalty and Security: Employment Tests in the United States.* New Haven, 1958.

2594 CHAMBERLAIN, Lawrence H. *Loyalty and Legislative Action: A Survey of Activity by the New York Legislature, 1919–1949.* Ithaca, N.Y., 1951.

2595 CHAPIN, Bradley. *The American Law of Treason. Revolutionary and Early National Origins.* Seattle, Wash., 1964.

2596 CHASE, Harold W. *Security and Liberty: The Problem of Native Communists, 1947–1955.* Garden City, N.Y., 1955.

2597 COMMAGER, Henry Steele. *Freedom, Loyalty, Dissent.* New York, 1954.

2598 "Conspiracy and the First Amendment." *Yale L J,* 79 (1970), 872–895.

2599 COOK, Thomas I. *Democratic Rights Versus Communist Activity.* Garden City, N.Y., 1954.

2600 DAVIS, David Brion. *Fear of Conspiracy: Images of Un-American Subversion from the Revolution to the Present.* Ithaca, N.Y., 1971.

2601 *Dennis v. United States.* 341 U.S. 494 (1951).

2602 "Developments in the Law—The National Security Interest and Civil Liberties." *Harv L Rev,* 85 (1972), 1130–1326.

2603 DOWELL, Eldridge F. *History of Criminal Syndicalism Legislation in the United States.* Baltimore, 1939.

2604 EHRMANN, Herbert B. *The Case That Will Not Die: Commonwealth vs. Sacco and Vanzetti.* Boston, 1969.

2605 EMERSON, Thomas I., and David M. HELFELD. "Loyalty among Government Employees." *Yale L J,* 58 (1948), 1–143.

2606 FITE, Gilbert C., and Horace C. PETERSON. *Opponents of War, 1917–1918.* Madison, Wis., 1957.

2607 FRAENKEL, O. K. "The Supreme Court and National Security." *Wash L Rev,* 33 (1958), 343–363.

2608 FRAENKEL, O. K. "War, Civil Liberties and the Supreme Court, 1941 to 1946." *Yale L J,* 55 (1946), 715–734.

2609 GARDINER, David P. *The California Oath Controversy.* Berkeley, Calif., 1967.

2610 GELLHORN, Walter. *Security, Loyalty and Science.* Ithaca, N.Y., 1950.

2611 GELLHORN, Walter, ed. *The States and Subversion.* Ithaca, N.Y., 1952.

2612 GREENBERG, Milton. "Loyalty Oaths: An Appraisal of the Legal Issues." *J Pol,* 20 (1958), 487–514.

2613 GRONER, Samuel B. "State Control of Subversive Activities in the United States." *Fed Bar J,* 9 (1947), 61–94.

2614 HURST, James Willard, ed. *The Law of Treason in the United States. Collected Essays.* Westport, Conn., 1971.

2615 HYMAN, Harold M. *To Try Men's Souls: Loyalty Tests in American History.* Berkeley, Calif., 1959.

2616 ISRAEL, Jerold H. "*Elfbrandt v. Russell,* the Demise of the Oath." *S Ct Rev* (1966), 193–252.

2617 JOUGHLIN, Louis, and Edmund M. MORGAN. *The Legacy of Sacco and Vanzetti.* New York, 1948.

2618 LASSWELL, Harold. *National Security and Individual Freedom.* New York, 1950.

2619 LEAHY, J. E. "Loyalty and the First Amendment—a Concept Emerges." *N D L Rev,* 43 (1966), 53–88.

2620 *Legal Concepts of Conspiracy: A Law Review Trilogy, 1922–1970.* New York, 1972.

2621 McCLOSKEY, Robert G. "Free Speech, Sedition and the Constitution." *Am Pol Sci Rev,* 45 (1951), 662–673.

2622 MILLER, Arthur S. "The Constitutional Law of the Security State." *Stan L Rev,* 10 (1958), 620–671.

2623 MOLLAN, Robert. "Smith Act Prosecution: The Effect of the Dennis and Yates Decisions." *U Pitt L Rev,* 26 (1965), 705–748.

2624 MORRIS, Arval A. "Academic Freedom and Loyalty Oaths." *L & Cont Prob,* 28 (1963), 487–514.

2625 PRITCHETT, C. Herman. *The Political Offender and the Warren Court.* Boston, 1958.

2626 *Scales v. United States.* 367 U.S. 203 (1961).

2627 SCHAAR, John H. *Loyalty in America.* Berkeley, Calif., 1957.

2628 SIMONS, Henry C. "Some Reflections on Syndicalism." *J Pol Econ,* 52 (1944), 1–15.

2629 SUTHERLAND, Arthur E. "Freedom and National Security." *Harv L Rev,* 64 (1951), 383–416.

2630 TARRANT, Catherine M. " 'To Insure Domestic Tranquility': Congress and the Law of Seditious Conspiracy, 1859–1861." *Am J Leg Hist,* 15 (1971), 107–123.

The Press

2631 BARRON, Jerome A. *Freedom of the Press for Whom? The Right of Access to the Mass Media.* Bloomington, Ind., 1973.

2632 BERNEY, Arthur L. "Libel and the First Amendment—A New Constitutional Privilege." *Va L Rev,* 51 (1965), 1–58.

2633 CLARK, David G., and Earl R. HUTCHINSON. *Mass Media and the Law: Freedom and Restraint.* New York, 1970.

2634 DEMBITZ, Nanette. "Congressional Investigations of Newspapermen, Authors, and Others in the Opinion Field—Its Legality under the First Amendment." *Minn L Rev,* 40 (1956), 517–560.

2635 DEVOL, Kenneth S. *Mass Media and the Supreme Court; The Legacy of the Warren Years.* New York, 1971.

2636 Georgetown Law Journal. *Media and the First Amendment in a Free Society.* Amherst, Mass., 1973.

2637 GERALD, Edward. *The Press and the Constitution, 1931–1937.* Minneapolis, 1948.

2638 GRAY, David L. *The Supreme Court and the News Media.* Evanston, Ill., 1968.

2639 HACHTEN, William A. *The Supreme Court on Freedom of the Press, Decisions and Dissents.* Ames, Iowa, 1968.

2640 HENKIN, Louis. "The Right to Know and the Duty to Withhold: The Case of the Pentagon Papers." *U Penn L Rev,* 120 (1971), 271–280.

2641 KALVEN, Harry, Jr. "The New York Times Case: A Note on 'The Central Meaning of the First Amendment.' " *S Ct Rev* (1964), 191–222.

2642 KALVEN, Harry, Jr. "The Reasonable Man and the First Amendment: Hill, Butts, and Walker." *S Ct Rev* (1967), 267–309.

2643 KELLY, Alfred H. "Constitutional Liberty and the Law of Libel: A Historian's View." *Am Hist Rev,* 74 (1968), 429–452.

2644 KEOGH, James. *President Nixon and the Press.* New York, 1972.

2645 LEVY, Leonard W., ed. *Freedom of the Press from Zenger to Jefferson: Early American Libertarian Theories.* Indianapolis, 1966.

2646 MERIN, Jerome L. "Libel and the Supreme Court." *Wm & M L Rev,* 11 (1969), 371–423.

2647 *Near v. Minnesota.* 283 U.S. 697 (1931).

2648 NELSON, Harold. "The Newsmen's Privilege Against Disclosure of Confidential Sources and Information." *Vand L Rev,* 24 (1971), 667–682.

2649 *New York Times Co. v. Sullivan.* 376 U.S. 254 (1964).

2650 *New York Times Co. v. United States.* 403 U.S. 713 (1971).

2651 NIMMER, Melville B. "The Right to Speak from *Times* to *Time:* First Amendment Theory Applied to Libel and Misapplied to Privacy." *Calif L Rev,* 56 (1968), 935–967.

2652 PEDRICK, William H. "Freedom of the Press and the Law of Libel: The Modern Revised Translation." *Corn L Q,* 49 (1964), 581–608.

2653 "The Right of the Press to Gather Information." *Colum L Rev,* 71 (1971), 838–864.

2654 ROSENBERG, Norman L. "The Law of Political Libel and Freedom of Press in Nineteenth Century America: An Interpretation." *Am J Leg Hist,* 17 (1973), 336–352.

2655 SHERWOOD, Margaret. "The Newsman's Privilege: Government Investigations, Criminal Prosecutions and Private Litigation." *Calif L Rev,* 58 (1970), 1198–1250.

2656 THAYER, Frank. *Legal Control of the Press.* Brooklyn, N.Y., 1962.

2657 WRIGHT, J. Skelly. "Defamation, Privacy, and the Public Right to Know: A National Problem and a New Approach." *Tex L Rev,* 46 (1968), 630–649.

Censorship and Obscenity

2658 AYER, Douglas, *et al.* "Self-Censorship in the Movie Industry: An Historical Perspective on Law and Social Change." *Wis L Rev,* 1970 (1970), 791–838.

2659 BOYER, Paul S. *Purity in Print: The Vice Movement and Book Censorship in America.* New York, 1968.

2660 CARMEN, Ira H. *Movies, Censorship, and the Law.* Ann Arbor, Mich., 1966.

2661 CHANDOS, John, ed. *To Deprave and Corrupt.* New York, 1962.

2662 CLOR, Harry. *Obscenity and Public Morality: Censorship in a Liberal Society.* Chicago, 1969.

2663 DENNETT, Mary Ware. *Who's Obscene?* New York, 1930.

2664 ENGDAHL, David E. "Requiem for Roth: Obscenity Doctrine Is Changing." *Mich L Rev,* 68 (1969), 185–236.

2665 ERNST, Morris L., and Alan U. SCHWARTZ. *Censorship: The Search for the Obscene.* New York, 1964.

2666 ERNST, Morris, and William SEAGLE. *To the Pure: A Study of Obscenity and the Censor.* New York, 1928.

2667 FRANK, John P. "Obscenity: Some Problems of Values and the Use of Experts." *Wash L Rev,* 41 (1966), 631–675.

2668 FRIEDMAN, Leon. *Obscenity; The Complete Oral Arguments Before the Supreme Court in the Major Obscenity Cases.* New York, 1970.

2669 FUNSTON, Richard. "Pornography and Politics: The Court, the Constitution, and the Commission." *West Pol Q,* 24 (1971), 635–652.

2670 GELLHORN, Walter. "Dirty Books, Disgusting Pictures, and Dreadful Laws." *Ga L Rev,* 8 (1974), 291–312.

2671 HANEY, Robert W. *Comstockery in America: Patterns of Censorship Control.* Boston, 1960.

2672 HENKIN, Louis. "Morals and the Constitution: The Sin of Obscenity." *Colum L Rev,* 63 (1963), 391–414.

2673 *Jacobellis v. Ohio.* 378 U.S. 184 (1964).

2674 KALVEN, Harry, Jr. "The Metaphysics of the Law of Obscenity." *S Ct Rev* (1960), 1–45.

2675 KUH, Richard H. *Foolish Figleaves? Pornography in—and out of—Court.* New York, 1967.

2676 LOCKHART, William B., and Robert C. McCLURE. "Censorship of Obscenity: The Developing Constitutional Standard." *Minn L Rev,* 45 (1960), 5–121.

2677 LOCKHART, William B., and Robert C. McCLURE. "Literature, the Law of Obscenity, and the Constitution." *Minn L Rev,* 38 (1954), 295–395.

2678 MAGRATH, C. Peter. "The Obscenity Cases: Grapes of *Roth.*" *S Ct Rev* (1966), 7–77.

2679 *Miller v. California.* 413 U.S. 15 (1973).

2680 MURPHY, Terrence J. *Censorship: Government and Obscenity.* Baltimore, 1963.

2681 NIMMER, Melville B. "The Constitutionality of Official Censorship of Motion Pictures." *U Chi L Rev,* 25 (1958), 625–657.

2682 PAUL, James C. N., and Murray L. SCHWARTZ. *Federal Censorship: Obscenity in the Mail.* New York, 1961.

2683 "Private Censorship of Movies." *Stan L Rev,* 22 (1970), 618–656.

2684 RANDALL, Richard S. *Censorship of the Movies: The Social and Political Control of a Mass Medium.* Madison, Wis., 1968.

2685 REMBAR, Charles. *The End of Obscenity: The Trials of "Lady Chatterley," "Tropic of Cancer," and "Fanny Hill."* New York, 1968.

2686 ROGGE, O. John. "The Obscenity Terms of the Court." *Vill L Rev,* 17 (1972), 393–462.

2687 *Roth v. United States.* 354 U.S. 476 (1957).

2688 SHAPIRO, Martin. "Obscenity Law: A Public Policy Analysis." *J Pub L,* 20 (1971), 503–522.

2689 STEPHENSON, D. Grier, Jr. "State Appellate Courts and the Judicial Process: Written Obscenity." *Wm & M L Rev,* 11 (1969), 106–137.

2690 STEPHENSON, D. Grier, Jr. "State Appellate Courts and Written Obscenity: The Georgia Experience." *Merc L Rev,* 19 (1968), 287–311.

2691 TEETER, Dwight L., Jr., and Don R. PEMBER. "Obscenity, 1971: The Rejuvenation of State Power and the Return to *Roth." Vill L Rev,* 17 (1971), 211–245.

2692 U.S. Commission on Obscenity and Pornography. *The Report.* Washington, D.C., 1970.

Freedom of Religion

General

2693 BETH, Loren P. *The American Theory of Church and State.* Gainesville, Fla., 1958.

2694 BUTTS, R. Freeman. *The American Tradition in Religion and Education.* Boston, 1950.

2695 DRINAN, Robert F. *Religion, the Courts, and Public Policy.* New York, 1963.

2696 FELLMAN, David. "Religion in American Public Law." *Bos U L Rev,* 44 (1964), 287–399.

2697 FRIEDRICH, Carl J. *Transcendent Justice: The Religious Dimensions of Constitutionalism.* Durham, N.C., 1964.

2698 GALENTER, Marc. "Religious Freedom in the United States: A Turning Point?" *Wis L Rev,* 1966 (1966), 217–296.

2699 GIANNELLA, Donald A. "Religious Liberty, Nonestablishment, and Doctrinal Development. Part I. The Religious Liberty Guarantee. Part II. The Nonestablishment Principle." *Harv L Rev,* 80 (1967), 1381–1431; 81 (1968), 513–590.

2700 HOWE, Mark A. DeWolfe. *The Garden and the Wilderness: Religion and Government in American Constitutional History.* Chicago, 1965.

2701 KATZ, Wilber G. *Religion and American Constitutions.* Evanston, Ill., 1964.

2702 KAUPER, Paul G. *Religion and the Constitution.* Baton Rouge, La., 1964.

2703 KURLAND, Philip B. *Religion and the Law: Of Church and State and the Supreme Court.* Chicago, 1962.

2704 MORGAN, Richard E. *The Supreme Court and Religion.* New York, 1972.

2705 NICHOLS, Roy F. *Religion and American Democracy.* Baton Rouge, La., 1959.

2706 PFEFFER, Leo. *Church, State and Freedom.* Boston, 1967.

2707 SMITH, Elwyn A. *Religious Liberty in the United States: The Development of Church-State Thought Since the Revolutionary Era.* Philadelphia, 1972.

2708 "Symposium: Expanding Concepts of Religious Freedom." *Wis L Rev,* 1966 (1966), 215–296.

2709 TORPEY, William G. *Judicial Doctrines of Religious Rights in America.* Chapel Hill, N.C., 1948.

Free Exercise

2710 "Black Muslims in Prison: Of Muslim Rites and Constitutional Rights." *Colum L Rev,* 62 (1962), 1488–1504.

2711 COBB, Sanford H. *The Rise of Religious Liberty in America: A History.* New York, 1970.

2712 DODGE, Joseph M., II. "The Free Exercise of Religion: A Sociological Approach." *Mich L Rev,* 67 (1969), 679–728.

2713 *Gillette v. United States.* 401 U.S. 437 (1971).

2714 HOCHSTADT, Theodore. "The Right to Exemption from Military Service of a Conscientious Objector to a Particular War." *Harv Civ R—Civ Lib L Rev,* 3 (1967), 1–66.

2715 JORGENSON, Lloyd P. "The Oregon School Law of 1922: Passage and Sequel." *Cath Hist Rev,* 54 (1968), 455–466.

2716 KELLOGG, Walter. *The Conscientious Objector.* New York, 1919.

2717 MALAMENT, David. "Selective Conscientious Objection and the *Gillette Decision.*" *Phil & Pub Aff,* 1 (1972), 363–386.

2718 MANWARING, David R. *Render unto Caesar: The Flag Salute Controversy.* Chicago, 1962.

2719 *Minersville School District v. Gobitis.* 310 U.S. 586 (1940).

2720 RABIN, R. L. "When Is a Religious Belief Religious: *United States v. Seeger* and the Scope of Free Exercise." *Corn L Q,* 51 (1966), 1–20.

2721 REDLICH, Norman, and Kenneth R. FEINBERG. "Individual Conscience and the Selective Conscientious Objector: The Right Not to Kill." *N Y U L Rev,* 44 (1969), 875–900.

2722 REGAN, Richard J. *Private Conscience and Public Law: The American Experience.* New York, 1972.

2723 SIBLEY, Mulford Q., and Phillip E. JACOB. *Conscription of Conscience: Conscientious Objectors, 1940–1947.* Ithaca, N.Y., 1952.

2724 STONE, Harlan Fiske. "The Conscientious Objector." *Colum U Q,* 21 (1919), 253–272.

2725 TYACK, Davis B. "The Perils of Pluralism: The Background of the Pierce Case." *Am Hist Rev,* 74 (1968), 74–98.

2726 *West Virginia State Board of Education v. Barnette.* 319 U.S. 624 (1943).

2727 *Wisconsin v. Yoder.* 406 U.S. 205 (1972).

Nonestablishment

2728 BARRON, Jerome A. "Sunday in North America." *Harv L Rev,* 79 (1965), 42–54.

2729 BETH, Loren P. "The Wall of Separation and the Supreme Court." *Minn L Rev,* 38 (1954), 215–227.

2730 BITTKER, Boris I. "Churches, Taxes and the Constitution." *Yale L J,* 78 (1969), 1285–1310.

2731 BOLES, Donald E. *The Bible, Religion and the Public Schools.* 3rd ed. Ames, Iowa, 1965.

2732 BROWN, Ernest J. "Quis Custodiet Custodes?—The School Prayer Cases." *S Ct Rev* (1963), 1–33.

2733 CAHN, Edmond. "The Establishment of Religion Puzzle." *N Y U L Rev,* 36 (1961), 1274–1297.

2734 CAHN, Edmond. "On Government and Prayer." *N Y U L Rev,* 37 (1962), 549–563.

2735 CORWIN, Edward S. "The Supreme Court as National School Board." *L & Cont Prob,* 14 (1949), 3–22.

2736 "Educational Vouchers: The Fruit of the *Lemon* Tree." *Stan L Rev,* 24 (1972), 687–711.

2737 FREUND, Paul A. "Public Aid to Parochial Schools." *Harv L Rev,* 82 (1969), 1680–1692.

2738 FREUND, Paul A. *Religion and the Public Schools.* Cambridge, Mass., 1965.

2739 HASKELL, Paul G. "The Prospects for Public Aid to Parochial Schools." *Minn L Rev,* 56 (1971), 159–187.

2740 JOHNSON, Alvin W., and Frank H. YOST. *Separation of Church and State in the United States.* Minneapolis, 1948.

2741 KAUPER, Paul G. "Church, State and Freedom: A Review." *Mich L Rev,* 52 (1954), 829–848.

2742 KAUPER, Paul G. "Prayer, Public Schools and the Supreme Court." *Mich L Rev,* 61 (1963), 219–282.

2743 KAUPER, Paul G. "The *Walz* Decision: More on the Religion Clauses of the First Amendment." *Mich L Rev,* 69 (1970), 179–210.

2744 KONVITZ, Milton R. *Religious Liberty and Conscience. A Constitutional Inquiry.* New York, 1968.

2745 KURLAND, Philip B. "The Regents' Prayer Case: 'Full of Sound and Fury, Signifying. . . .' " *S Ct Rev* (1962), 1–33.

2746 LAUBACH, John H. *School Prayers: Congress, the Courts and the Public.* Washington, D. C., 1969.

2747 *Lemon v. Kurtzman.* 403 U.S. 602 (1971).

2748 McCOLLUM, Vashti Cromwell. *One Woman's Fight.* Rev. ed. Boston, 1961.

2749 *McCollum v. Board of Education.* 333 U.S. 203 (1948).

2750 *McGowan v. Maryland.* 366 U.S. 420 (1961).

2751 McLOUGHLIN, William G. *New England Dissent, 1630–1833: The Baptists and the Separation of Church and State.* 2 vols. Cambridge, Mass., 1971.

2752 MOEHLMAN, Conrad H. *The Wall of Separation Between Church and State: An Historical Study of Recent Criticism of the Religious Clause of the First Amendment.* Boston, 1951.

2753 POWELL, Theodore. *The School Bus Law: A Case Study in Education, Religion and Politics.* Middletown, Conn., 1960.

2754 *School District of Abington Township v. Schempp.* 374 U.S. 203 (1963).

Privacy

2755 BEANEY, William M. "The Constitutional Right to Privacy in the Supreme Court." *S Ct Rev* (1962), 212–251.

2756 BEANEY, William M. "The Griswold Case and the Expanded Right to Privacy." *Wis L Rev,* 1966 (1966), 979–998.

2757 *Berger v. New York.* 388 U.S. 41 (1967).

2758 CALLAHAN, Daniel J. *Abortion: Law, Choice and Morality.* New York, 1970.

2759 CHRISTIE, George C. "Government Surveillance and Individual Freedom: A Proposed Statutory Response to *Laird v. Tatum* and the Broader Problem of Government Surveillance of the Individual." *N Y U L Rev,* 47 (1972), 871–902.

2760 DASH, Samuel. *The Eavesdroppers.* New Brunswick, N.J., 1959.

2761 DIXON, Robert G., Jr. "The Griswold Penumbra: Constitutional Charter for an Expanded Law of Privacy?" *Mich L Rev,* 64 (1965), 197–218.

2762 EMERSON, Thomas I. "Nine Justices in Search of a Doctrine." *Mich L Rev,* 64 (1965), 219–234.

2763 "Foreign Security Surveillance and the Fourth Amendment." *Harv L Rev,* 87 (1974), 976–1000.

2764 GEIS, Gilbert. *Not the Law's Business? An Examination of Homosexuality, Abortion, Prostitution, Narcotics, and Gambling in the United States.* Washington, D.C., 1972.

2765 *Griswold v. Connecticut.* 381 U.S. 479 (1965).

2766 KATIN, Ernest. "*Griswold v. Connecticut:* The Justices and Connecticut's 'Uncommonly Silly Law.' " *Not Dame Law,* 42 (1967), 680–706.

2767 KATZ, A. "Privacy and Pornography: *Stanley v. Georgia.* " *S Ct Rev* (1969), 203–218.

2768 *Katz v. United States.* 389 U.S. 347 (1967).

2769 KITCH, Edmund W. "Katz v. United States: The Limits of the Fourth Amendment." *S Ct Rev* (1968), 133–152.

2770 KITTRIE, Nicholas N. *The Right to Be Different: Deviance and Enforced Therapy.* Baltimore, 1971.

2771 LONG, Edward V. *The Intruders: The Invasion of Privacy by Government and Industry.* New York, 1967.

2772 LUSKY, Louis. "Invasion of Privacy: A Clarification of Concepts." *Colum L Rev,* 72 (1972), 693–711.

2773 McKAY, Robert B. "Self-Incrimination and the New Privacy." *S Ct Rev* (1967), 193–232.

2774 MAYER, Michael F. *Rights of Privacy.* New York, 1972.

2775 MEISEL, Alan. "Political Surveillance and the Fourth Amendment." *U Pitt L Rev,* 35 (1973) 53–72.

2776 MILLER, Arthur R. *The Assault on Privacy: Computers, Data Banks, and Dossiers.* Ann Arbor, Mich., 1971.

2777 MILLER, Arthur S. "Privacy in the Corporate State: A Constitutional Value of Dwindling Significance." *J Pub L,* 22 (1973), 3–35.

2778 MORELAND, Roy. "The Right of Privacy Today." *Ky L J,* 19 (1931), 101–136.

2779 MURPHY, Walter F. *Wiretapping on Trial. A Case Study in the Judicial Process.* New York, 1965.

2780 *Olmstead v. United States.* 277 U.S. 438 (1928).

2781 "On Privacy: Constitutional Protections for Personal Liberty." *N Y U L Rev,* 48 (1973), 670–773.

2782 *Pavesich v. New England Mutual Life Insurance Co.* 122 Ga. 190 (1905).

2783 PEMBER, Don R. *Privacy and the Press; The Law, the Mass Media, and the First Amendment.* Seattle, Wash., 1972.

2784 *Roe v. Wade.* 410 U.S. 113 (1973).

2785 SCHWARTZ, Herman. "The Legitimation of Electronic Eavesdropping: The Politics of 'Law and Order.' " *Mich L Rev,* 67 (1969), 455–510.

2786 SPRITZER, Ralph S. "Electronic Surveillance by Leave of the Magistrate: The Case in Opposition." *U Penn L Rev,* 118 (1969), 169–201.

2787 *Stanley v. Georgia.* 394 U.S. 557 (1969).

2788 *United States v. U.S. District Court.* 407 U.S. 297 (1972).

2789 WARREN, Samuel D., and Louis D. BRANDEIS. "The Right to Privacy." *Harv L Rev,* 4 (1890), 193–220.

2790 WESTIN, Alan F. *Privacy and Freedom.* New York, 1967.

2791 WESTIN, Alan F., and Michael BAKER. *Databanks in a Free Society.* New York, 1972.

2792 YANKWICH, Leon R. "The Right of Privacy: Its Development, Scope and Limitations." *Not Dame Law,* 27 (1952), 499–528.

Equal Protection of the Laws

General

2793 BERGER, Morroe. "The Supreme Court and Group Discrimination Since 1937." *Colum L Rev,* 49 (1949), 201–230.

2794 "Developments in the Law—Equal Protection." *Harv L Rev,* 82 (1969), 1065–1192.

2795 "The Evolution of Equal Protection: Education, Municipal Services, and Wealth." *Harv Civ R—Civ Lib L Rev,* 7 (1972), 103–213.

2796 FRANK, John P., and Robert F. MUNROE. "The Original Understanding of 'Equal Protection of the Law.' " *Colum L Rev,* 50 (1950), 131–169.

2797 GUNTHER, Gerald. "Foreward: In Search of Evolving Doctrine on a Changing Court: A Model for a Newer Equal Protection." *Harv L Rev,* 86 (1972), 1–48.

2798 HARRIS, Robert J. *The Quest for Equality: The Constitution, Congress, and the Supreme Court.* Baton Rouge, La., 1960.

2799 HOROWITZ, Harold W., and Kenneth L. KARST. *Law, Lawyers and Social Change; Cases and Materials on the Abolition of Slavery, Racial Segregation, and Inequality of Educational Opportunity.* Indianapolis, 1969.

2800 JENCKS, Christopher, *et al. Inequality: A Reassessment of the Effect of Family and Schooling in America.* New York, 1972.

2801 KURLAND, Philip B. "Egalitarianism and the Warren Court." *Mich L Rev,* 68 (1970), 629–682.

2802 LAPENCE, J. A. *Protection of Minorities.* Berkeley, Calif., 1960.

2803 MENDELSON, Wallace. "From Warren to Burger: The Rise and Decline of Substantive Equal Protection." *Am Pol Sci Rev,* 66 (1972), 1226–1233.

2804 MICHELMAN, Frank I. "Foreward: On Protecting the Poor Through the Fourteenth Amendment." *Harv L Rev,* 83 (1969), 7–59.

2805 SCHOETTLE, Ferdinand P. "The Equal Protection Clause in Public Education." *Colum L Rev,* 71 (1971), 1355–1419.

2806 SILVERMAN, William. "Equal Protection, Economic Legislation, and Racial Discrimination." *Vand L Rev,* 25 (1972), 1183–1204.

Racial Equality

2807 "Affirmative Integration: Studies of Efforts to Overcome De Facto Segregation in the Public Schools." *L & Soc Rev,* 2 (1967), 11–104.

2808 APPLEBAUM, Harvey M. "Miscegenation Statutes: A Constitutional and Social Problem." *Geo L J,* 53 (1964), 49–92.

2809 BERMAN, Daniel M. *It Is So Ordered.* New York, 1966.

2810 BERMAN, William C. *The Politics of Civil Rights in the Truman Administration.* Columbus, Ohio, 1970.

2811 BICKEL, Alexander M. "The Decade of School Desegregation: Progress and Prospects." *Colum L Rev,* 64 (1964), 193–229.

2812 BICKEL, Alexander M. "The Original Understanding and the Segregation Decision." *Harv L Rev,* 69 (1955), 1–65.

2813 BLACK, Charles L., Jr. "Foreward: State Action, Equal Protection, and California's Proposition 14." *Harv L Rev,* 81 (1967), 69–109.

2814 BLACK, Charles L., Jr. "The Lawfulness of the Segregation Decisions." *Yale L J,* 69 (1960), 421–430.

2815 BLAUSTEIN, Albert P., and C. C. FERGUSON, Jr. *Desegregation and the Law: The Meaning and Effect of the School Segregation Cases.* 2nd ed. New York, 1964.

2816 BLOCH, Charles J. "The School Segregation Cases: A Legal Error." *Am Bar Assoc J,* 45 (1959), 27–30.

2817 BOUDIN, Louis B. "The Supreme Court and Civil Rights." *Sci & Soc,* 1 (1937), 273–309.

2818 *Brown v. Board of Education.* 347 U.S. 483 (1954).

2819 Bureau of National Affairs. *State Fair Employment Practice Laws and Their Administration.* Washington, D.C., 1964.

2820 CATTERALL, H. T. *Judicial Cases Concerning American Slaves and the Negro.* 5 vols. New York, 1968 (reprint of 1926 ed.).

2821 "Civil Rights in the South: A Symposium." *N C L Rev,* 42 (1963), 1–178.

2822 CLARK, Kenneth B. "Desegregation: An Appraisal of the Evidence." *J Soc Iss,* 9 (1953), 1–76.

2823 COLEMAN, James S., *et al. Equality of Educational Opportunity.* Washington, D.C., 1966.

2824 "The Courts, HEW, and Southern School Desegregation." *Yale L J,* 77 (1967), 321–365.

2825 CRAIN, Robert, and David KIRBY. *Political Strategies in Northern Desegregation.* Lexington, Mass., 1973.

2826 "Developments in the Law—Employment Discrimination and Title VII of the Civil Rights Act of 1964." *Harv L Rev,* 84 (1971), 1109–1316.

2827 DIMOND, Paul R. "School Segregation in the North: There Is But One Constitution." *Harv Civ R—Civ Lib L Rev,* 7 (1972), 1–55.

2828 DIXON, Robert G., Jr. "Civil Rights in Transportation and the I.C.C." *Geo Wash L Rev,* 31 (1962), 198–241.

2829 DORSEN, Norman. *Discrimination and Civil Rights.* Boston, 1969.

2830 DULLES, Foster Rhea. *The Civil Rights Commission, 1957–1965.* East Lansing, Mich., 1968.

2831 DUNN, James R. "Title VI, the Guidelines and School Desegregation in the South." *Va L Rev,* 53 (1967), 42–88.

2832 "Equality Before the Law: A Symposium on Civil Rights." *Northw U L Rev,* 14 (1959), 330–404.

2833 FISS, Owen M. "Racial Intolerance in the Public Schools: The Constitutional Concepts." *Harv L Rev,* 78 (1965), 564–617.

2834 FORPOSCH, Morris D. "The Desegregation Opinion Revisited: Legal or Sociological." *Vand L Rev,* 21 (1967), 47–76.

2835 FRIEDMAN, Leon, ed. *Argument: The Oral Argument Before the Supreme Court in Brown v. Board of Education of Topeka.* New York, 1969.

2836 GARFINKEL, Herbert. "Social Science Evidence and the School Segregation Cases." *J Pol,* 21 (1959), 37–59.

2837 GIBSON, William M. *Aliens and the Law.* Chapel Hill, N.C., 1940.

2838 GOULD, William B. "Racial Equality in Jobs and Unions, Collective Bargaining, and the Burger Court." *Mich L Rev,* 68 (1969), 237–258.

2839 GRAHAM, Howard Jay. "The Fourteenth Amendment and School Segregation." *Buff L Rev,* 3 (1953), 1–24.

2840 GRAHAM, Hugh D. *Crisis in Print: Desegregation and the Press.* Nashville, Tenn., 1967.

2841 GREENBERG, Jack. *Race Relations and American Law.* New York, 1959.

2842 HOROWITZ, Harold W., and Kenneth L. KARST. "Reitman v. Mulkey: A Telophase of Substantive Equal Protection." *S Ct Rev,* (1967), 39–80.

2843 HOWARD, A. E. Dick. "Mr. Justice Black: The Negro Protest Movement and the Rule of Law." *Va L Rev,* 53 (1967), 1030–1091.

2844 KAPLAN, John. "Equal Justice in an Unequal World: Equality for the Negro—The Problem of Special Treatment." *Northw U L Rev,* 61 (1966), 363–410.

2845 KAPLAN, John. "Segregation Litigation and the Schools." *Northw U L Rev,* 58 (1963), 1–72, 157–214; 59 (1964), 121–170.

2846 KELLY, Alfred H. "The Congressional Controversy over School Segregation, 1867–1875." *Am Hist Rev,* 64 (1959), 537–563.

2847 KELLY, Alfred H. "The Fourteenth Amendment Reconsidered: The Segregation Question." *Mich L Rev,* 54 (1956), 1049–1086.

2848 KILPATRICK, James J. *The Southern Case for School Segregation.* New York, 1962.

2849 KING, Donald B., and Charles W. QUICK, eds. *Legal Aspects of the Civil Rights Movement.* Detroit, Mich., 1965.

2850 KONVITZ, Milton R. *The Alien and the Asiatic in American Law.* Ithaca, N.Y., 1946.

2851 KONVITZ, Milton R. *A Century of Civil Rights.* Ithaca, N.Y., 1965.

2852 KONVITZ, Milton R. *Civil Rights in Immigration.* Ithaca, N.Y., 1953.

2853 KONVITZ, Milton R. *The Constitution and Civil Rights.* New York, 1947.

2854 KRISLOV, Samuel. *The Negro in Federal Employment: The Quest for Equal Opportunity.* Minneapolis, 1967.

2855 LEVY, Leonard W., and Harlan B. PHILLIPS. "The Roberts Case; Source of the Separate But Equal Doctrine." *Am Hist Rev,* 56 (1951), 510–518.

2856 LOCKARD, Duane. *Toward Equal Opportunity: A Study of State and Local Anti-Discrimination Laws.* New York, 1968.

2857 McAULIFFE, Daniel J. "School Desegregation: The Problem of Compensatory Discrimination." *Va L Rev,* 57 (1971), 65–96.

2858 McCORD, John H., ed. *With All Deliberate Speed: Civil Rights Theory and Reality.* Urbana, Ill., 1969.

2859 MANGUM, Charles S., Jr. *The Legal Status of the Negro.* Chapel Hill, N.C., 1940.

2860 MARSHALL, Thurgood. "Mr. Justice Murphy and Civil Rights." *Nat Bar J,* 9 (1951), 1–25.

2861 MENDELSON, Wallace. *Discrimination.* Englewood Cliffs, N.J., 1962.

2862 MILLER, Arthur S. *Racial Discrimination and Private Education: A Legal Analysis.* Chapel Hill, N.C., 1957.

2863 MILLER, Loren. *The Petitioners: The Story of the Supreme Court of the United States and the Negro.* Cleveland, Ohio, 1966.

2864 *Milliken v. Bradley.* 418 U.S. 717 (1974).

2865 MURPHY, Walter F. "Desegregation in Education: A Generation of Future Litigation." *Md L Rev,* 15 (1955), 221–243.

2866 MUSE, Benjamin. *Ten Years of Prelude: The Story of Integration Since the Supreme Court's 1954 Decision.* New York, 1964.

2867 MYRDAL, Gunnar. *An American Dilemma: The Negro Problem and Modern Democracy.* New York, 1944.

2868 NASH, A. E. Keir. "Fairness and Formalism in the Trials of Blacks in the State Supreme Courts of the Old South." *Va L Rev,* 56 (1970), 64–100.

2869 NATHAN, Richard P. *Jobs and Civil Rights: The Role of the Federal Government in Promoting Equal Opportunity in Employment and Training.* Washington, D.C., 1969.

2870 NELSON, Bernard H. *The Fourteenth Amendment and the Negro Since 1920.* 2nd ed. New York, 1967.

2871 NEWBY, I. A. *Challenge to the Court: Social Scientists and the Defense of Segregation, 1954–1966.* Baton Rouge, La., 1969.

2872 NORTHRUP, Herbert R., and Richard L. ROWAN. *The Negro and Employment Opportunity.* Ann Arbor, Mich., 1965.

2873 OLSON, Otto H., ed. *The Thin Disguise: Turning Point in Negro History. Plessy v. Ferguson: A Documentary Presentation, 1864–1896.* New York, 1967.

2874 ORFIELD, Gary. *The Reconstruction of Southern Education: The Schools and the 1964 Civil Rights Act.* New York, 1969.

2875 PANETTA, Leon E., and Peter GALL. *Bring Us Together—The Nixon Team and the Civil Rights Retreat.* Philadelphia, 1971.

2876 *Plessy v. Ferguson.* 163 U.S. 537 (1896).

2877 President's Committee on Civil Rights. *To Secure These Rights.* Washington, D.C., 1947.

2878 PRICE, Monroe E. *Law and the American Indian.* Indianapolis, 1973.

2879 RANSMEIER, Joseph S. "The Fourteenth Amendment and the 'Separate but Equal' Doctrine." *Mich L Rev,* 50 (1951), 203–260.

2880 REPPY, Alison. *Civil Rights in the United States.* New York, 1951.

2881 RICE, Roger L. "Residential Segregation by Law, 1910–1917." *J So Hist,* 34 (1968), 179–199.

2882 ROCHE, John P. "Education, Segregation and the Supreme Court—A Political Analysis." *U Penn L Rev,* 99 (1951), 949–959.

2883 ROCHE, John P. "The Future of 'Separate but Equal.' " *Phylon,* 12 (1951), 219–226.

2884 ROCHE, John P. *The Quest for the Dream: The Development of Civil Rights and Human Relations in Modern America.* New York, 1964.

2885 RODGERS, Harrell R., Jr., and Charles S. BULLOCK, III. *Law and Social Change: Civil Rights Laws and Their Consequences.* New York, 1972.

2886 ROSEN, Sanford J. "The Law and Racial Discrimination in Employment." *Calif L Rev,* 53 (1965), 729–799.

2887 RUCHAMES, Louis. *Race, Jobs and Politics; The Story of FEPC.* New York, 1953.

2888 "School Desegregration after Swann: A Theory of Government Responsibility." *U Chi L Rev,* 39 (1972), 421–447.

2889 "Schools, Busing and Desegregation: The Post-*Swann* Era." *N Y U L Rev,* 46 (1971), 1078–1127.

2890 "School Desegregation and the Office of Education Guidelines." *Geo L J,* 55 (1966), 325–351.

2891 SEELEY, James J. "The Public Referendum and Minority Group Legislation: Postscript to *Reitman v. Mulkey.*" *Corn L Rev,* 55 (1970), 881–910.

2892 "Segregation in the Public Schools; A Symposium." *J Pub L,* 3 (1954), 5–170.

2893 "Segregation in Public Schools—A Violation of 'Equal Protection of the Laws.' " *Yale L J,* 56 (1947), 1059–1067.

2894 "Segregation of Poor and Minority Children into Classes for the Mentally Retarded by Use of I.Q. Tests." *Mich L Rev,* 71 (1973), 1212–1250.

2895 *Shelley v. Kraemer.* 334 U.S. 1 (1948).

2896 SICKELS, Robert J. *Race, Marriage and the Law.* Albuquerque, N.M., 1972.

2897 SMITH, Robert C. *They Closed Their Schools: Prince Edward County, Virginia, 1951–1964.* Chapel Hill, N.C., 1965.

2898 SOVERN, Michael I. *Legal Restraints on Racial Discrimination in Employment.* New York, 1966.

2899 STEPHENSON, Gilbert T. *Race Distinctions in American Law.* New York, 1910.

2900 *Swann v. Charlotte-Mecklenburg Board of Education.* 402 U.S. 1 (1971).

2901 *Sweatt v. Painter.* 339 U.S. 629 (1950).

2902 "Symposium on Race Relations." *Vand L Rev,* 26 (1973), 394–584.

2903 ULMER, S. Sidney. "Earl Warren and the Brown Decision." *J Pol,* 33 (1971), 689–702.

2904 U.S. Commission on Civil Rights. *Report.* Washington, D.C., 1959–.

2905 VIEIRA, Norman. "Racial Imbalance, Black Separatism, and Permissible Classification by Race." *Mich L Rev,* 67 (1969), 1553–1626.

2906 VINES, Kenneth N. "Federal District Judges and Race Relations Cases in the South." *J Pol,* 26 (1964), 337–357.

2907 VOSE, Clement E. *Caucasians Only: The Supreme Court, the NAACP and the Restrictive Covenant Cases.* Berkeley, Calif., 1959.

2908 WADLINGTON, Walter. "The Loving Case: Virginia's Anti-Miscegenation Statute in Historical Perspective." *Va L Rev,* 52 (1966), 1189–1223.

2909 WAITE, Edward F. "The Negro in the Supreme Court." *Minn L Rev,* 30 (1946), 219–304.

2910 WASHBURN, Wilcomb E. *Red Man's Land, White Man's Law, a Study of the Past and Present Status of the American Indian.* New York, 1971.

2911 WOODWARD, C. Vann. *The Strange Career of Jim Crow.* New York, 1957.

2912 WORKMAN, William D. *The Case for the South.* New York, 1960.

Sexual Equality

2913 ALTBACH, Edith H., ed. *From Feminism to Liberation.* Cambridge, Mass., 1971.

2914 BARNETT, Walter. *Sexual Freedom and the Constitution; An Inquiry into the Constitutionality of Repressive Sex Laws.* Albuquerque, N.M., 1973.

2915 BROWN, Barbara A., *et al.* "The Equal Rights Amendment: A Constitutional Basis for Equal Rights for Women." *Yale L J,* 80 (1971), 871–985.

2916 "Equal Rights for Women: A Symposium on the Proposed Constitutional Amendment." *Harv Civ R—Civ Lib L Rev,* 6 (1971), 215–288.

2917 FLEXNER, Eleanor. *A Century of Struggle: The Women's Rights Movement in the United States.* Cambridge, Mass., 1959.

2918 JOHNSTON, John D., Jr., and Charles L. KNAPP. "Sex Discrimination by Law: A Study in Judicial Perspective." *N Y U L Rev,* 46 (1971), 675–747.

2919 KANOWITZ, Leo. *Sex Roles in Law and Society: Cases and Materials.* Albuquerque, N.M., 1973.

2920 KANOWITZ, Leo. *Women and the Law: The Unfinished Revolution.* Albuquerque, N.M., 1969.

2921 "Sex Discrimination and Equal Protection: Do We Need a Constitutional Amendment?" *Harv L Rev,* 84 (1971), 1499–1524.

Governmental Services

2922 ALEXANDER, Kern, and K. Forbis JORDAN. *Constitutional Reform of School Finance.* Lexington, Mass., 1973.

2923 BERKE, Joel S., and John J. CALLAHAN. "*Serrano v. Priest:* Milestone or Millstone?" *J Pub L,* 21 (1972), 23–72.

2924 BURT, Robert A. "Forcing Protection on Children and Their Parents: The Impact of *Wyman v. James.*" *Mich L Rev,* 69 (1971), 1259–1310.

2925 "The Constitutionality of Local Zoning." *Yale L J,* 79 (1970), 896–925.

2926 DIENES, C. Thomas. "To Feed the Hungry: Judicial Retrenchment in Welfare Adjudication." *Calif L Rev,* 58 (1970), 555–627.

2927 GRUBB, W. Norton, and Stephan MICHELSON. "Public School Finance in a Post-*Serrano* World." *Harv Civ R—Civ Lib L Rev,* 8 (1973), 550–570.

2928 KRAUSE, Harry D. "Legitimate and Illegitimate Offspring of *Levy v. Louisiana*—First Decisions on Equal Protection and Paternity." *U Chi L Rev,* 36 (1969), 338–363.

2929 KRISLOV, Samuel. "The OEO Lawyers Fail to Constitutionalize a Right to Welfare: A Study in the Uses and Limits of the Judicial Process." *Minn L Rev,* 58 (1973), 211–245.

2930 KURLAND, Philip B. "Equal Educational Opportunity: The Limits of Constitutional Jurisprudence Undefined." *U Chi L Rev,* 35 (1968), 583–600.

2931 LAFRANCE, Arthur, *et al. Law of the Poor.* St. Paul, Minn., 1973.

2932 LEFCOE, George. "The Public Housing Referendum Case, Zoning, and the Supreme Court." *Calif L Rev,* 59 (1971), 1384–1458.

2933 NICHOLSON, Marlene Arnold. "Campaign Financing and Equal Protection." *Stan L Rev,* 26 (1974), 815–854.

2934 REISCHAUER, Robert D., and Robert W. HARTMAN. *Reforming School Finance.* Washington, D.C., 1973.

2935 RICHARDS, David A. J. "Equal Opportunity and School Financing: Towards a Moral Theory of Constitutional Adjudication." *U Chi L Rev,* 41 (1973), 32–71.

2936 "Symposium: Law of the Poor." *Calif L Rev,* 54 (1966), 319–1014.

2937 WISE, Arthur E. *Rich Schools, Poor Schools; The Promise of Equal Educational Opportunity.* Chicago, 1972.

Individual Rights and the Military

2938 BISHOP, Joseph W., Jr. *Justice under Fire; A Study of Military Law.* New York, 1974.

2939 DiMONA, Joseph. *Great Court-Martial Cases.* New York, 1972.

2940 FAIRMAN, Charles. "The Supreme Court on Military Jurisdiction: Martial Rule in Hawaii and the Yamashita Case." *Harv L Rev,* 59 (1946), 833–882.

2941 HENDERSON, Gordon D. "Courts-Martial and the Constitution; The Original Understanding." *Harv L Rev,* 71 (1957), 293–324.

2942 IMWINKELREID, Edward J., and Francis A. GILLIGAN. "The Unconstitutional Burden of Article 15: A Rebuttal." *Yale L J,* 83 (1974), 534–552.

2943 KLAUS, Samuel. *Milligan Case.* New York, 1970 (reprint of 1929 ed.).

2944 *Ex parte Merryman.* 17 Federal Cases 9487 (1861).

2945 *Ex parte Milligan.* 4 Wallace (71 U.S.) 2 (1866).

2946 MINEAR, Richard H. *Victor's Justice, the Tokyo War Crimes Trial.* Princeton, N.J., 1971.

2947 MOYER, Homer E., Jr. *Justice and the Military.* Washington, D.C., 1972.

2948 *Ex parte Quirin.* 317 U.S. 1 (1942).

2949 REEL, A. F. *The Case of General Yamashita.* Chicago, 1949.

2950 SCHUG, Willis E., ed. *United States Law and the Armed Forces: Cases and Materials on Constitutional Law, Courts-Martial, and the Rights of Servicemen.* New York, 1972.

2951 ULMER, S. Sidney. *Military Justice and the Right to Counsel.* Lexington, Ky., 1970.

2952 "The Unconstitutional Burden of Article 15." *Yale L J,* 82 (1973), 1481–1494.

2953 *United States ex rel. Toth v. Quarles.* 350 U.S. 11 (1955).

2954 *Wade v. Hunter.* 336 U.S. 684 (1949).

2955 WARREN, Earl. "The Bill of Rights and the Military." *N Y U L Rev,* 37 (1962), 181–203.

2956 WEST, Luther C. "A History of Command Influence on the Military Judicial System." *UCLA L Rev,* 18 (1970), 1–156.

2957 WIENER, Frederick B. "Courts-Martial and the Bill of Rights: The Original Practice." *Harv L Rev,* 72 (1958), 1–49, 266–304.

2958 *In re Yamashita.* 327 U.S. 1 (1946).

F. The Franchise and the Political Process

2959 BICKEL, Alexander M. "The Voting Rights Cases." *S Ct Rev* (1966), 79–166.

2960 BLUMSTEIN, James F. "Party Reform, the Winner-Take-All Primary, and the California Delegate Challenge: The Gold Rush Revisited." *Vand L Rev,* 25 (1972), 952–1021.

2961 CHRISTOPHER, Warren. "The Constitutionality of the Voting Rights Act of 1965." *Stan L Rev,* 18 (1965), 1–37.

2962 CHUTE, Marchette. *The First Liberty. A History of the Right to Vote in America, 1619–1850.* New York, 1969.

2963 CLAUDE, Richard. *The Supreme Court and the Electoral Process.* Baltimore, 1970.

2964 "The Constitutionality of Qualifying Fees for Political Candidates." *U Penn L Rev,* 120 (1971), 109–142.

2965 "Democracy in the New Towns: The Limits of Private Government." *U Chi L Rev,* 36 (1969), 379–412.

2966 ELLIOTT, Wade E. Y. *The Rise of Guardian Democracy: The Supreme Court's Role in Voting Rights Disputes, 1845–1969.* Cambridge, Mass., 1974.

2967 FREDMAN, L. E. *The Australian Ballot.* East Lansing, Mich., 1968.

2968 *Gomillion v. Lightfoot.* 364 U.S. 339 (1960).

2969 GRANTHAM, Dewey W., Jr. "The White Primary and the Supreme Court." *S Atl Q,* 48 (1949), 529–538.

2970 GUIDO, Kenneth J., Jr. "Student Voting and Residency Qualifications: The Aftermath of the Twenty-Sixth Amendment." *N Y U L Rev,* 47 (1972), 32–58.

2971 HAMILTON, Charles V. *The Bench and the Ballot. Southern Federal Judges and Black Voters.* New York, 1973.

2972 HAMILTON, Howard D. "Direct Legislation: Some Implications of Open Housing Referenda." *Am Pol Sci Rev,* 64 (1970), 124–137.

2973 *Harper v. Virginia State Board of Elections.* 383 U.S. 663 (1966).

2974 HEYMAN, Ira M. "Federal Remedies for Voteless Negroes." *Calif L Rev,* 48 (1960), 190–215.

2975 "Judicial Intervention in National Political Conventions: An Idea Whose Time Has Come." *Corn L Rev,* 59 (1973), 107–132.

2976 *Katzenbach v. Morgan.* 384 U.S. 641 (1966).

2977 KIRBY, James C., Jr. "The Constitutional Right to Vote." *N Y U L Rev,* 45 (1970), 995–1014.

2978 LEWINSON, Paul. *Race, Class, and Party: A History of Negro Suffrage and White Politics in the South.* New York, 1959 (reprint of 1932 ed.).

2979 LUCAS, Jo D. "Dragon in the Thicket: A Perusal of *Gomillion v. Lightfoot.*" *S Ct Rev* (1961), 194–244.

2980 McCARTY, L. Thorne, and Russell B. STEVENSON, Jr. "The Voting Rights Act of 1965: An Evaluation." *Harv Civ R—Civ Lib L Rev,* 3 (1968), 357–412.

2981 McKINLEY, A. E. *The Suffrage Franchise in the Thirteen English Colonies in America.* Boston, 1905.

2982 McLAUGHLIN, Andrew C. *The Courts, the Constitution and Parties.* Chicago, 1912.

2983 MATHEWS, J. M. *Legislative and Judicial History of the Fifteenth Amendment.* Baltimore, 1909.

2984 *O'Brien v. Brown.* 409 U.S. 1 (1972).

2985 OGDEN, Frederick D. *The Poll Tax in the South.* University, Ala., 1968.

2986 PORTER, Kirk H. *A History of Suffrage in the United States.* Chicago, 1918.

2987 *Smith v. Allwright.* 321 U.S. 649 (1944).

2988 *South Carolina v. Katzenbach.* 383 U.S. 301 (1966).

2989 STANTON, Elizabeth Cady, *et al. The History of Woman Suffrage.* 6 vols. New York, 1881–1922.

2990 STRONG, Donald S. *Negroes, Ballots, and Judges: National Voting Rights Legislation in the Federal Courts.* Norman, Okla., 1968.

2991 SWINNEY, Everett. "Enforcing the Fifteenth Amendment, 1870–1877." *J So Hist,* 28 (1962), 202–218.

2992 TAPER, Bernard. *Gomillion v. Lightfoot: The Tuskegee Gerrymander Case.* New York, 1962.

2993 TUTTLE, Elbert P. "Equality and the Vote." *N Y U L Rev,* 41 (1966), 245–266.

2994 *United States v. Classic.* 313 U.S. 299 (1941).

2995 "Voting Rights: A Case Study of Madison Parish, Louisiana." *U Chi L Rev,* 38 (1971), 726–787.

2996 WILLIAMSON, Chilton. *American Suffrage from Property to Democracy, 1760–1860.* Princeton, N.J., 1960.

G. Travel and Expatriation

2997 Association of the Bar of the City of New York. Special Committee to Study Passport Procedures. *Freedom to Travel.* New York, 1958.

2998 BOUDIN, Leonard B. "The Constitutional Right to Travel." *Colum L Rev,* 56 (1956), 47–75.

2999 DIONISOPOULOS, P. Allan. "Afroyim v. Rusk: The Evolution, Uncertainty and Implications of a Constitutional Principle." *Minn L Rev,* 55 (1970), 235–257.

3000 "The Right to Travel: Another Constitutional Standard for Local Land Use Regulations?" *U Chi L Rev,* 39 (1972), 612–638.

3001 ROCHE, John P. "The Expatriation Cases: 'Breathes There the Man with Soul So Dead . . . '?" *S Ct Rev* (1963), 325–356.

3002 ROCHE, John P. "The Loss of American Nationality: The Development of Statutory Expatriation." *U Penn L Rev,* 99 (1950), 25–71.

3003 VELVEL, Lawrence R. "Geographic Restrictions on Travel: The Real World and the First Amendment." *Kan L Rev,* 15 (1966), 35–67.

INDEX

INDEX

B-B

130

INDEX

INDEX

INDEX

INDEX

INDEX

INDEX

INDEX

INDEX

INDEX

INDEX

INDEX

INDEX

INDEX

NOTES

NOTES

Supplement

I. General Sources

B. Reference Works and Public Documents

46a BAIN, Richard C., and Judith H. PARRIS. *Convention Decisions and Voting Records.* 2nd ed. Washington, D.C., 1973.

68a KURLAND, Philip B., and Gerhard CASPER, eds. *Landmark Briefs and Arguments of the Supreme Court of the United States: Constitutional Law.* Arlington, Va., 1975–.

76a SINGER, Aaron. *Campaign Speeches of American Presidential Candidates, 1928–1972.* New York, 1976.

76b *The Third Branch; Bulletin of the Federal Courts.* Washington, D.C., 1969–.

77a TUFTE, Edward R. "Political Statistics for the United States: Observations on Some Major Data Sources." *Am Pol Sci Rev,* 71 (1977), 305–314.

II. Origins

169a COLEMAN, Frank M. "The Hobbesian Basis of American Constitutionalism." *Polity,* 7 (1974), 57–89.

192a NOLAN, Dennis R. "Sir William Blackstone and the New American Republic: A Study in Intellectual Impact." *NYUL Rev,* 51 (1976), 731–768.

NOTE: This supplement has been added because of an unavoidable delay in publication, and recent years have been especially significant in American constitutional development. The supplement entries are keyed to their appropriate placement in the bibliography proper, with section headings and with exact alphabetical position by entry number and letter. An index to the supplement follows.

III. Political, Social, Economic and Intellectual Context

A. General

219a BOYD, Julian P. "On the Need for 'Frequent Recurrence to Fundamental Principles." *Va L Rev,* 62 (1976), 859–871.

244a GILMORE, Grant. *The Ages of American Law.* New Haven, 1977.

255a HART, H. L. A. "Law in the Perspective of Philosophy: 1776–1976." *NYUL Rev,* 51 (1976), 538–551.

277a MASON, Alpheus T. "America's Political Heritage—A Bicentennial Salute." *Pol Sci Q,* 91 (1976), 193–217.

278a MASON, Alpheus T. "Free Government's Balance Wheel." *Wilson Q,* 1 (1977), 93–108.

279a MASON, Alpheus T. "Security Through Freedom: A Bicentennial Legacy." *NY State Bar J,* 48 (1976), 601–604.

300a UNGAR, Sanford J. *FBI.* Boston, 1975.

B. 1607–1775

317a BLACK, Barbara A. "The Constitution of Empire: The Case for the Colonists." *U Penn L Rev,* 124 (1976), 1157–1211.

C. 1775–1790

405a D'ELIA, Donald J. *Benjamin Rush: Philosopher of the American Revolution.* Transactions of the American Philosophical Society, New Series, vol. 64, pt. 5. Philadelphia, 1974.

405b DIAMOND, Martin. "The Declaration and the Constitution: Liberty, Democracy, and the Founders." *Public Interest,* No. 41 (Fall, 1973), 39–55.

424a GRIMES, Alan P. "Conservative Revolution and Liberal Rhetoric: The Declaration of Independence." *J Pol,* 38 (1976), 1–19.

430a IREDELL, James. *The Papers of James Iredell.* Ed. Don Higgenbotham. Raleigh, N.C., 1976–.

431a JAY, John. *John Jay: The Making of a Revolutionary—Unpublished Papers.* Ed. Richard B. Morris. New York, 1975–.

432a JENSEN, Merrill, ed. *The Documentary History of the Ratification of the Constitution.* Madison, 1976–.

461a MORGAN, Robert J. "Madison's Theory of Representation in the Tenth Federalist." *J Pol,* 36 (1974), 852–885.

470a OSTROM, Vincent. "The American Contribution to a Theory of Constitutional Choice." *J Pol,* 38 (1976), 56–78.

470b PETERSON, Merrill D. *Adams and Jefferson: A Revolutionary Dialogue.* Athens, Ga., 1976.

485a "Symposium on the Formative Period." *Political Science Reviewer,* 6 (1976) 1–420.

D. 1790–1860

543a DE PAUW, Linda G., ed. *Documentary History of the First Federal Congress of the United States of America, March 4, 1789–March 3, 1791.* Baltimore, 1972–.

568a HORWITZ, Morton J. *The Transformation of American Law, 1780–1860.* Cambridge, Mass., 1977.

634a WEBSTER, Daniel. *The Papers of Daniel Webster.* Eds. Charles M. Wiltse and Harold D. Moser. Hanover, N.H., 1974–.

E. 1929–1941

817a GROSS, James. A. *The Making of the National Labor Relations Board.* Albany, N.Y., 1974.

F. 1941–1961

851a BLACK, Earl. *Southern Governors and Civil Rights: Racial Segregation as a Campaign Issue in the Second Reconstruction.* Cambridge, Mass., 1976.

857a ELY, James W., Jr. *The Crisis of Conservative Virginia; The Byrd Organization and the Politics of Massive Resistance.* Knoxville, 1976.

G. 1961–

889a "American Political Institutions after Watergate—A Discussion." *Pol Sci Q,* 89 (1974), 713–749.

896a BICKEL, Alexander M. *The Morality of Consent.* New Haven, 1975.

904a FAIRLIE, Henry. *The Kennedy Promise; the Politics of Expectation.* Garden City, N.Y., 1973.

922a "Justice: A Spectrum of Responses to John Rawl's Theory." *Am Pol Sci Rev,* 69 (1975), 588–674.

934a NIE, Norman H., Sidney VERBA, and John R. PETROCIK. *The Changing American Voter.* Cambridge, Mass., 1976.

934b NUECHTERLEIN, James A. "Arthur M. Schlesinger, Jr., and the Discontents of Postwar American Liberalism." *Rev Pol,* 39 (1977), 3–40.

945a Symposium, "East-West Dispute and North-South Gap: The Emerging Relationship." *Orbis,* 20 (1977), 841–1101.

IV. Political Institutions

A. The Congress

972a HUITT, Ralph K. "Congress: Retrospect and Prospect." *J Pol*, 38 (1976), 209–227.

992a WISE, Sidney. "The Democratic Caucus: A Cardboard Tiger." *Intellect*, 105 (1976), 149–152.

B. The Presidency

993a ARNOLD, Peri E. "The First Hoover Commission and the Managerial Presidency." *J Pol*, 38 (1976), 46–70.

996a CALIFANO, Joseph A., Jr. *A Presidential Nation.* New York, 1975.

1018a JAWORSKI, Leon. *The Right and the Power: The Prosecution of Watergate.* New York, 1976.

1022a KEARNS, Doris. *Lyndon Johnson and the American Dream.* New York, 1976.

1022b KIRKPATRICK, Jeane. *The New Presidential Elite; Men and Women in National Politics.* New York, 1976.

1031a MANKIEWICZ, Frank. *U.S. v. Richard M. Nixon; The Final Crisis.* New York, 1975.

1052a SEIDMAN, Harold. *Politics, Position and Power: The Dynamics of Federal Organization.* 2nd ed. New York, 1975.

1071a WILDAVSKY, Aaron. *The Politics of the Budgetary Process.* 2nd ed. Boston, 1974.

C. The Federal Judiciary

General

1079a CASPER, Jonathan D. "The Supreme Court and National Policy Making." *Am Pol Sci Rev*, 70 (1976), 50–63.

1082a FUNSTON, Richard. "The Supreme Court and Critical Elections." *Am Pol Sci Rev*, 69 (1975), 795–811.

1082b GOULDEN, Joseph C. *The Benchwarmers; The Private World of Powerful Federal Judges.* New York, 1974.

1096a SMITH, Joseph H. "An Independent Judiciary: The Colonial Background." *U Penn L Rev*, 124 (1976) 1104–1156.

1103a WHITE, G. Edward. *The American Judicial Tradition; Profiles of Leading American Judges.* New York, 1976.

1104a *Yearbook; Supreme Court Historical Society.* Washington, D.C., 1976–.

1790–1864

1133a HALL, Kermit L. "240 Men: The Antebellum Lower Federal Judiciary, 1829–1861." *Vand L Rev,* 29 (1976), 1089–1129.

1166a SEDDIG, Robert G. "John Marshall and the Origins of Supreme Court Leadership." *U Pitt L Rev,* 36 (1975), 785–833.

1864–1941

1225a GLENNON, Robert J., Jr. "Justice Henry Billings Brown: Values in Tension." *Colorado L Rev,* 44 (1973), 553–604.

1225b "Governor on the Bench: Charles Evans Hughes as Associate Justice." *Harv L Rev,* 89 (1976), 961–997.

1941–

1312a BLACK, Hugo, Jr. *My Father: A Remembrance.* New York, 1975.

1323a DUNNE, Gerald T. *Hugo Black and the Judicial Revolution.* New York, 1977.

1326a FORTAS, Abe. "Chief Justice Warren: The Enigma of Leadership." *Yale L J,* 84 (1975), 405–412.

1338a HOWARD, A. E. Dick. "From Warren to Burger: Activism and Restraint." *Wilson Q,* 1 (1977), 109–121.

1349a LAMB, Charles M. "The Making of a Chief Justice: Warren Burger on Criminal Procedure, 1956–1969." *Corn L Rev,* 60 (1975), 743–788.

1349b LASH, Joseph P. *From the Diaries of Felix Frankfurter.* New York, 1975.

1358a MENDELSON, Wallace. "Mr. Justice Douglas and Government by the Judiciary." *J Pol,* 38 (1976), 918–937.

1362a "The One Hundred and First Justice: An Analysis of the Opinions of Justice John Paul Stevens, Sitting as Judge on the Seventh Circuit Court of Appeals." *Vand L Rev,* 29 (1976), 125–209.

1372a SHAPIRO, David L. "Mr. Justice Rehnquist: A Preliminary View." *Harv L Rev,* 90 (1976), 293–357.

1384a WARREN, Earl. *The Memoirs of Earl Warren.* Garden City, N.Y., 1977.

D. *Political Parties*

1389a ADAMANY, David. "Money, Politics, and Democracy: A Review Essay." *Am Pol Sci Rev,* 71 (1977), 289–304.

1392a BURNHAM, Walter Dean. "Revitalization and Decay: Looking Toward the Third Century of American Electoral Politics." *J Pol,* 38 (1976), 146–172.

1393a CHASE, James S. *Emergence of the Presidential Nominating Convention, 1798–1832.* Urbana, 1973.

1410a RANNEY, Austin. *Curing the Mischiefs of Faction; Party Reform in America.* Berkeley, 1975.

1411a SCHIER, Richard F. "Money, the Media, and the Man Who." *Intellect,* 105 (1976), 146–148.

1411b SCHIER, Richard F. "The Real Minority: Intellectuals and Democratic Politics." *Intellect,* 103 (1975), 496–500.

·1412a SUNDQUIST, James L. *The Dynamics of the Party System: Alignment and Realignment of Political Parties in the United States.* Washington, D.C., 1973.

E. State and Local Institutions

1416a BANFIELD, Edward C. *The Unheavenly City; The Nature and Future of Our Urban Crisis.* Boston, 1970.

1416b BANFIELD, Edward C. *The Unheavenly City Revisited.* Boston, 1974.

1418a DANIELSON, Michael N. *The Politics of Exclusion.* New York, 1976.

1444a RAKOVE, Milton L. *Don't Make No Waves—Don't Back No Losers: An Insider's Analysis of the Daley Machine.* Bloomington, Ind., 1975.

1454a TEAFORD, Jon C. *The Municipal Revolution in America: Origins of Modern Urban Government, 1650–1825.* Chicago, 1975.

V. Doctrines and Politics

A. Separation and Sharing of Powers

General

1457a FELLMAN, David. "The Separation of Powers and the Judiciary." *Rev Pol,* 37 (1975), 357–376.

1462a LEVI, Edward H. "Some Aspects of Separation of Powers." *Colum L Rev,* 76 (1976), 371–391.

The Congress

Legislative Power

1506a BARBER, Sotirios A. *The Constitution and the Delegation of Congressional Power.* Chicago, 1975.

The Presidency

General

1640a CORWIN, Edward S. *Presidential Power and the Constitution.* Ithaca, N.Y., 1976.

1649a STEPHENSON, D. Grier, Jr. " 'The Mild Magistracy of the Law': *U.S. v. Richard Nixon.*" *Intellect,* 103 (1975), 288–292.

Appointments and Nominations

1665a HALPER, Thomas. "Supreme Court Appointments: Criteria and Consequences." *NY Law Forum,* 21 (1976), 563–584.

Foreign Affairs and the Military Power

1752a Symposium. "Organizing the Government to Conduct Foreign Policy: The Constitutional Questions." *Va L Rev,* 61 (1975), 747–806.

B. The Judicial Process:
The Supreme Court, the Lower Federal
Courts, and the State Courts

General

1792a ADAMANY, David, and Philip DUBOIS. "Electing State Judges." *Wis L Rev,* 1976 (1976), 731–779.

1810a DWORKIN, Ronald. "Hard Cases." *Harv L Rev,* 88 (1975), 1057–1109.

1873a SEDLER, Robert Allen. "The Summary Contempt Power and the Constitution: The View from Without and Within." *NYUL Rev,* 51 (1976), 34–92.

1882a VANDERBILT, Arthur T., II. *Changing Law: A Biography of Arthur T. Vanderbilt.* New Brunswick, N.J., 1976.

Organization and Jurisdiction

1887a BERG, Larry L., *et al.* "The Consequences of Judicial Reform: A Comparative Analysis of the California and Iowa Appellate Systems." *West Pol Q,* 28 (1975), 263–280.

1892a "Developments in the Law—Class Actions." *Harv L Rev,* 89 (1976), 1319–1644.

1896a EARLY, Stephen J. *Constitutional Courts of the United States.* Totowa, N.J., 1977.

1909a HENKIN, Louis. "Is There a 'Political Question' Doctrine?" *Yale L J,* 85 (1976), 597–625.

1913a KAUFMAN, Irving R. "Judicial Reform in the Next Century." *Stan L Rev,* 29 (1976), 1–26.

1913b LAMB, Charles M. "Judicial Policy-Making and Information Flow to the Supreme Court." *Vand L Rev,* 29 (1976), 45–124.

1917a MILLER, Arthur S., and Jerome A. BARRON. "The Supreme Court, the Adversary System, and the Flow of Information to the Justices: A Preliminary Inquiry." *Va L Rev,* 61 (1975), 1187–1245.

1918a "The 100th Anniversary of the 1875 Judiciary Act: Federal Jurisdiction Symposium." *Wis L Rev,* 1975 (1975), 295–596.

1918b ORREN, Karen. "Standing to Sue: Interest Group Conflict in the Federal Courts." *Am Pol Sci Rev,* 70 (1976), 723–741.

1919a REDISH, Martin H., and Curtis E. WOODS. "Congressional Power to Control the Jurisdiction of Lower Federal Courts: A Critical Review and a New Synthesis." *U Penn L Rev,* 124 (1975), 45–109.

1923a *Stone v. Powell,* 49 L. ed. 2nd 1067 (U.S. Sup. Ct., 1976).

Judicial Review, Constitutional Interpretation, and the Judicial Role

1936a BLACKMUN, Harry A. "Thoughts About Ethics." *Emory L J,* 24 (1975), 3–20.

1953a COX, Archibald. *The Role of the Supreme Court in American Government.* New York, 1976.

1970a GLENNON, Robert J., Jr. "Portrait of the Judge As an Activist: Jerome Frank and the Supreme Court." *Corn L Rev,* 61 (1976), 950–984.

1979a HARRIS, Robert J. "Judicial Review: Vagaries and Varieties." *J Pol,* 38 (1976), 173–208.

1990a LUSKY, Louis. *By What Right?* Indianapolis, Ind., 1976.

1999a MENDELSON, Wallace. "The Politics of Judicial Activism." *Emory L J,* 24 (1975), 43–66.

The Bar

2065a AUERBACH, Jerold S. *Unequal Justice: Lawyers and Social Change in Modern America.* New York, 1976.

2073a GEORGE, Warren E. "Development of the Legal Services Corporation." *Corn L Rev,* 61 (1976), 681–730.

2088a SCHEINGOLD, Stuart A. *The Politics of Rights: Lawyers, Public Policy, and Political Change.* New Haven, 1974.

Judicial Federalism

2093a BARTELS, Robert. "Avoiding a Comity of Errors: A Model for Adjudicating Federal Civil Rights Suits that 'Interfere' with State Civil Proceedings." *Stan L Rev,* 29 (1976), 27–92.

C. Federalism

2130a "Dialogues on Decentralization." *Publius,* 6 (1976), 1–193.

2155a NATHAN, Richard P., *et al. Monitoring Revenue Sharing.* Washington, D.C., 1975.

E. Civil Liberties and Civil Rights

General

2203a "The American Indian and the Law." *L & Cont Prob,* 40 (1976), 1–223.

2217a BRENNAN, William J., Jr. "State Constitutions and the Protection of Individual Rights." *Harv L Rev,* 90 (1977), 489–504.

2226a "Children and the Law." *L & Cont Prob,* 39 (1975), 1–293.

2246a HOWARD, A. E. Dick. "State Courts and Constitutional Rights in the Day of the Burger Court." *Va L Rev,* 62 (1976), 873–944.

2259a NOWAK, John E. "The Scope of Congressional Power to Create Causes of Action Against State Governments and the History of the Eleventh and Fourteenth Amendments." *Colum L Rev,* 75 (1975), 1413–1469.

Property Rights and Police Power

2271a ACKERMAN, Bruce A. *Private Property and the Constitution.* New Haven, 1977.

2304a McCURDY, Charles W. "Justice Field and the Jurisprudence of Government-Business Relations: Some Parameters of Laissez-Faire Constitutionalism, 1863–1897." *J Am His,* 61 (1975), 970–1005.

2325a SCHEIBER, Harry N. "Instrumentalism and Property Rights: A Reconsideration of American 'Styles of Judicial Reasoning' in the 19th Century." *Wis L Rev,* 1976 (1976), 1–18.

2327a STEPHENSON, D. Grier, Jr. "The Supreme Court and Constitutional Change: *Lochner v. New York* Revisited." *Vill L Rev,* 21 (1976), 217–243.

Due Process of Law: Procedural Rights

General

2379a ALSCHULER, Albert W. "The Trial Judge's Role in Plea Bargaining, Part I." *Colum L Rev,* 76 (1976), 1059–1154.

2393a FRIENDLY, Henry J. "Some Kind of Hearing." *U Penn L Rev,* 123 (1975), 1267–1317.

2394a GROSSMAN, Joel B. "Political Justice in the Democratic State." *Polity,* 8 (1976), 358–388.

2396a *Imbler v. Pachtman.* 47 L. ed. 2nd 128 (U.S. Sup. Ct., 1976).

2396b JACOB, Herbert. *Felony Justice; An Organizational Analysis of Criminal Courts.* Boston, 1976.

2401a LEVY, Leonard W. *Against the Law; The Nixon Court and Criminal Justice.* New York, 1974.

2407a ROSETT, Arthur and Donald R. CRESSEY. *Justice by Consent: Plea Bargaining in the American Courthouse.* Philadelphia, 1976.

Search and Seizure and the Exclusionary Rule

2420a CANON, Bradley C. "Testing the Effectiveness of Civil Liberties Policies at the State and Federal Levels: The Case of the Exclusionary Rule." *American Politics Q,* 5 (1977), 57–82.

2434a SCHROCK, Thomas S., and Robert C. WELSH. "Up from Calandra: The Exclusionary Rule as a Constitutional Requirement." *Minn L Rev,* 59 (1974), 251–383.

2436a *United States v. Martinez-Fuerte.* 49 L. ed. 2nd 1116 (U.S. Sup. Ct., 1976).

2437a WEINREB, Lloyd L. "Generalities of the Fourth Amendment." *U Chi L Rev,* 42 (1974), 47–85.

Interrogations, Confessions, and Right to Counsel

2453a LEVINE, James P. "The Impact of 'Gideon': The Performance of Public & Private Criminal Defense Lawyers." *Polity,* 8 (1975), 215–240.

Fair Trial

2477a *Nebraska Press Association v. Stuart.* 49 L. ed. 2nd 683 (U.S. Sup. Ct., 1976).

2485a U.S. Senate. Committee on the Judiciary. Subcommittee on Constitutional Rights. Staff Report. *Free Press—Fair Trial.* 94th Cong., 2nd sess., 1976. Washington, D.C., 1976.

2485b U.S. Senate. Committee on the Judiciary. Subcommittee on Constitutional Rights and the Subcommittee on Improvements in Judicial Machinery. *Free Press and Fair Trial.* Parts 1 and 2. 89th Cong., 1st sess., 1965. Washington, D.C., 1965.

Double Jeopardy, Detention, and Punishment

2494a GOLDFARB, Ronald L. *Jails: The Ultimate Ghetto of the Criminal Justice System.* Garden City, N.Y., 1975.

2495a *Gregg v. Georgia.* 49 L. Ed. 2nd 859 (U.S. Sup. Ct., 1976).

2503a THOMAS, Wayne H., Jr. *Bail Reform in America.* Berkeley, 1976.

2504a   VAN DEN HAAG, Ernest. *Punishing Criminals.* New York, 1975.

2505a   WILSON, James Q. *Thinking About Crime.* New York, 1975.

Freedom of Expression and Association

General

2555a   SHAMAN, Jeffrey M. "Revitalizing the Clear-and-Present-Danger Test: Toward a Principled Interpretation of the First Amendment." *Vill L Rev,* 22 (1976–1977), 60–82.

The Press

2632a   BOLLINGER, Lee C., Jr. "Freedom of the Press and Public Access: Toward a Theory of Partial Regulation of the Mass Media." *Mich L Rev,* 75 (1976), 1–42.

2655a   SIMONS, Howard, and Joseph A. CALIFANO, Jr. *The Media and the Law.* New York, 1976.

Censorship and Obscenity

2672a   HOLBROOK, David. "The Politics of Pornography." *Political Q,* 48 (1977), 44–53.

2685a   RICHARDS, David A. J. "Free Speech and Obscenity Law: Toward a Moral Theory of the First Amendment." *U Penn L Rev,* 123 (1974), 45–91.

Freedom of Religion

General

2707a   SORAUF, Frank J. *The Wall of Separation; The Constitutional Politics of Church and State.* Princeton, N.J., 1976.

Nonestablishment

2751a   *Meek v. Pittenger.* 421 U.S. 349 (1975).

Privacy

2759a   *Cox Broadcasting Corp. v. Cohn.* 420 U.S. 469 (1975).

Equal Protection of the Laws

General

2806a   WILKINSON, J. Harvie, III. "The Supreme Court, The Equal Protection Clause, and the Three Faces of Constitutional Equality." *Va L Rev,* 61 (1975), 945–1018.

Racial Equality

2808a *Arlington Heights v. Metropolitan Housing Corp.* 50 L. ed. 2nd 450 (U.S. Sup. Ct., 1977).

2817a BREST, Paul. "Foreword: In Defense of the Antidiscrimination Principle." *Harv L Rev,* 90 (1976), 1–54.

2824a "The Courts, Social Science, and School Desegregation, Parts I and II." *L & Cont Prob,* 39 (1975), 1–432.

2824b COVER, Robert M. *Justice Accused: Antislavery and the Judicial Process.* New Haven, 1975.

2825a *De Funis* Symposium. *Colum L Rev,* 75 (1975), 485–602.

2837a GLAZER, Nathan. *Affirmative Discrimination: Ethnic Inequality and Public Policy.* New York, 1975.

2838a GRAGLIA, Lino A. *Disaster by Decree; The Supreme Court Decisions on Race and the Schools.* Ithaca, N.Y., 1976.

2849a KLUGER, Richard. *Simple Justice; The History of* Brown v. Board of Education *and Black America's Struggle for Equality.* New York, 1976.

2854a LEFBERG, Irving F. "Chief Justice Vinson and the Politics of Desegregation." *Emory L J,* 24 (1975), 243–312.

2875a PERRY, Michael J. "The Disproportionate Impact Theory of Racial Discrimination." *U Penn L Rev,* 125 (1977), 540–589.

2878a RABINOWITZ, Howard N. "From Exclusion to Segregation: Southern Race Relations, 1865–1890." *J Am Hist,* 63 (1976), 325–350.

2886a ROSSUM, Ralph A. "Ameliorative Racial Preferences and the Fourteenth Amendment: Some Constitutional Problems." *J Pol,* 38 (1976), 346–366.

2887a SANDALOW, Terrance. "Racial Preferences in Higher Education: Political Responsibility and the Judicial Role." *U Chi L Rev,* 42 (1975), 653–703.

2899a STEPHENSON, Mason W., and D. Grier STEPHENSON, Jr. " 'To Protect and Defend': Joseph Henry Lumpkin, The Supreme Court of Georgia, and Slavery." *Emory L J,* 25 (1976), 579–608.

Sexual Equality

2917a JOHNSTON, John D., Jr. "Sex Discrimination and the Supreme Court, 1971–1974." *NYUL Rev,* 49 (1974), 617–692.

Governmental Services

2926a "Future Directions for School Finance Reform." *L & Cont Prob,* 38 (1974), 293–581.

F. The Franchise and the Political Process

2965a "Developments in the Law—Elections." *Harv L Rev,* 88 (1975), 1111–1339.

2989a STARR, Kenneth W. "Federal Judicial Invalidation as a Remedy for Irregularities in State Elections." *NYUL Rev,* 49 (1974), 1092–1129.

Index to the Supplement